GOING PART-TIME

GOING PART-TIME

THE INSIDER'S GUIDE FOR PROFESSIONAL WOMEN WHO WANT A CAREER *AND* A LIFE

CINDY TOLLIVER AND
NANCY CHAMBERS

AVON BOOKS NEW YORK

AVON BOOKS
A division of
The Hearst Corporation
1350 Avenue of the Americas
New York, New York 10019

Copyright © 1997 by Cindy Tolliver and Nancy Chambers Urbonas
Interior design by Kellan Peck
Published by arrangement with the authors
Visit our website at **http://AvonBooks.com**
ISBN: 0-380-78834-9

Library of Congress Cataloging in Publication Data:

Tolliver, Cindy, 1951–
   Going part-time : the insider's guide for professional women who want a career and a life / Cindy Tolliver and Nancy Chambers.
      p.   cm.
   Includes bibliographical references (p.) and index.
   1. Part-time employment—Handbooks, manuals, etc. 2.Women—Employment—Handbooks, manuals, etc. 3. Women in the professions—Handbooks, manuals, etc. 4. Career development—Handbooks, manuals, etc. 5. Vocational guidance for women. I. Chambers, Nancy. II. Title.
HD5110.T65   1997   97-1496
331.4'2572—dc21   CIP

First Avon Books Trade Printing: August 1997

AVON TRADEMARK REG. U.S. PAT. OFF. AND IN OTHER COUNTRIES, MARCA REGISTRADA, HECHO EN U.S.A.

Printed in the U.S.A.

OPM   10 9 8 7 6 5 4 3 2 1

◼ Contents

Preface

I have wrestled with the work/family equation for years and from both perspectives. During the five years I tried to combine working full-time with rearing two young daughters, life felt like a vaudeville act, an endless round of "catch it before it hits the ground." After my third daughter was born in 1990, I decided to stay home full-time. I couldn't add one more ball to my juggling act and still keep them up in the air, and I certainly didn't want to drop the ball when the ball in question was one of my children!

I loved the domestic tranquillity and quality time with my children and husband. But as those of you who have stayed home full-time with children know, you get no pay raises, no pats on the back for a job well done, and no performance evaluations. I admit I got a little bored, not to mention the fact that my self-esteem started flying south. I missed the pressure of deadlines, the office gossip, and even the commute in heavy traffic with my coffee and news radio.

Eventually my dissatisfaction led to a part-time writing career. In addition to my own book projects, I worked on contract with a small publishing house editing several manuscripts a year. My new job met my needs for intellectual stimulation and personal growth. The money—about $4,000 a year—hardly made a dent in the grocery bill for a family of five, but it gave me an opportunity to keep my skills sharp and my networking line in the water. It offered me the security of knowing that if I had to bring in more income, I was ready to spring into action.

I haven't always been bullish on part-time professionals. Ironically, the subject first came to my attention several years ago when I was giving talks promoting my first book about "sequencing" women who were making the transition from full-time work to staying home with the kids. It seemed to be just a matter of time—be it two months or ten years—before these professional women at home began to get antsy. They didn't want full-time work. Nor would they settle for a jobette that earned little more than minimum wage. They weren't worried about being on the mommy track. They just wanted to get on the train. Yet they were only half of the equation. For every woman at home who wanted more, there was a woman working full-time who wanted something less. For both groups—the "too much" and the "too little"—part-time seemed to be "just right."

I didn't have a solution to the equation, but I was hooked on finding some answers. I collaborated with Mary Ann Alwan, herself a part-time professional in the computer industry. We were able to tap into a network of part-time professionals as well as human resources and hiring managers in Silicon Valley high-tech companies. We decided that the Silicon Valley region south of San Francisco was the perfect place to start. Many believe that Silicon Valley has been and still is a microcosm of what the workplace will look like ten years from now.

From there we branched out. We talked to women all over the country who worked in a variety of fields, including business, finance, law, medicine, education, publishing, engineering, and veterinary medicine, to name a few. We talked to women in all phases of the life/work cycle: women who after a short maternity leave went back to work part-time; women who started back full-time, then scaled down to part-time; women who found part-time jobs after years away from their work; at-home mothers planning part-time careers, and so forth. We particularly sought interviews with women in previously male-dominated fields to learn how they pioneered part-time work where it had never existed.

To gain insight into the part-time professional market, we also listened to experts from various work/life organizations such as New Ways to Work in San Francisco, Families and Work Institute in New York, and Catalyst, also in New York. Consulting firms, part-time temporary agencies, professional business women's associations such as the National Association of Female Executives and the Assocation of Part-Time Professionals and workplace gurus like Nancy Austin and Milt Moskowitz, contributing editors of *Working Woman* and *Working Mother*, all shared their ideas.

In short, we interviewed our brains out. The thick stacks of over 100 in-depth interviews with women who prove that it is possible to get it "just right" contained a gold mine of information. The problem was that each of these women had by and large needed to reinvent the part-time wheel with each of their jobs. Nobody was talking to anybody else. And no one had collected their stories and the strategies they used to do what they did and codified it in a book just for part-time professionals. That became our job and the overarching purpose of *Going Part-time*.

Writing this book became an object lesson in "If I knew then what I know now." First of all, like many part-time professionals, we had grossly underestimated the number of unexpected events that could interrupt the work flow. Family crises too numerous to describe here occurred and, as the balancers in the family, had to be attended to. One surprise development that changed the project came just at the point when Mary Ann and I had finished interviewing and had begun the writing process. She and her husband were blessed with an unexpected opportunity to adopt a baby, an event that would end their years-long struggle to expand their family. Mary Ann had to make a choice and went with what she valued the most.

Second and also typical of the part-time professional experience, estimates of the amount of work the project would take were low. So, with the book's deadline looming five months away (three of those months being in the summer with all three kids home), three-quarters of the book left to write, and panic setting in, I was fortunate enough to connect with Nancy Chambers. At that time, Nancy worked as an assistant editor at *Working Woman* in New York. Her knowledge of work/life issues, her ace skills using Lexis/Nexis on-line research software, and her talent for editing have been invaluable in finishing off three final chapters and the resource section.

Our new eleventh-hour job share represented telecommuting at its best. In the morning I would fax Nancy an outline of a chapter from my house in Saratoga, California. She received it in the seventh floor of her midtown Manhattan office. She would then work late into the night, like a computer Rumpelstiltskin spinning the straw bullet points into gold.

The project was on schedule. The book is better for all the twists and turns involved in the process. And ultimately, the three people involved got what they wanted the most—which is what flexible work arrangements are all about.

HOW TO USE THIS BOOK

This book is organized in five parts. At the beginning of each part is a personal interview that we hope focuses you on the information following. Part One, *You and the Decision,* explores the work options and financial and career trade-offs involved in making the decision to work part-time. Part Two, *You and Management,* describes the manager's point of view, with a discussion of the research showing why part-time professionals are good for business and the most common objections to part-time workers made by managers and how you can overcome these objections. Part Three, *Strategies for Getting It— From the Inside,* details the practical process of preparing to convert to part-time with your current employer, including writing a killer proposal, negotiating your deal, and how to set up a job share. Part Four, *Strategies for Getting It—From the Outside,* includes separate chapters for those who are coming into a company from the outside, for women who are returning to the workforce part-time after a period at home full-time, and for those who decide to set up their own shops as part-time independent contractors. Part Five, *Making It Work,* outlines strategies for making the most of your part-time professional work at the office and at home. And finally, Part Six discusses what needs to change for professional part-time to fulfill its potential in the future. In addition the Resource section offers books, publications, associations, on-line support, and phone numbers that will be useful to you as part-time professionals.

—Cindy Tolliver

INTRODUCTION
The New Part-time Professional

"In spite of talk about a future in management, a side of me could never see holding a job that might mean I would get home from work hours after our kids got home from school."

—Anna Quindlen, "Why I Quit," *Working Woman*

One fall afternoon in 1995, Susan Burke's warm, intelligent voice spoke to us over the phone. Her story described the basic problem we were trying to solve. Like so many women we know, Burke had planned to balance a full-time career and child rearing—until she had children. Once her daughter was born, her maternal feelings struck "like a bolt of lightning" and she found she couldn't—or didn't want to—make the full-time balancing act work. She felt stuck. Either way she tipped, she ended up cheating her job or her children or herself. She believed professional part-time was the answer. But the marketing manager at Norwest Direct wanted a real career, not just a chance to earn a few bucks doing whatever.

But how?

The great challenge for Burke—and for many women today—is to see how much they can achieve in their careers *and* still have a life. In some ways, it's like driving your car on the freeway when you hit that certain optimal cruising speed: Exceed it and the car starts to shimmy and shake. Similarly, women today are reaching for work arrangements that allow them to achieve that certain glorious

1

point of balance between speed and stability where prosperous careers and a rich personal life converge.

The quest for balance has given rise to a new breed of player in the workplace: the part-time professional. Highly skilled, experienced, and savvy, new part-time professionals are trading off fifty-plus-hour workweeks, ''second shifts,'' and child-care dilemmas for more time for family dinners, Little League games, homework assistance, and community projects.

These women are downshifting their hours, but they remain serious, committed professionals. They understand the bottom-line business needs of the workplace and want to make a significant contribution there. But on *their* terms. Less ambivalent than their forerunners about the need to spend time with their families, they insist on flexibility and are willing to take a career detour—but not a derailment—in order to get it. They want a legitimate career path and are unwilling to relinquish the chance to go for the glory at the office. They want to compete for and win meaty work assignments and career development opportunities that bring top benefits, promotions, and pay.

Are they asking too much?

We don't think so. Over two years of research and interviews with over 100 women who are holding down part-time professional jobs has convinced us that top-flight part-time professional work that pays is both feasible and practical. Millions of women, by virtue of their own ingenuity, skills, and grit, have done it. And so can you. Between them, these women have accumulated a great store of wisdom. We have collected their stories and strategies and will share them with you.

We don't offer naive, glib formulas. But we do deliberately choose to view the glass as half full. We choose to focus on what you *can* do to span the chasm between current workplace conditions and top-notch part-time professional work.

What we've gleaned from the research and from the interviews can be condensed into three broad statements that form the underlying premises of this book:

1. You can find part-time professional work that pays—*now!*
2. Part-time professional opportunities exist in all industries, in all types of companies, and at all levels.
3. Any professional willing to be flexible and to work hard can create satisfying part-time work.

REDEFINING PROFESSIONAL PART-TIME: NOT JUST FEWER HOURS

Part-time doesn't even have to mean less than forty hours a week. Whittling the workload down from seventy to forty hours and making it home for dinner can be a major step toward sanity for employees in pressure-cooker environments. In the case of seasonal jobs such as tax accounting, part-time could mean working full-time for only part of the year. And finally, consultants doing project-based work generally vary their part-time hours as the project load dictates.

Part-time Professional Jobs Are Out There—Right Now

A lot of people are already doing what you want to do: More than 4.7 million professionals worked part-time in 1995, a statistic that is probably low because it only reflects employer-employee relationships. The significant number of freelancers, independent contractors, self-employed doctors, lawyers, and accountants who work limited hours or on a seasonal basis are not included in this figure.

Moreover, opportunities for part-time professional work are growing at a record-breaking pace. While the overall workforce, including the nonprofessional part-timers, has grown less than 2 percent from 1989 to 1995, the number of part-time professionals has jumped 50 percent, from 3 million to 4.7 million. This means that part-time professional opportunities are growing twenty-five times faster than other full-time or nonprofessional part-time jobs!

And these part-time professionals are not just working for pin money. Catalyst, the New York research firm specializing in women in the workplace, surveyed thirty-eight companies and found that 29 percent of corporate part-timers earned salaries ranging from $35,000 to over $100,000 a year. Lawyers and accountants earned even more, with two-thirds in the $80,000 to over $100,000 salary range. Part-time professionals who work as independent contractors frequently earn $50 to $250 an hour.

Part-time Professional Profile

Catalyst reports that 97 percent of those using flexible policies within corporations are mothers who want to spend more time with their children. But parenting issues are not the only driving force. A growing number of professionals are cutting back to care for aging parents—7 to 10 percent of workers today report having some responsibility for an older relative. And some workers of retirement age want to work part-time as an escape from at-home boredom or to make up for savings shortfalls. Yet other childless workers are tired of the high-stress, one-dimensional lifestyle that full-time careers often demand. More and more of them are willing to forgo a few rungs on the career ladder in order to have a life outside the office.

While there is nothing intrinsically female about part-time professional work, women are definitely at the forefront of the part-time professional movement. Although the media frequently feature high-powered fathers who scale back their careers to savor the pleasures of fatherhood, most experts don't see significant numbers of men switching to part-time schedules. The exception is independent contractors. Some experts suggest that 28 percent of these part-time professionals are men.

THIS BOOK IS NOT FOR WOMEN ONLY

We address our book to women readers because they are the overwhelming majority of those seeking professional part-time work. Assuming you are a woman also allows us to avoid the awkward "he/shes" and "his/hers" that litter paragraphs when writers try to cover the gender bases. However, the information in this book applies equally to men and women interested in part-time professional work. The strategies for success are universal and gender-neutral.

Where to Find It

As a sampling of what's hot for professional part-timers (see sidebar) shows, you can find it in all industries. Even industries that appear inhospitable may welcome you if you have specialized skills. Within part-time friendly industries, opportunities for part-time vary widely. The health-care industry is a good example. You may find a part-time nursing position easily, but as jobs move further away from traditional clinically oriented nursing tasks toward managerial responsibilities, part-time positions quickly thin out.

Here are six industries with the most part-time potential:

1. At your service: Law, health-care, hospitality, financial, and business services provide a rich source of part-time work. The service industries are now responsible for most new jobs and are still experiencing explosive growth. Hard-pressed managers who lack the time to hire replacements will honor requests for part-time employment from highly skilled applicants with good performance records.

2. High-tech connections: Telecommunications, electronics, and manufacturers of chemical, pharmaceutical, and biotechnology products depend on top professionals. Flexible policies enable these companies to hold on to valued employees and, with them, a competitive edge.

3. Uncle Sam: A 1978 law requires federal agencies to expand professional-level part-time positions and to prorate salaries and benefits for federal employees who have been onboard for three years or more. State and local governments tend to follow suit.

4. Open minds at nonprofits: Universities, libraries, and charitable organizations are experts at and advocates of a flexible workplace.

5. Projects, big or small: Nurses have long been successful working part-time because their days consist of a series of projects with finite time requirements. Also, the media, including publishing, television, film, and radio, rely on writers and editors who work on independent, self-directed projects.

6. Smaller, flatter, better: Part-time professionals stymied by the inflexible policies of big corporations often find smaller companies much more willing to bend. Small companies may not be able to afford the same salary and benefits packages as larger corporations but they can offer flexibility. One variation of the small, flat organization is the professional partnership. This type of company readily allows diverse professionals—physicians, veterinarians, accountants, executive search recruiters, lawyers, physical therapists—to practice their professions part-time.

■ **WHAT'S HOT FOR PART-TIME PROFESSIONALS**

Groundbreaking part-timers, business gurus, and those who have "been there, done that" let you in on where the flexibility is.

"Part-time would work in most medical specialties . . . especially in gynecology, pediatrics, toxicology and radiology."
    —Dr. Susan Davis, part-time pediatrician, Indianapolis

"Definitely telecommunications . . . So much is happening there—developing technologies, rapid growth—that part-time is available for really talented leaders."
    —Amy Rothwell, part-time executive search consultant, Yardley, Pennsylvania

"The development field is booming, especially in education. Most development jobs are already part-time since nonprofits can't afford full-time."

> —Judy Chang, part-time coordinator of alumni affairs and development, University of Illinois, Champaign-Urbana

"Everybody in the field knows if you go into physical therapy you can work part-time for good money."

> —Nancy Siegal, part-time physical therapist, Northboro, Massachusetts

"Try work that's project-based. The media industry is nothing but a string of projects—every film, every movie, every CD-ROM, every script."

> —Kathryn Linehan, media consultant, Hollywood

"Financial services are more open to part-time, whether it's accounting, banking, or financial management . . . I want to say high-tech, but it's such a workaholic culture . . ."

> —Milton Moskowitz, author of *Working Mother*'s 100 Best Companies list

"Engineering . . . good engineers are hard to find so we are going to have to offer flexibility if we want to stay competitive."

> —Larry Potter, vice president of Hewlett-Packard, Palo Alto, California

"Venture capital is perfect . . . especially if you're far enough along in your career . . . I didn't lose anything in terms of the scope of my responsibilities. If my partners are making investments in three or four companies a year, I might do two."

> —Mary Jane Elmore, part-time venture capitalist, Palo Alto, California

"Banking. I think that an industry in change is a good place to look for part-time professional work because churning breeds opportunity."

> —Karen Stoeller, work/life manager, Harris Bank, Chicago

"Lawyers with a niche specialty like licensing or trusts and estates. There's also a growing market for lawyers who work on a contract basis."
—Cynthia Cannady, senior director of law,
Apple Computers, Cupertino, California

"Human resources. They're selling it, they've got to know how to do it."
—Kimetha Firpo, consultant with Work/Family
Directions in Chicago

"Insurance is good. At least here at Aetna, part-time is a given."
—Lisa Bradway, compensation/benefits analyst at Aetna
Life and Casualty, Trenton, New Jersey

"Big companies have got the money so they are more willing to experiment off in some division."
—Nancy Austin, management expert, Aptos, California

"Professional services are ideal. You work full-time on particular clients—you just have fewer clients."
—Carol Meyer, partner, Andersen Consulting, New York

TOP TEN REASONS THE FUTURE LOOKS BRIGHT FOR PART-TIME PROFESSIONALS

Continual changes in what author Peter Vaill calls the "permanent white waters" of the American workplace carry profound implications for your part-time professional prospects. The following ten big trends comprise a unique combination of acceptability, availability, and demand that are fueling further growth and will open the door of opportunity for you.

1. The stigma once associated with part-time work is diminishing. More and more professionals in high-profile, high-status fields such as medicine, law, accounting, and engineering have chosen to downshift from full-throttle careerism to a kinder, gentler workload. From their success, colleagues are learning that a lower-gear career provides an opportunity to enjoy the scenery and is by no means a trip to nowhere.

2. The growing number of professional women with children

will force a change in the workplace mentality. By the year 2000, two-thirds of new workers will be women. Of those women, three out of four will become pregnant during their working years and many will probably want to cut back their hours to care for their families. Already, a full one-third of working mothers with children thirteen and under would sacrifice advancement for the advantages of part-time work. One-fourth would even change employers to reduce their hours. Young women especially want more balance. Based on a Catalyst study of women MBA candidates at seven top business schools, Catalyst President Sheila Wellington says that no matter what their age,'' Today's businesswoman wants both career and family.'' And many of them plan on having both by working part-time for at least a portion of a forty-year work life. If employers hope to have anything resembling an experienced, skilled workforce to carry out their strategies, they will have to accommodate the child-care needs of women.

3. A diminishing pool of skilled workers will create a buyer's market for those that remain. Fewer skilled professionals will be available for positions in fast-growing managerial, professional, and technical fields as a result of the aging baby boomer population and the falling birth rate. In addition, as just mentioned, professional and highly skilled women with young children comprise the fastest growing segments of the workforce. The dictum "talent talks" means professionals with the right skills will be able to write their own part-time tickets. Worldwide, the United States ranks third in dependence on women in the workplace, behind Scandinavia and Canada, and it's getting more dependent on their skills with every passing year.

4. The contingent workforce is here to stay. The trend toward maintaining a small core of employees and temporarily augmenting the staff during periods of peak customer demand looks to continue for the foreseeable future. This practice allows an employer to avoid the high costs of permanent employee salaries and benefits as well as the time-consuming and expensive hiring-and-firing cycles, but it also benefits the professional interested in part-time work because it opens the door to professional temping and independent contractors.

5. The global marketplace often requires a nonstandard work-day. Businesses with national and international operations need employees willing to work flexible hours so they can field opposite coast calls or answer odd-hour requests from Tokyo or Madrid. In addition, many businesses such as insurance companies and banks use part-time staff to provide customer service around the clock.

6. Technology facilitates part-time work. First of all, the technology industry, young and unburdened by hidebound management practices, creates fresh niches for part-time professionals. At the same time, the computerization of administrative tasks makes it easier and more cost-effective for corporations to manage the complexities of varied work schedules and benefits adjustments and compensation prorations. Technology itself—personal and portable computers, fax machines, voice mail, electronic mail systems, and high-speed ISDN lines—facilitate flexible work arrangements for off-site employees, a.k.a. telecommuters.

7. Work/life benefits emerge as a competitive tool. Fueled by the groundbreaking research of private work/life consulting and research groups, it is now understood that if companies offer employees an assortment of "family-friendly" programs for employees, including child care, elder care, extended maternity leaves, sabbaticals, and flexible scheduling, then they earn a more competitive reputation. Companies are already responding to the need to compete for and retain critical workers. In 1995, more than 400 U.S. corporations had work/life managers to design and implement family-friendly policies, compared to only 200 in 1990.

8. Generation Xers want more of a life outside work. The younger crowd, having observed parents and older siblings toiling from dawn till beyond dusk only to be rewarded with a pink slip, are not eager to follow in workaholic footsteps. Younger professionals tend to think more like independent contractors in that they expect to manage their own careers and schedules and obtain their own continuing education and upgrading of skills rather than entrusting such things to an employer.

9. The pro-flexibility research keeps rolling in. The sheer volume of research showing that offering part-time improves productivity and morale and allows companies to retain valued employees will prove too much even for resistant managers to ignore. And as managers begin granting part-time on a case-by-case basis, the success of the experiment will convert them to believers in the cause. Eventually, the benefits of offering part-time will become as normal a part of company benefits as vacation days.

10. Society perceives more parental supervision as one cure for societal ills. Worried about the spread of teenage gangs and violent crime, highly placed officials are speaking out on the need for parents to supervise their children. This "return to family" focus is bipartisan and nationwide, and only flexible hours and more time at home can cure it. Two more luminaries who are indirect evangelists for part-time work: Hillary Clinton has used the First Lady bully pulpit to preach the gospel of more time with the family in her 1996 book *It Takes a Village*. Education Secretary Richard Riley, in a speech to the Washington Press Club on September 8, 1994, also tackled the subject: "Many parents and other family members are stretched to the limit juggling jobs and putting food on the table, but we are missing something far deeper in all this rushing around—we are letting our children grow up almost alone and disconnected."

WHAT IT TAKES

Despite the trends, it's too early to celebrate. A meager 2 percent of workers take advantage of flexible options when clearly many more want and need to. While the good ideas are already there, says Fran Rodgers, CEO of Work/Family Directions, "The focus for the nineties must be on the implementation of these ideas." While acknowledging the challenges ahead, the bottom line is that there's never been a better time to find part-time professional work.

We don't pretend that tapping into the part-time professional gold mine is easy, but it can be done. We do contend that any professional willing to be flexible and to work with the business needs of the job can create highly paid, professional part-time work.

This is the first book to cover in-depth *all* the professional part-time options you have and how to get them. With the information in the following chapters you will be able to research, understand, and articulate how the part-time professional job you want fits in with the business needs of your target company. We are confident that with time and hard work you will be able to achieve the point of balance that is right for your life.

WHAT THIS BOOK WILL DO FOR YOU

This book will help you to:

- understand why companies are willing to offer part-time professional opportunities;

- identify desirable part-time professional jobs you may wish to pursue;
- assess the risks and trade-offs of going part-time;
- assess your goals in relation to your values and the demands of the part-time professional job market;
- use the employer's point of view to write and sell your part-time work proposal;
- identify your present interests and skills as well as skills you'll need to compete in the part-time professional job market;
- understand the personal and professional habits, attitudes, and practices that promote success as a part-time professional;
- interview and write résumés and proposals that will win part-time professional work;
- turn your current full-time job into a part-time one;
- find a professional part-time job coming in from the outside or after a stint at home;
- set up your own shop as a consultant or independent contractor;
- identify future trends and maintain your part-time success into the twenty-first century.

PART ONE

YOU AND THE DECISION TO WORK PART-TIME

Success with Twinges of Regret:

An Interview with Nancy Anderson

Nancy Anderson shocked the business community in 1989 when she opted out of her position as general manager of Hewlett-Packard's commercial systems division—the first woman to attain such a rank—to be with her three-year-old son full-time. Fifteen months later, Anderson resurfaced as a part-time executive at a small software start-up. Currently, she is the part-time CEO of San Mateo, California–based T.R.A.D.E., Inc., another software start-up.

Q: *Was it very difficult to find such a senior-level part-time arrangement?*

A: I feel very fortunate. I was vice president of marketing at a start-up working three hours a day before this job. When I started looking around, a lot of people weren't open to a part-time arrangement, at least initially. Later, they changed their minds because there were too few qualified candidates for the CEO slot.

Q: *T.R.A.D.E. is much smaller than the division you managed at HP. Do you feel challenged?*

A: Getting this company off the ground has definitely been a challenge. When I came onboard, we had some serious problems with the product strategy and the distribution channel. We had to make significant changes to turn the company around. My first part-time job, however, was a different story. I probably wouldn't have done that job if I hadn't wanted part-time hours so badly. As vice president of marketing, I was doing things I had done fifteen years before. Because of the reduced hours, I stayed with that job for two years. In the end, it worked out well because I learned a lot about start-ups. If I had gone right from HP to not working, then straight to having a demanding job like my current one, it would have been hard.

Q: *Have you had any negative experiences working part-time?*

A: I believe managers judge you by your results. Part-time or full-time, if you get results, your management is happy. And my management—the board of directors—is happy. The negatives of part-time tend to be much more personal, like the pressure of constantly balancing things. That's the downside for most of the women I know in this situation. For example, my ten-year-old son doesn't have a key to the house. Why? Because I know that if I give him a key, I'll be tempted to stay at the office after 3:00 P.M. If I know he's waiting at the doorstep, I'll get out of the office.

Q: *How do you manage a business on a part-time basis?*

A: My management style is to push decisions down as far as I can in the organization, to hire great people, and to give them as much responsibility as they can take. Consequently, I have an outstanding team here. They're very independent, so they get a lot done. Plus, I am really clear about letting people know that I want them to call me at home. And when they call, I want them to treat me the same way they do at the office.

Q: *What kind of trade-offs have you made?*

A: I don't feel I've compromised my career that much. I was already pretty far along in my career when I had my son. Yet at times I do feel a twinge of regret. The other day, for example, I got a call from a head-hunter looking for suggestions for a CEO of a $140-million-dollar company. Five years ago, this same headhunter used to call me trying to get *me* for those jobs. Now he just wants to tap into my network. He said, "I know you wouldn't be right for this job because you're trying to balance your life." When he said that, I definitely felt that twinge. But, you know, life has a lot of trade-offs, and what I am getting in return is something I enjoy a lot more. Not everybody feels that way. Some women work part-time not because they love being home but because they don't feel they can handle the demands of full-time office and full-time family. Those women face tougher adjustments.

Q: *Is there anybody besides yourself working part-time at your current company?*

A: We have a few other part-time professionals. In addition, most of our engineers telecommute one or two days a week. They're very good engineers, and they clearly get a lot done on the days they're home. Because working at home saves them a couple hours of driving time, they view it as a huge benefit. Someone just did a survey for us and found employee satisfaction to be very, very high. People liked the fact that the company seems balanced about family and work. I think the fact that I work part-time makes them all feel more comfortable about balancing their own lives.

Q: *Some people may hear your story and say, ''She's obviously a superstar. I could never do what she has done.''*

A: I think no matter where you are in your career, you're judged by the value you bring to your employer. Regardless of the job, really competent people are always scarce. However, it's hard for me to tell someone they could duplicate my situation. I was fortunate to have worked at HP, a hugely visible company. I gained a lot of credibility from that. Also, my division was a very visible part of HP—one of the largest and most profitable—so I ended up knowing a lot of people. Somebody might be very talented and competent, but if she lacks the right connections, gaining access to part-time work might be hard. A lot of it depends on whether you're fortunate enough to be involved with people who are open to alternative job structures.

ONE

Part-time Professional Options, Finances, and Values

"The much-heralded new choices for women now seem like hard decisions . . . Full-time, part-time, mommy track, child care, one paycheck or two—each option comes with an elaborate and unsettling cost accounting that goes to the psyche as well as the pocketbook."

—Ellen Goodman, *Value Judgments*

After returning from a fleeting six-week maternity leave, 32-year-old banker Susan Burke, whom we introduced to you at the beginning of the book, approached her employer about converting her job into a part-time position. Her boss dismissed Burke's request outright, saying "We've never done that here." In fact, her hours escalated. Just when she wanted to cut back her hours, Burke's workload soon became so heavy she often toiled at the office until 10:00 P.M. to keep from falling behind.

The intolerable hours propelled the new mother to look for a job that would allow her to better balance work and family. With nine years of solid experience in the banking industry, Burke wanted work that was professionally satisfying and that made financial sense. A month later she connected with a small bank desperate for someone with her skills and level of expertise, but unable to pay a full-time salary. They offered her the equivalent of workplace nirvana: a three-day schedule, a promotion, and a staff. Since that first position, Burke has negotiated two more part-time professional jobs. "I don't think good part-time jobs remain static for five years,'' she says referring to the difficulty of staying in the part-time saddle amid corporate restructuring and downsizings.

Since 1994, Susan Burke has co-chaired the presidency of the Twin Cities Part-Time Professionals Association, a networking organization that meets every other month to exchange part-time professional information and swap job lead tips. Members agree, says Burke, that the hardest thing about part-time professional work is *finding* it. She also observes that many new members come in having no idea that so many professionals are working part-time. "And if they do, they're only aware of the twenty-hours-a-week garden-variety, but it quickly dawns on them that that's just Part-time-101,'' says Burke.

FIVE PART-TIME OPTIONS DEFINED

There is a truism that one size doesn't fit all, whether it's panty hose, classroom learning styles, or ergonomically correct office furniture. It's especially true for part-time work arrangements. A new generation of options—job sharing, telecommuting, freelancing, independent contracting, temping, and every conceivable combination in between—allows men and women to work in ways that pre–baby boomers never dreamed of.

This section discusses the five basic part-time job options available to you: (1) standard part-time, (2) job sharing, (3) telecommuting, (4) self-employment, and (5) temping. What are the salient features of each option? How prevalent is it? How does it work? What happens to your salary and benefits? What are the advantages and disadvantages? What do managers think about it? What kind of professionals have successfully used these work models? The answers will prepare you to design a work option that best fits the details of the work you do and the life you would love to lead.

1. Standard Part-time

You'll work a reduced schedule. Although three days a week is the most common, part-time may mean one to four days a week, five short days, two ten-hour days. *Note:* Changing your *shift* so that you work long days, on weekends or evenings, rather than during standard work hours is called flextime. It can be used as part of a part-time scheduling option. In some high-stress jobs, a maximum of forty hours a week with a guarantee that you'll leave by 5:00 P.M. every day is considered part-time.

PREVALENCE

Standard part-time is the oldest and by far the most widely accepted of your options. Nationwide, 57 percent of all employees work for companies that offer standard part-time. In the Fortune 1000 companies, 88 percent offer it.

Standard part-time is probably the most popular option because it is "the easiest option" according to part-time banking veteran Susan Burke. Easiest because you don't have to find, marry, and set up housekeeping with a compatible job-share partner—a distinctly uneasy task. Easiest, because you can find the widest range of scheduling possibilities. And last, easiest because your manager may be less resistant to a "known quantity" like standard part-time than to its more flamboyant cousin, job sharing.

WHAT HAPPENS TO PAY AND BENEFITS

Permanent part-time pay varies widely from company to company and from case to case. In general, salaries tend to be in proportion to full-time earnings, based on the reduction in hours. If a part-time employee reduces her hours by half, for example, she receives half her full-time salary. Some enlightened employers allow part-time employees to compete for prorated bonuses as well, a strategy which encourages them to log in extra hours for special projects or during hectic times.

ADVANTAGES

- You have more time for family and outside interests.
- You have a wide range of scheduling possibilities.
- You aren't dependent on a partner.
- You often receive prorated pay and benefits.
- Your manager is probably more comfortable with this schedule.
- Standard part-time is relatively easy to implement, especially if you're with a company where you have a good track record.

DISADVANTAGES

- Your job may be difficult to narrow down to a part-time schedule.
- You might be "mommy tracked," receive less frequent promotions, and be viewed as less committed.

- You may have to give up higher-level job responsibilities you love.
- You may be the first to go in a layoff.
- You may have less time to interact with coworkers.
- You may miss out on opportunities or important information if you are not present at critical times.

2. Job Sharing

An innovative outgrowth of standard part-time, job sharing allows two people to share the duties of one full-time position. Job sharers can design schedules in a number of ways depending on the type of work the partners do, the needs of the coworkers and managers, and the personal needs of the team members. Job sharers can work three to four full days a week with one day a week overlapping or they can work partial days every week. Others work one week on and one week off. It's up to you.

PREVALENCE

Although less common than standard part-time and still considered experimental, job sharing is fast becoming part of mainstream corporate policy and practice. Of 505 corporations polled nationwide in 1994 by human resource consultants Hewitt and Associates, 37 percent offered job sharing, compared with only 28 percent in a 1990 poll.

■ In a job-sharing study of 155 companies conducted by the Conference Board, a business research organization in New York City, 79 percent of employers said job sharing helps them retain valuable employees and 48 percent said it increases productivity.

The popularity of job sharing is growing for two big reasons. First, it can minimize damage to a career for women who want to work part-time. And second, it offers a solution for a knotty management problem brought on by the 1993 Family Medical Leave Act. This law guarantees eight weeks of maternity leave to employees in companies with over fifty employees. Job sharing provides a built-in insurance policy for coverage during such absences. In fact, in some cases job-share partners even plan their pregnancies to facilitate smooth coverage of the job.

One of the biggest surprises for us was the discovery that job sharing is red hot at large corporations with workaholic cultures that do not normally support people trying to work *less*. The continuity of job sharing offers the only viable part-time route for women who want to maintain high-level management positions, where standard part-time is *verboten*. While most job sharers still work at the clerical/administrative level, an impressive number of high-powered and visible professionals—vice presidents, physicians, senior executives—who want to stay on the fast track are breaking ground and setting precedents.

It wasn't long ago, in a 1989 study, that the research organization Catalyst found no job sharers earning more than $35,000 a year, a salary suggesting that no one above middle management had a job-share position. None of the job sharers in the study were in supervisory roles.

But that was then. At the same corporations today, upper level job sharers crop up with increasing regularity. At Hewlett-Packard, for example, several job-share pairs share senior executive-level management positions. Significantly, each drives her own company Ford Taurus, a perquisite holding great symbolic power according to HP insiders. Another job-share team at Norwest Financial Corporation shares a vice presidency and manages fifty people between them. These job sharers in high places are by no means unique. The list grows longer and more impressive each year.

WHAT HAPPENS TO PAY AND BENEFITS

Often both partners split one full-time salary, or, if partners have different skills and experience, each partner's salary can be prorated independently. Fringe benefits can be split in a number of ways depending on company policy. Partners can split the standard fringe benefits package right down the middle or according to the hours worked. With cafeteria-style plans, job sharers can tailor benefits. For example, if one partner is covered under her husband's medical plan, she can choose vision care or dental coverage in lieu of medical coverage.

ADVANTAGES

- You'll have more time outside work.
- You can stay in a job that requires full-time coverage and/or management responsibilities.
- You can retain the seniority, status, and pay scale of a high-level position.

- You can relax more on days off knowing someone else is at the helm.
- You have the opportunity to concentrate on the parts of the job where you have the most skills.
- The "buddy system" offers you mutual support in bad times and someone with whom to celebrate your successes.
- You have your partner to use as a sounding board, feedback you normally wouldn't get.
- You can resolve problems more effectively because you have two people to brainstorm solutions and act on them.
- You have someone who can cover for you in an emergency.

DISADVANTAGES

- You have the added pressure of being a role model in a relatively new way of working.
- You may find it difficult to share the power, authority, decision-making, and credit of a high status job.
- You must spend a great deal of time communicating with your partner as well as making sure customers, managers, and coworkers don't experience any communication glitches because of your job share.
- Your performance will depend on the performance of someone else.
- You may have to work full-time to cover for your partner if she goes on maternity leave, vacation, disability, or to a new job.
- As you move up the ladder, it becomes increasingly difficult to find a suitable job-share partner with commensurate experience and skills.
- Your job is at risk if your partner moves or quits.

SELF-ASSESSMENT: AM I A GOOD CANDIDATE FOR JOB SHARING?

- Does your job require full-time coverage or management responsibilities that can't be done away from the office?
- How difficult would it be to find someone with complementary skills who could share a job with you?
- How good are your organizational and communication skills?
- How comfortable would you be sharing a workspace with someone else?
- How flexible are you?
- Would you be willing to do the extra work necessary to present

a "seamless" front to managers and customers if that's what the job entails?

- Are you willing to tie your own performance to another person's?
- Will you be comfortable sharing the decision-making authority and credit for the work with someone else?
- Are you willing to take a chance on a job-share partnership not working out, and potentially jeopardizing your personal credibility?

3. Telecommuting

Often used as part of a part-time work arrangement, telecommuting—also called flexiplace, work-at-home, and teleworking—allows employees to work all or a portion of their scheduled work hours from home or at a satellite facility. They "commute" via telephone, e-mail, or fax machines. Many part-time professionals feel they strike a more fluid balance between work and family by spending a day or two in a central office and a third at home. Self-employed telecommuters such as writers, graphic designers, marketing consultants, and stockbrokers, however, may work mostly at home with only the occasional meeting with clients or bosses. In many cases, telecommuters never meet the people they work with in the flesh. Actually, the authors of this book never met until after the manuscript was turned in.

PREVALENCE

The prevalence of telecommuting is turning the old real estate pitch "location, location, location" on its head. Telecommuting enables people to live in less expensive, less congested areas no matter where their office is headquartered. Companies in Northern California began using telecommuting extensively in 1989 when the Loma Prieta earthquake damaged the freeways. Since that time, telecommuting statistics have gone through the roof. Consider the following:

- According to Work/Family Directions, 85 percent of the nation's biggest companies offer some form of telecommuting.
- According to a 1994 LINK Resource survey, 8.8 million workers in the United States currently telecommute.
- LINK further estimates that by 2000 that number will soar to *25 million.*

Several factors account for this astonishing growth. First and foremost is the increasing affordability of technology. According to LINK, in 1983 the cost to equip a home with a PC, phone, fax, telephone, printer, e-mail, etc., was over $10,000. In 1994 the cost was less than $3,000. Making the home PC as powerful as the office's helps, too. In fact, ISDN "fast cable" lines, previously only available at offices, are now available for your home. A second factor is the increasing number of "knowledge professionals," such as writers, graphic designers, and computer programmers. These workers can complete work that calls for thinking, writing, and planning more efficiently away from the distractions of the office. And finally, even managers can't dispute the mutual benefits of telecommuting. Working from home, professionals can work during the time normally committed to commuting and, at the same time, satisfy the need for more time at home. The physical separation from workers bothers managers less than usual when they see the amount of real work that can get done via telecommuting. While some so-called "line-of-sight" managers remain uncomfortable if they cannot see their employees working, new technology promises to squelch that objection. In Microsoft CEO Bill Gate's best-seller *The Road Ahead,* Gates described technology that would allow workers to log on and log off so that employers could track the exact amount of time an employee works. Says Gates, "If the baby started crying, Dad or Mom would click 'not available' and take care of the child with unpaid minutes away from the job."

FORMAL VS INFORMAL TELECOMMUTING

More than 90 percent of the millions of telecommuters do so informally as "closet" telecommuters. For example, years ago author Nancy Austin worked for Hewlett-Packard, which had open-cubicle office spaces, an arrangement designed to facilitate the free flow of ideas and to encourage teamwork. However, an environment so open to interruptions and distractions would drive her insane when she was working on something that required intense concentration. Her manager agreed informally to let her work at home, but made it clear that it was a short-term arrangement.

Formal telecommuting agreements are becoming more common today. Lori Johnson, a training specialist for Shell Oil who does almost 40 percent of her work from home, insisted on an official telecommuting agreement. Johnson wanted it in writing because she didn't want to worry about her "face not sitting in the office" for any specified amount of time. She wanted expectations clearly spelled out. Her agreement basically says that if it's more efficient to work from home, she can work from home. She loves this arrangement because it gives her the flexibility to drive in her kids' carpool and do other kid stuff during traditional work hours. On hectic days, she makes up for lost time by working at night after the kids are in bed.

WHAT HAPPENS TO PAY AND BENEFITS

Usually, telecommuting has no effect on pay and benefits, although in some cases, firms categorize telecommuters as contractors and drop benefits. In some cases, telecommuters foot the whole bill for their equipment. You may be able to expense your paper and phone bill costs.

ADVANTAGES

- You can control your own schedule, working before the rest of the family gets up or late at night or before and after dental appointments, errands, and carpool shifts.
- If your children are in school, you can eliminate the need for child care by accomplishing the bulk of your work during school hours.
- You save time and money on commuting.
- Every day is casual day.
- You are not distracted by interruptions from coworkers when you're doing work that requires intense concentration.
- You can maintain the same pay and benefits.
- You can save travel time and expenses, as well as cut the amount of money you spend on lunch and wardrobe expenses.

DISADVANTAGES

- You won't get the immediate feedback, the opportunity to bounce ideas off coworkers, or the camaraderie of an office environment.
- You may find it hard to separate work and family because each may beg for your attention at the same time.
- You must deal with friends and neighbors who think that because you're working at home, you're not really working and can watch their kids, pick up their packages, or come over for coffee.
- You may miss unplanned meetings where important decisions are made.
- You are responsible for the home office equipment you have and won't enjoy the on-site support services available at the office.

- You may incur hidden expenses such as increased heating, lighting, and electricity costs.
- You may lose important networking opportunities.

The following questions are adapted from the "Telecommuters Screening Survey" used by the Southern California Association of Governments as found in *The Telecommuters Handbook* by Brad Schepp.

- How much do you need supervision, pats on the back, and other feedback?
- How strong are your organizational and planning skills?
- How important is office input to your work function?
- Will you take the initiative in requesting input when you need it?
- How self-disciplined are you?
- Will you be able to force yourself to put in the required number of hours in the home environment?
- How computer literate are you?
- How much of a need for social interaction do you have?
- How much experience do you have in your current job?
- How much scheduling flexibility do you need to meet your family responsibilities?
- Will your physical presence cause inconvenience and friction at home?
- Will you have children at home for all or part of the normal workday?
- Do you have access to child care during times when children are there?
- Do you have adequate space in your home to dedicate to your work?
- How long is your commute?

4. Self-Employment

Whatever you call them—independent contractors, consultants, home-based entrepreneurs, freelancers—these part-time professionals have decided to go solo and turn their own skills and ideas into profit. The beauty of part-time self-employment is that as your own boss, you can set your own part-time hours. In fact, the number of hours you work depends entirely on how much money you want to earn.

PREVALENCE

If corporate America can't give you what you want professionally or personally, you are in good company. In 1992, 23.8 million people worked at home running their own businesses. Of these, 12.1 million were full-time, 11.7 million part-time. And most of these small businessmen were small businesswomen. In fact, women are forming small businesses at twice the rate of men. By the end of the decade it is projected that 40 percent to 50 percent of all businesses will be owned by women.

Recently, a new corporate trend has been identified that provides new opportunities for entrepreneurs: It's called outsourcing. Outsourcing takes place when a company contracts for the responsibilities of certain departments in order to cut costs. For example, payroll, accounting, post room, secretarial, and food services can all be farmed out to independent third parties. This creates job opportunities for enterprising individuals who can pick up this work that is no longer being done internally by the company. The new outsourcing trend is fueling small business growth in America and around the world.

An increasing number of professionals looking for flexible schedules are exploiting this trend. And both women and men are finding that self-employment suits their personal requirements.

• **Master of your own daytimer.** When Angie Nandor's boss refused to let her keep a long-scheduled dental appointment, ordering her to make future medical and dental appointments on Saturdays, she said enough. Nandor quit her full-time job as a graphic designer in Columbus, Ohio, to become a freelance graphic designer and desktop publisher. Her new career gave her the flexibility to plan her own appointments when she wants them.

• **No more coffee talks, no more kissy face, no more pink slip threats.** The amount of energy that goes into the politics of a permanent job can be draining, asserts Betsy Mace, a marketing consultant. Now, as her own boss, she spends almost 100 percent of her time getting the job done. "I was never any good at 'kissing up.' I hate corporate politics. This way, I'm no longer subject to the vagaries of the corporation. Once you're established, you're not part of the reorganizations, layoffs, or restructuring."

• **Choosy never sounded so good.** Tired of working on Dilbertlike ungratifying dead-end projects, independent contractors can apply their energies to areas they find interesting and challenging. Elaine Kearney, a consultant specializing in establishing nonprofit consortiums, seeks out her own opportunities, sells her services, and solves the client's problem with her own creative ideas. "I've never gotten fulfillment out of a job the way I do as an independent contractor. I like working with teams, but I prefer the closure of working on independent projects. I like to start it, complete it, then on to the next one."

• **The Gloria Gainer Principle: I will survive.** Suzanne Ely, a general partner of a management consulting company in Los Gatos, California, that specializes in voice technologies, epitomizes the passion that causes many entrepreneurs to take the plunge. Says Ely, "I'm quite independent and a huge control freak. I don't want to work for somebody else." She loves the excitement of working without a safety net. "Only when you walk away from the infrastructure of a company do you truly find out what you're capable of accomplishing. As long as you have that infrastructure, you're never sure if you pulled it off or not."

WHAT HAPPENS TO PAY AND BENEFITS

The self-employed have the potential to earn more than their full-time counterparts—but the key word here is *potential*. This potential for big earnings depends largely on the type of work you do, the current market for your skills, how effectively you can tap into the market, and on how good you are at what you do. A few extraordinary part-time professionals, usually independent contractors, have found that, financially speaking, they can have their cake and eat it too. At the top of their professions, these aces are so good and have become so well-known and so in demand that customers line up for their services. Billing a high hourly rate, they earn even more than what they made working full-time. Marilyn Murphy, for example, made $60,000 in her last full-time job as a public relations manager. As a contractor, her $100/hour rate nets her six figures, an income well above her prior one even if you don't include the value of company benefits.

Similarly, Laurie Garda, a former part-time Bell Communications Research (Bellcore) engineer, was in the right place at the right time in the right industry. She now works part-time as a consultant with a telecommunications firm working roughly 400 hours a year (one-fourth a standard full-time job) making half her full-time annual salary. "In effect, I doubled my full-time hourly rate," says Garda.

According to business consultant David Nye, self-employed professionals in many fields earn more than anybody else. His research suggests that "job shoppers" (Nye's term for independent contractors who work on short-term projects) receive hourly compensation that tends to be 25 percent to 50 percent higher than that received by regular staff in similar positions. This sunny financial scenario, however, contradicts other cloudier salary statistics for the self-employed. According to Richard Bolles, author of *What Color Is Your Parachute?*, home-based self-employed workers earn only 70 percent of their full-time office equals.

You should also know that two out of every three new businesses fail within the first five years of operation. For the owners of these failed businesses, observes Bolles, the word *entrepreneur* can quickly become a glamorous synonym for starving. The good news, however, is that if you survive the initial two years, the risk of failure decreases dramatically. And it is worth noting that according to *Business Week*, the failure rate of women-owned businesses is one-fifth that of men because they are better at research and planning.

ADVANTAGES
- You can find great satisfaction working for yourself and meeting the challenges of running a business.
- You can maintain a career.
- You choose your own work.
- You have the potential to earn more money.
- You don't have to play office politics and corporate reorganizations won't affect you.
- You have a good bridge back to full-time work.
- You set your own hours.

DISADVANTAGES
- Your income may be irregular.
- You may have to foot the bills for benefits if you are not covered by an employed spouse.
- You may have fewer opportunities for feedback and networking.
- You no longer have access to in-house training and development opportunities.
- You may experience ongoing stress from not knowing where your next job is coming from.

SELF-ASSESSMENT: DO I HAVE THE RIGHT STUFF TO START MY OWN BUSINESS?
- How important is autonomy to you?

- Can you work with periods of intense activity followed by sudden lulls?
- Do you excel at organization?
- How well do you persevere in the face of opposition and frustration?
- Are you prepared to take on the scutwork of running a business?
- Do you need a lot of feedback and encouragement?
- How passionate do you feel about the kind of work you will be doing?
- Can you handle working in isolation?
- Can you sell yourself?
- How do you feel about taking risks and living with uncertainty?
- How good are your skills in all the areas needed for your proposed business?
- Can you meet needs for child care?
- Will running a business from home affect other family members?
- How will you integrate your new business with the demands of family life?
- Can you afford the financial risk?
- Can you see your way clear to set aside living expenses for the first six months when you probably will earn nothing?
- Can you afford the upfront expenses involved in purchasing the necessary equipment and office supplies?
- Does your husband's salary provide the family with a base income?

5. Temping

Temps sign up with a temporary professional agency which, for a percentage fee, matches them and their skills with a client company. Temps then work at the company even though they usually receive their paychecks from the temp agency. Temps can choose which projects they work on and in that way can control their own schedules.

Women who want to work part-time hours register their requests in the agency's database. They can sign up for only certain days or hours. Or they can work full-time for several months at a clip, turning down work when they want to spend time at home. When a client request matches the temp's, the agency sends her to the job site. Andrea Meltzer of Executive Options, an executive search firm in the Chicago area that places temporary professionals, says, "You'd be amazed at what employers want. One small company last week wanted someone for just one day a week, and we matched them up.''

PREVALENCE

The growth of temporaries is nothing short of spectacular. Historically, temporary agencies like Kelly Girls have specialized in clerical/administrative positions. But in larger metropolitan areas, you can now find temp agencies in almost every professional flavor—accountants, engineers, management executives, physicians, lawyers, sales and marketing people, insurance specialists, financial services, computer programmers.

Temping, like contracting, allows employers to size their workforce to their current needs. Although they pay a surcharge to the agency in addition to the temp's salary, it's still less expensive than hiring an employee with full benefits.

Consider these facts about the temping of America:

- Manpower, Inc., the largest temp agency in the United States, is now the nation's largest private employer, employing almost twice as many people as General Motors.
- According to the National Association of Temporary Staffing Services (NATSS), there are 1.3 million people working as temps today. That's three times as many as ten years ago.
- The temporary worker population has risen 250 percent since 1982, while the nation's total workforce has increased by only 20 percent.

■ According to NATSS, the National Association of Temporary Staffing Services, 38 percent of temporaries report receiving full-time offers when working on temp assignments.

ADVANTAGES

- You can pick and choose assignments to create your ideal schedule.
- It's a good way to move back into the workforce because you can test and improve your skills and try out employers.
- Many temp agencies provide training.
- You don't have the paperwork hassles of billing and tax reports.
- Someone else finds the work for you.
- If you temp regularly at one company, they sometimes extend in-house training and development opportunities to you.

DISADVANTAGES

- Temping lacks job security.
- Temps sometimes work at a lower rate than full-time employees for doing the same work.
- You may feel like a second-class citizen in your workplace.
- Usually there are no health or other fringe benefits.
- Companies concerned about security issues often limit temps to "noncritical" projects.
- You may end up doing the work no one else wants to do.
- You may not feel part of the team.
- As a temp, you may miss out on training and reward infrastructures.
- Temp agencies may place you in a job unsuited to your skills.
- You can arrange for periods of time off, but usually you must adhere to the client's business hours.
- Temping arrangements normally do not include working at home.

SELF-ASSESSMENT: WOULD TEMPING WORK FOR ME?

- Do you have marketable skills?
- Will you be able to handle not feeling like part of the team?
- Do you need health benefits?
- Temps tend to be assigned to peripheral projects. Would you be okay with this?
- Will your child-care plan be flexible enough to accommodate various working hours?
- Are you comfortable with the feast-or-famine aspects of temping?

PART-TIME SCHEDULES

In determining the type of option that suits your needs, think about your scheduling needs:

- Do you need to pick up children before and/or after school?
- How much personal time do you need for errands, to make phone calls, etc.?
- What kind of school volunteer activities, work with civic organizations, or continuing educational commitments do you have?
- Would three days per week give you enough time at home or at work?
- Would just one day off do the trick?

- Would a five-day schedule that allows you to be there after school eliminate most child-care needs?
- If you've been working sixty hours a week, is what you need a standard forty-hour week?
- Would flextime (early mornings, evenings, weekends) solve the problem?
- Do you have child-care backup for crunch times or when you're working at home?
- Would your husband help out if you have to stay late at work?
- How long is your commute?
- Is there a set number of hours you must work to obtain company benefits?

Part-time Money and Benefits—What You Can Count On, What You Can't

The "Can we afford it?" exercise is an essential step in the decision-making process. Cutting the cord to your full-time job prematurely might mean exchanging the stresses of Superwoman for the even greater strain of worrying about potential insolvency. Not everyone can afford to work less. You have to estimate your part-time paycheck and benefits and carefully assess whether you can swing it.

Benefits

Statutory benefits—those required by law—continue whether a person is employed full-time or not. Employers must pay half of an employee's Social Security liability and pay for unemployment insurance premiums for all employees regardless of hours worked. In addition, employers who offer a 401(k) plan to full-time employees must, by law, include part-time employees in the program as long as the part-time employee works 1,000 hours a year, is twenty-one years old, and has at least one year of service with the company.

Beyond these few obligatory benefits, part-time benefits go all over the map. A study by Hewitt Associates in 1995 reveals that the more hours a part-time employee works, the more likely she is to receive a given benefit. Some lucky part-timers receive full benefits at no additional cost for working as few as twenty hours a week. In other cases, employers prorate the costs of providing benefits based on the number of hours the employee works. A half-time employee would therefore foot half of the cost for medical coverage, for example. This price may sound steep for part-time employees, but it is still a bargain compared with the cost of an individual policy. A medium to large company can almost always secure a better rate. Other companies offer reduced service levels instead. For example, a company may offer part-time employees access to an HMO but make private physician choice programs available only to full-timers.

Some employers refuse to offer part-time employees any benefits whatsoever. The company may see this as a cost-control measure. Or, in some cases, antiquated computer systems cannot accommodate exceptions, and reprogramming systems for perhaps as little as 2 percent of the employee population is not worth the effort. Paradoxically, the inability to reprogram systems for part-timers sometimes results in employers paying full benefits to part-timers at no extra cost to them. They figure it's just easier to give them full benefits.

THE BENEFITS GAP:
PERCENT OF EMPLOYERS AWARDING BENEFITS TO PART-TIMERS

Number of hours per week	Full time 40 %	Part-time 30 %	Part-time 20-29 %	Part-Time under 20 %
Medical insurance	100	76	62	25
Dental insurance	96	69	56	23
Life insurance	99	70	55	23
Long-term disability	95	53	36	11

Source: Hewitt Associates, A Survey of Part-Time Benefits, 1995.

Coming to Terms with Financial Trade-offs

Wrestling with the hard financial questions that come with a shrinking paycheck and benefits package is not easy. Can you adjust to earning less if your lifestyle depends on two full-time salaries? Can you and your family do without the extra compensation when you reduce your hours? After taxes and child care, is your take-home pay worth it? One woman commented, "It was a tough decision. My husband and I could agree on things like giving up the winter ski vacation, but where do you draw the line? Does going part-time mean I can't afford tickets to the circus?"

If your earnings have gone for paying the rent and putting food in the pantry, your answers will be different from those of someone whose income has paid for nonessentials such as family trips to Disneyland or home renovations. Furthermore, a woman's paycheck often represents more than what it can buy. For many women, the size of the paycheck represents status and success, freedom, and a sense of security. These emotional factors shouldn't be overlooked when evaluating the trade-offs.

If your husband earns a hefty income, you may be able to take a substantial financial hit in order to pursue work you are passionate about or to attain increased flexibility. Karen Markus, an attorney and registered nurse, left her law firm to work part-time teaching health law at a local university. Even with occasional speaking engagements and writing opportunities, Markus now earns only about *one-tenth* her former salary. But the choice was hers. A four-day-a-week position with prorated salary awaited her at her law firm—the biggest in the state of California—when she returned from maternity leave. While on leave, she simply decided she liked being a mom better than practicing law. Referring to her unexpected newfound joy of motherhood, Markus happily declares, "I never want to look another billable hour in the face again!"

Others work primarily for the fringe benefits. Fifty-two-year-old Lois Kalafus works twenty hours per week as a licensed clinical social worker in a medical clinic. She knows she could perform the same work in private practice and earn *four times* the pay. Yet, Kalafus feels she's way ahead of her private practice associates. Her employer provides health benefits, paid vacations, a retirement plan, no-effort referrals, and—her personal favorite—freedom from billing patients. Adds Kalafus, "On most weekday mornings I can make an eight A.M. exercise class or take an early walk with a friend. It's a good way to live."

Use the worksheet on page 36 as a guide to determine your financial needs. Also use it to target an acceptable salary when you go job hunting or when you're in negotiations.

THE EVER-LOOMING "PRACTICAL" ARGUMENT AGAINST
PART-TIME WORK: LONG-TERM FINANCIAL TRADE-OFFS

Chances are, if you're reading this book, you've already thought about the long-term financial consequences, and you're willing to go for the part-time adventure in spite of them. But we have to say this or we wouldn't be doing our job. Working for less money over time coupled with fewer promotions than full-time counterparts may mean a permanent lag in income and a smaller retirement account. Even with regular raises, a part-timer will have a tough time keeping pace with full-time peers who are advancing at a relatively faster rate.

■ CAN I AFFORD TO WORK PART-TIME?

Calculate how much you would lose in income and benefits compared with how much you would save on taxes, child care, and other work-related expenses.

The Costs

Some employers offer benefits to part-time employees; others don't. If benefits are lost or scaled back and must be replaced by the employee, that cost must be added to the lost wages to determine the overall cost of switching to part-time work.

Current employer-paid benefits	Would benefits continue?	Cost to replace
Health insurance	__ Yes __ No	$_____
Life insurance	__ Yes __ No	_____
Disability insurance	__ Yes __ No	_____
401(k) contribution	__ Yes __ No	_____
Pension	__ Yes __ No	_____
Overtime pay	__ Yes __ No	_____
Sick pay	__ Yes __ No	_____
Vacation days	__ Yes __ No	_____
Other	__ Yes __ No	_____
Total Benefit Cost*:		$_____

Generally speaking, if you're working a three-fifths shift, you'll earn three-fifths (60 percent) of your previous monthly salary. In other words, if 100 percent of your income in $1,000, you'll earn $600 monthly if you go to a three-day-a-week schedule.

The Savings

There are some savings involved in working less, but exactly how much and where will depend on you. Some families will reduce the number of hours their children are in day care. Others will do more of their own housekeeping and laundry or spend less on work clothes. Determine the areas in which you are likely to save and estimate the monthly dollar amount:

Tax savings (Multiply the decrease in monthly income by your marginal tax rate [15, 28, 31, or 36 percent, etc].
Use the joint marginal rate if you are married filing jointly.)

$_____

Child care $_____
Bought lunches $_____
Bought dinners $_____
Transportation/parking $_____
Hired household help $_____
Wardrobe $_____
Other $_____

Total Monthly Savings: $_____
Monthly Cost: $_____
Monthly Savings: $_____
Net Cost: $_____

Subtract the **Net Cost** from your new salary to find what you would clear each month.

*Reprinted with permission from the *Los Angeles Times*, part-time careers section.

Studies reveal that career women who exit the workforce even briefly never regain the earnings or savings power of their peers who never left. This holds true even after they've been back to work for twenty years. On the positive side, part-timers feel their long-term financial outlook is much stronger than it would be if they had quit work altogether.

LET YOUR GUT AND YOUR VALUES BE YOUR GUIDE

Coming to terms with part-time trade-offs involves reconciling a welter of conflicting factors, including your lifestyle, your love for your profession, your child-care situation, your husband, your ambitions, the ages of your children, and so on. In the end, no matter how many pro and con lists you make, the decision to go part-time will come down to personal values. That's because the one little argument on the "pro" list—more time for your family—may be so weighted in your heart that it's worth fifty "con" arguments.

Personal coach Gail Faris recommends that you write down the things that you value most. Then rank them. Your list might include items such as family, job content, title, salary, long-term financial security, health, friends, exercise, vacation, hobbies, home, etc. Don't try to fit other people's models of the "right" priorities. Only *you* can properly evaluate whether working part-time will suffice in your life. This priority ranking exercise will help you identify not just

■ FIVE WAYS TO KEEP THE BOOKS—AND YOUR LIFE—BALANCED

- *Tally up all your expenses once a year.* According to financial analyst Lynn Ballou, the awareness that results from analyzing where the dollars have gone can net a 10 percent fatter checkbook.
- *Check your tax bracket.* In a progressive tax system like ours, the last dollar in the pot is the most expensive. In 1995, the highest federal marginal tax rate was 38 percent. That, coupled with state and other taxes, might be devouring the portion of salary you are proposing to give up. Conversely, your part-time salary might leave you with almost as much take-home pay because you are taxed at a lower rate.
- *Manage your investments more closely.* Traditional savings accounts barely outpace inflation. Smartly managed investments in mutual funds, bonds, and the stock market, on the other hand, can boost your bottom line and close the gap on the salary you are giving up.
- *Avoid paying taxes whenever possible.* Employers often provide pretax dependent care and health-care spending accounts. Astonishingly, very few eligible employees take advantage of this free money.
- *Defer taxes whenever you get the chance.* Use retirement accounts such as 401(k), IRA, SEP IRA, and Keogh accounts to help slash a tax bill.

what is important to you, but what is *most* important to you. Placing a copy of this priority list in your daytimer or posting it conspicuously on the refrigerator door will serve as daily reinforcement on those days when regret sets in. Says Faris, "If in time you still don't feel satisfied with what you're getting out of your decision, maybe you were fooling yourself. Maybe the flexibility you *thought* was so important is not so important to you after all."

Remember that while choices you make now undoubtedly impact the future, you are not shackled to them forever. Your choices are dynamic. At different phases of life, women recalibrate their priorities because the trade-offs women want to make between profession and children change as careers evolve and families grow up or move away. Going part-time is often a temporary solution, a detour not a derailment, that serves as a bridge back to full-time work.

TWO

Part-time Career Trade-offs

"The mommy track was for wimps, in my less than generous estimation, or for the rare retro gal who had a millionaire husband to support her. Real women died at their desks, one hand still gripping the computer mouse and the other a cup of double espresso."

—Barbara Ehrenreich, "In Search of a Simpler Life," *Working Woman*

Historically, professionals have paid a steep price for their choice to work part-time. Often denied promotions, partnerships, and manager status, part-time "mommy-trackers" have been perceived as marginal players in their organizations. Today employers can and do use part-time employment as a business strategy to gain a competitive edge. Has the price tag for part-time gone down? Clearly, a growing number of extraordinary part-time professionals like part-time CEO Nancy Anderson are playing hardball with the glass ceiling. Their examples alone serve as proof positive that working fewer hours does not necessarily derail a career.

IS THE WORKPLACE WARMING UP TO PART-TIME?

Most of us peer up through seven layers of management to the lofty perch from which CEO Anderson leads her company. What about the merely competent professional? Can she still make it as a part-time professional? Our research suggests the answer is yes. The workplace, while far from embracing part-time, shows definite signs of warming up to it. And not just for superstars.

• A Johnson and Johnson study found that the number of employees who felt they paid a price for using flexible work and flexible leave policies—both of which include part-time components—fell from almost one-half to one-third in just two years.
• Catalyst reports that nearly half of the female participants in another study were promoted while working flexibly, and most felt that they had opportunities for professional development.

But studies and superstars aside, career risks still loom large for most would-be part-time professionals. In a compelling 1993 study of 902 graduates of Harvard's Law, Medical, and Business schools, Deborah Swiss and Judith Walker found that 88 percent of the women surveyed felt that working part-time would be detrimental to their careers. In spite of these perceived career risks, however, most of these women were willing to take on the odds: 70 percent went on to reduce their hours after the birth of a child.

What career trade-offs might a professional expect to face? Are they necessary losses? If so, it's better to know upfront in order to avoid being blindsided later by unpleasant realities. And if the trade-offs are not necessary, how can you avoid them?

THE CAREER SLOWDOWN

It's true. Part-time professionals may lose career momentum when they downshift their hours. They may end up performing more routine professional tasks—litigation support rather than courtroom litigation, a corporate staff job instead of line management. Mimi Thomas, a part-time financial analyst at Intel Corporation, even lost her office after she cut her part-time deal. She walked in one day to find that she shared a new cubicle with another part-timer. Her old office with the mountain view was now inhabited by someone else, a full-timer.

Many ratchet down their jobs by choice. They're more than happy to relinquish a grueling travel schedule and the breakneck pace of full-time office hours followed by an endless string of after-hour business dinners and meetings. New mothers in particular expend so much mental and physical energy adjusting to the demands of a baby that finding a job where they're not totally stretched can be a lifesaver.

Kim Reed willingly agreed to step down from her position as a full-time market communications manager to a "smaller" job. Now she handles only her company's direct mail efforts, one piece of her former job. Although Reed concedes that working part-time has stalled her professional advancement—her new position "feels more like a job than a career"—she's still happy with the trade-off. Says Reed, "With three small children, I don't need more of a challenge. It's enough for now to concentrate on raising my three children at the time when they need me the most."

Karen Bursic, who holds a Ph.D. in Industrial Engineering from the University of Pittsburgh, has experienced firsthand the ultimate career slowdown as a result of working part-time—being the first to go in a downsizing. When the business school at the University of Pittsburgh, where Bursic was teaching part-time, cut back its curriculum, Bursic was among the first to lose her classes. Bursic observes that from a strictly bottom-line point of view, keeping competent part-timers would make more financial sense than more expensive full-timers. "However," explains Bursic, "there is a sense that companies owe more loyalty to their full-time employees."

But her story has a happy ending. Getting laid off from the business school gave her a chance to go back to the industrial engineering school, where her real interest lies. Bursic currently teaches part-time there while also working on leading-edge research in engineering education. As a part-timer she is off the tenure track. "Tenure track professors put in a lot of night and weekend time," says the mother of two preschoolers, "In addition to research and course work, they advise students, sit on various committees, and work under the gun of the 'publish or perish' dictum. I simply cannot do all that right now." She adds, "I will probably be working for forty years and can certainly afford to give up six while my kids are young."

HOW TO SLOW DOWN *AND* STAY ON THE FAST TRACK

Before distance runner Roger Bannister broke the four-minute mile record in 1954, people considered it physically impossible for humans to run a mile in under four minutes. Since Bannister's record-setting breakthrough, however, top runners the world over developed quickly, as if by magic, the physical capability to run sub-four-minute times at competitions fairly regularly. The year after Bannister broke four minutes, 37 other runners broke four minutes. The year after that, 300. What happened was a lesson in mental conditioning. Once Bannister's sub-four time made competitors see that such speed was possible, runners reset their expectations and training and, consequently, achieved new peak levels. The four-minute mile effect holds true for the part-time professional career track as well. As a cadre of all-star leaders breaks part-time career barriers, refusing to accept invisibility or underachievement as a part-time way of life, they raise your expectations for what you can achieve to new heights.

CHERYL LAFLEUR, GENERAL COUNSEL

Forty-one-year-old Cheryl LaFleur burned up the part-time fast track from 1986 to the end of 1991. LaFleur had been a trial attorney with eight years of experience with a top Boston law firm when she had her first child in 1985. Although LaFleur found working part-time incompatible with a heavy trial docket, she couldn't accept stepping off the partner track, the only alternative then available at her firm. Hoping that a large corporation might offer her professional fulfillment as well as some slack, LaFleur networked extensively, eventually landing a job with New England Electric Company System. Says LaFleur, "I compromised and took a slightly lower position with lower pay in exchange for the flexibility I needed as a new mother." Once settled in at the utility giant, LaFleur rose rapidly. Her work as a litigation manager and assistant to the president and chairman were enviable positions even by full-time standards. The only glitch in her part-time career was a one-year delay in getting promoted to senior counsel, a decision which LaFleur thought "quite fair" considering her intervening maternity leave. Says LaFleur, "I went through moments of resentment interspersed with moments of deep gratitude. I'd start feeling like 'Gosh, I'm working just as hard as all the full-timers, so why am I not getting paid as much.' But then the kids would get chicken pox or something or I'd hit a string of snow days, and I'd feel very lucky. All in all, I felt very fortunate." LaFleur returned to full-time when she was promoted to vice-president and general counsel of the $2.2-billion company.

MORE COMPANIES ARE MOVING
INTO THE LEFT LANE

As high-caliber, highly visible part-time professionals like LaFleur penetrate the upper echelons of businesses, managers experience firsthand the valuable contributions part-timers can make. As a result, businesses that normally adhere to hard and fast promotion structures are beginning to make way for them. Andersen Consulting, for example, a worldwide firm specializing in management and technology consulting, traditionally an "up-or-out" industry, has recently changed the way it hands out promotions. In the past, failing to make manager after four or five years sent a strong signal that an employee should move on. Today, Andersen Consulting still demands the requisite skill set for promotions, but has relaxed the time criteria. Says Carol Meyer, partner in charge of Andersen Consulting's worldwide human resources, "Today's policy allows for the different rate at which people develop skills and tries to accommodate what might be happening in their personal lives." Andersen Consulting also makes sure its part-time staff gets an equal crack at more desirable, more visible projects. Adds Meyer, "I think we do a good job of ensuring that part-timers don't just get the leftovers."

THE MOST OUTRAGEOUS OBSTACLE: BEING
PERCEIVED AS LESS COMMITTED

An almost universal complaint of part-timers is that managers and coworkers view them as less committed. One reason for this misperception is that many corporate cultures place a premium on face time. "Be the first in and the last out" is stock how-to-succeed advice given to executives in corporations. Putting in long hours, working through dinner, staying later than the boss, and showing up on Saturday mornings—even if they're practicing their golf swings in the corner or twiddling their thumbs—are viewed by employers as signs of dedication and promotability. Not surprisingly, such face-time management styles lay stiff penalties on part-timers because the whole point of going part-time is to reduce the hours at work.

Karen Nussbaum, former director of the Women's Bureau of the U.S. Department of Labor who is currently the director of the Working Woman's Department of the AFL-CIO, feels that face time poses an unnecessary roadblock for women seeking part-time work.

"There's nothing inherent about the way most organizations operate that requires employees to work endless hours and be on call all the time," says Nussbaum. "The focus should be on productivity and quality." Although face time is an antiquated Industrial Age concept, the woman who has always been considered a rising star will find cold comfort in knowing it. She realizes that as soon as she reduces her hours, her star will lose much of its luster in the eyes of her boss.

A second reason for this perception problem is the corporate penchant for rewarding and promoting slavish devotion to work. Almost by definition, a part-time employee has another major priority to which she is devoted. Ellen Bravo, executive director of 9to5, the National Association of Working Women and author of *The Job/ Family Challenge*, comments, "The expectation that an employee should be willing to meet, move, or travel at a moment's notice puts a woman with family responsibilities at a severe disadvantage. How can a part-timer possibly maintain that type of love affair with her employer? Is it any wonder that 91 percent of senior executives have wives who stay at home? Unless you've got another parent at home or unless you don't have a life outside work, you simply can't drop everything for your job."

Deborah Swiss and Judith Walker, the authors of *Women and the Work/Family Dilemma,* found that working mothers *in general*—not just part-timers—suffered from the perception of being less committed. Their study of women educated in Harvard's professional graduate schools revealed what they describe as a "maternal wall," whereby women with proven dedication to their professions find their commitment questioned by bosses and coworkers as soon as they decide to become mothers. A working mother who then opts for part-time has two strikes against her.

SLOWLY, THE NEGATIVE STIGMA IS DIMINISHING

Fortunately, the perception that part-timers are less committed shows signs of diminishing. Pam Craig, a pioneer of part-time work at Andersen Consulting, has witnessed a virtual transformation of how her organization views flexible work arrangements since she went part-time in 1989. Says Craig, "Back then, before people would even say hello to me, they would blurt out, 'You're part-time?' They were really incredulous. I honestly do not hear comments like that today.

Part-time is a more accepted, common, and positively viewed activity." Now back to full-time as a partner, Craig herself has granted part-time opportunities to several people in the regional industry group she manages. Adds Craig, "Part-time is a wonderful career path, even for the long term. No one questions our part-timers' commitment after years of doing quality work." However, colleagues' initial "I can't believe you're throwing it all away" reaction is still typical for organizations just beginning to experiment with part-time.

Years ago, you wouldn't find *promotion* and *part-time* in the same sentence. In 1989, Hewlett-Packard granted Susan Bockus and Carol Olson one of HP's first management job-share positions as business planning managers. Says Bockus, "Our management may have figured we were so happy with the flexibility, we were no longer interested in being promoted." But they were interested. Their division wasn't growing at the time, but Bockus and Olson pursued their own interest in growth by expanding the size of their group as well as taking on large marketing development projects. Eventually, the pair decided to start their own business and apply what they had learned at HP. They now help small companies figure out how to pursue new markets with new technology.

In contrast to male-dominated professions such as the computer industry, traditionally female-dominated professions—nursing, teaching, and the arts—have long accepted and respected part-timers as committed professionals. Women like Inez McDermott, who works fifteen hours a week as a director of The New England College art gallery in New Hampshire (except when she's changing an exhibit and works forty hours a week), has never suffered from a lack of respect from colleagues. Being part-time is irrelevant in a field where part-time is standard operating procedure. "I don't have to explain anything to anybody," says McDermott of her prestigious art curator and gallery director's position. She organizes and presents nationally recognized exhibits, her gallery schedule is as active as that of any other college gallery, and in spite of the fifteen hours a week, McDermott is considered one of the art leaders in the state.

I'M A MANAGER—I CAN'T WORK PART-TIME

- Forty-one percent of companies surveyed by Catalyst would not permit their managers to work part-time.

• A full one-third of employees surveyed were forced to switch to nonsupervisory positions to get their part-time jobs.

Why do part-timers have such a hard time hanging on to hard-won management duties? The answer lies in part with the nature of the management beast itself. The complex and subtle people issues that form the core of the job require a great deal of time. Managers, at least the good ones, make themselves available to coach, supervise, answer questions, trouble shoot, and do public relations for those they supervise. They travel on company business and serve as career coaches. When employees leave, managers cover for the missing person and jump in to interview and hire replacements, train new team members and monitor them until they get up to speed. Sometimes the role demands nothing less than being there full-time.

At the peak of her full-time career with Houston-based Shell Oil, Lori Johnson managed more than fifty Ph.D. scientists who themselves put in very long hours. Says Johnson, "I couldn't come close to doing justice to that job just working forty hours a week. To be able to hang in there and compete, I had to work long hours. My husband didn't like it, but that's the way the job was." After Johnson had children, she couldn't see her way clear to manage on a part-time basis. "As the person who was asking them to do work and was setting the example, I would have felt guilty about working forty hours, let alone thirty." Instead, she opted for a less demanding, more independent job as an internal consultant and trainer, a position for which Shell had a clear business need and one that she could easily do part-time.

WHEN MANAGING WORKS BEST

Despite the obstacles, managing part-time can work in certain situations:

1. The independent types: It can work if subordinates are self-motivated. CEO Anderson, for example, can manage her company part-time because she has assembled a top-notch team of experienced senior executives requiring little or no hand-holding. Ironically, a key element in her part-time management strategy is a full-time senior management staff that provides the continual face-to-face interaction that more junior level employees require to remain productive.

2. Less is better: Catalyst suggests that a part-time manager should supervise only one to four employees.

3. The client-based organization: At Andersen Consulting, for example, full-time managers and associate partners typically manage several clients. Each client, then, becomes a separate part-time job. To reduce hours, a manager simply cuts back on the number of clients she takes on. From the client's perspective, the level of service remains constant. Andersen Consulting currently limits its part-time program to managers and associate partners who work with clients. More junior consultants who have day-to-day supervisory responsibilities within the firm can only get part-time on a case-by-case basis. Says Andersen Consulting partner Carol Meyer, "Junior people have a much harder time making a full-time contribution in part-time hours."

4. If you have a partner in part-time: Job sharing also opens up management possibilities. Shelly Smith and Patty O'Brien currently share a business planning management job at Hewlett-Packard. Together, they manage six people and are responsible for market strategies and long-range product planning for their division. Smith and O'Brien's manager, Janice Chaffin, feels that their management position is uniquely suited to job sharing for several reasons. First, the job itself is a full-time position and could never be done part-time. Second, an important management function, strategic problem solving, is enhanced by having two brains bearing down on a problem. Says Chaffin, "Together, they develop very creative solutions to complex business problems. One person working in their job might have a harder time."

Business consultant Barbara Miller, suggests that part-time managers offer a hidden bonus to employers. Their part-time schedules encourage coworkers to learn to make decisions in their absence, to learn new skills and new areas of the business, and to build new relationships with clients. Such "empowering" cross-training is not likely to happen with a full-time manager in charge.

ASSESSING YOUR OWN WORKPLACE CULTURE

Despite the possibility for career setbacks, the potential for topflight part-time work is growing. Part-timers can and do travel, they manage, they win promotions and raises, and they earn the utmost respect of managers, colleagues, and clients. It doesn't matter whether you are a never-say-die Harvard-educated superstar who steadfastly refuses to defer dreams of making it to the top or whether you are a competent professional who wants to keep a hand in a much-loved profession while your children are young. The potential is there.

Yet few offer an unqualified yes when asked if they are completely happy with their part-time careers. Many feel they suffer career penalties as a result of their choice. They are often frustrated by an intractable work culture that undervalues the efforts of part-timers and overlooks them when the time comes for promotions and for handing out plum assignments.

On balance, part-time status seems better than the full-time alternative with its attendant full load of guilt, stress, fatigue, and burnout to most of the women we talked to. For them, "having it all" has evolved to the more realistic concept that Catalyst founder Felice Schwartz describes: "You can't have it all. Today, having it all means having what you value most."

How can you minimize the risk of career penalties? Learn the politics of your office and company so that you make informed choices. Ask yourself: Who gets the attention? Who gets the great assignments? Who are the lesser vessels and what are they doing? Who was granted a part-time position and what are they doing? If some part-time requests were rejected, how many and were the requests made by top performers or only marginal ones? Network with other part-timers to find out their stories. You may discover that your company doesn't play fair. Still, forewarned is forearmed.

Once you assess what career penalties (if any) might be imposed, you can figure out your course of action: (1) You can decide to stay at your company and make the necessary trade-offs, (2) You can look elsewhere or go out on your own. Or, there's a third option that's not for the faint-hearted, but may still be the best choice if you need more flexibility now and don't have time to establish yourself elsewhere. (3) You can decide to stay on and persevere in teaching your company a new way of doing things. Whatever your choice, you will need to learn more about what managers think about part-time professionals, the subject of the next two chapters.

PART TWO

YOU AND MANAGEMENT

Working with the System:

An Interview with Sandra Sullivan

In 1989, Sandra Sullivan sold her manager at Aetna Life & Casualty on setting up a compressed workweek with a telecommuting agreement. When word of her innovative work arrangement leaked out, curious co-workers, managers, and even people outside the company barraged her with excited phone calls asking her, "How'd you do it?" Impressed by the high interest, the enterprising Sullivan saw a business opportunity in the making. When Aetna downsized and eliminated her business unit, Sullivan grabbed her severance check, finished up her masters in human resource management, and launched Flex-It, a consulting firm based in Southington, Connecticut, that specializes in flexibility know-how.

Q: *Who are your clients and what do you do for them?*

A: I work mostly with large corporations. Besides the standard fare of helping them design and implement flexible work policies, I train managers in flexibility. I help them make the mental shift from a management style that's stuck in the Industrial Age to one that capitalizes on the Information Age.

Q: *What do you mean by "capitalizing on the Information Age"?*

A: How you measure performance, for one thing. In the Industrial Age it was valid to expect that if a worker spent forty hours running a machine, you'd get twice as much work than from the worker spending twenty hours at the machine. But this is the Information Age. If a worker can use technology and use it well, that worker may produce as much sitting at a computer in twenty hours as somebody who spends forty hours at it. It's the productivity that should be measured, not the hours at the desk.

Q: *How do you help them make this shift?*

A: Not easily. You can't really tell them anything—you can't tell them that Industrial Age paradigms don't work anymore. So my specialty is devising creative little exercises that allow managers to see for themselves.

Q: *Can you give me an example of one of these exercises?*

A: I do a "popcorn experiment." I hand three volunteers a spoon, a set of chopsticks, or a knife. Then I time them while they eat a cup of popcorn. When they're finished, I ask the group, "So who won?" Invariably, the group picks the person with the spoon because he finished the popcorn first. Nobody ever picks the chopsticks person because that person always finishes the task last. The connection eventually dawns on the group that based on the Industrial Age paradigm of "time on the job equals productivity," the person with the chopsticks would always win. They begin to see the flaws in the old "he who sits at his desk the longest is the most productive" thinking.

Q: *What's the most common objection you hear?*

A: It's the manager who says to me, "My God, how am I supposed to keep track of all these employees on flexible schedules." And I say, you can't, of course. But if you are trying to keep track of all these schedules, you're not managing, you're policing. As long as you don't try to micromanage the whole process, you can have five thousand different work arrangements. Then I say to HR, if you want your managers to be policemen, that's up to you. But if you don't, then you've got a training issue on your hands.

THREE

Why Your Company Should Say Yes

"Nothing but good has happened to any company because of adopting flexible benefits. Not one case in all these years."

—Milton Moskowitz author of the *Working Mother 100,* on his ten years of interviewing companies about flexible benefits

It's important for you to understand why managers should say yes to your part-time professional proposal. Why is it so critical that you understand why your part-time work arrangement is good for business? It's important so that you don't commit that most common of part-time errors: thinking of yourself as a supplicant asking for a big favor. The knowledge that your part-time position is justified by legitimate business reasons—and sometimes even saves the company a bundle—should boost your confidence as you approach the negotiation table. You will *know* you are not asking for any favors. A confident attitude, along with an airtight proposal based on business needs alone, make for an unbeatable combination for not only getting your part-time job but also for making it work over the long term.

PART-TIMERS ARE GOOD FOR BUSINESS

Here are six big reasons why part-time professionals are good for business.

1. Your company retains an experienced employee. By virtue of your training and experience as a current employee you are best suited to achieve the company's business goals. When employees want flexibility and can't get it from their current employer, they often leave. The resulting holes in the organization—even when eventually filled in by new employees—hurt a company's overall ability to compete in the marketplace, not to mention the huge expense of such turnover.

Exactly how much could it cost your company to refuse you a part-time position? Think about these numbers: Standard industry estimates put the replacement costs of salaried employees at 150 percent of salary, a figure that reflects recruiting, hiring, and some initial training costs. Pacific Bell, for instance, estimates that it costs $110,000 to recruit, hire, and train a new programmer. Similarly, a San Jose law firm spends approximately $100,000 when they hire a new lawyer.

And that's just for one employee. Multiply that by the total number of employees who leave because employers refused a part-time request, and suddenly not granting it seems fiscally irresponsible. Chubb Corporation, a New Jersey insurance provider, counted all the employees who quit over two years because they couldn't get a flexible schedule. Estimated replacement costs for these lost employees for 1992–1993 totaled a whopping $3.3 million.

But these heavy replacement costs don't even tell the whole story. By the time an experienced employee leaves, a company's investment in that employee's development is a major one. Consider the ten-year veteran of a company currently making $80,000. According to the international consulting firm Towers Perrin, her employer may well have invested more than $1 million on salary and benefits alone. If a company refuses her request for part-time, they put a sizable investment at risk. And that doesn't even include training. You could argue that another ten-year veteran representing another company's $1-million investment could replace the employee who quit. But a new employee will probably not be as cost-effective as holding on to the current one. New employees, however skilled and experienced, take time to get up to speed. Their coworkers and supervisors also require a period of adjustment to mesh as a team.

Companies that sell "thoughtware"—the ideas and expertise of their employees—face incalculable losses when their people walk out the door. For example, people and their expertise are Bell Labs Research's single largest asset. Bell Communications Research, the research-and-development arm of the seven now independent regional telephone companies, automatically enrolls new hires in postgraduate programs while still on salary. This hefty initial cash outlay for continuing education is followed up by several years of intensive, highly specialized on-the-job training. Bell understands the critical role employees play in executing their business strategies and appreciates employees as a source of sustainable competitive advantage. Laurie Garda, a former Bellcore part-timer, maintains that Bellcore didn't hesitate for a second to offer her a part-time position. Says Garda, "My boss had a business need and I filled it. You just don't go walking around and find people who know this business. The trained minds of their people are their biggest investment, so they go to great lengths to keep them."

2. Companies need experienced employees in order to offer customers value-added services. For many companies, staying competitive means providing the business savvy of experienced, long-term personnel to their customers. Investment bankers Hambrecht & Quist are turning to part-time as a way to retain experienced people, a surprising move in a male-dominated field famous for long hours. Investment banking is a relationship business. Because customers like to work with people they already know, losing employees who have established these relationships hurts. Besides, the more seasoned the people are, the better quality advice they can deliver to clients. Says Hambrecht & Quist CEO Dave Case, "Young people give you energy and intensity, but not necessarily wisdom. And the people with wisdom don't necessarily want to keep pushing hard forever."

Public accounting firm Ernst & Young is also tapping the potential of part-time programs to enhance its own emphasis on "value-added" services. Like all CPA firms, Ernst & Young supplements its bread-and-butter auditing services with advice on how to improve the client's business. But, as Ernst & Young partner Dave Ward points out, "In order to deliver the ten best ideas on how to grow business, you need people who know the client's industry inside and out." This new demand for experience is changing the way the accounting firm thinks about the needs of employees. Says Ward, "We still need young people right out of college to grow up within the organization, but we need to expand our staffing model to keep and bring more people who have acquired business acumen—a lot of whom are women who have flexibility needs—who can really bring something to the table." Ward predicts, "The way we're going, it's not inconceivable that you're going to be able to walk in here

■ THE GOLDEN HANDCUFFS OF FLEXIBILITY

Top companies and important studies show that flexibility works if you want to keep your employees:

• Seventy-one percent of people on flexible work schedules at Johnson and Johnson in 1993 said that flexibility was "very important" to their decision to stay at J&J.

• A random sample of IBM employees in 1992 found that work/family programs ranked sixth in their decision to stay with Big Blue. Among top performers, however, such benefits were the *second* most important reason for staying with the company.

• A 1990 survey study done for *Working Woman* showed that women who worked for bosses who accommodated requests for flexible work arrangements were seven times more likely to stay.

• After the First Tennessee Bank introduced a policy allowing full-time workers to switch to part-time without giving up benefits in 1993, 85 percent of full-time employees who had planned to quit because of family reasons decided to stay.

• In the early 1990s, the accounting firm Deloitte and Touche noticed a disturbing trend: Its most promising women often quit just before they were about to become partners. After researching the problem, the firm introduced a series of work/family benefits in an effort to reduce turnover. The strategy, which included part-time hours for partners and the opportunity to be made partner while on a part-time schedule, has paid off. The percentage of women admitted to partnership in 1995 was 21 percent, versus 8 percent in 1991. And the turnover rate for female senior managers dropped eight percentage points between 1993 and 1995.

in five years and see one-third of the people working in flexible work arrangements."

3. Your company can use part-time opportunities as a recruiting tool. Part-time and other flexible benefits help companies compete for the best and brightest. A part-time option may make a difference to a candidate who is entertaining different job offers, explains Amy Rothwell, executive search recruiter from Yardley, Pennsylvania, if the job is a good career move and if she thinks it might help her balance work and family in the future. Says Rothwell, "Let's just say it greases the skids—it's not necessarily a dealmaker."

Even job candidates who don't want part-time work now—and may never want it—will ask about it as evidence of how the company treats its people. Today, in the interview process, managers expect questions about part-time possibilities, a topic that was formerly considered taboo. Both new graduates and more experienced hires want an environment that appreciates diversity and the need for flexibility. Says Andersen Consulting's Carol Meyer, "Historically, our partners and recruiters may have been turned off by the topic, but now they're used to it. They see the long-term value in these flexible initiatives and are responding appropriately."

4. Part-timers can increase the productivity of the company. Forty percent of the U.S. workforce is struggling with work and family responsibilities according to the American Management Association. At times, many of these individuals function poorly because they are distracted by family concerns, resulting in an estimated $3 billion annual loss in productivity.

Part-timers have negotiated their personal time upfront. As a result, they can focus their full attention on work when they are on the job. Management consultant Barbara Miller calls surreptitiously juggling family concerns at work "working under the radar." In one cubicle you might have a daughter spending hours on the phone trying to find living arrangements for her mother who has Alzheimer's while down the corridor a father is slipping away to check on a sick child at home under the guise of making a sales call. It's a common problem for full-timers and a real drain on productivity.

A compelling study of part-time employment in Germany conducted by the McKinsey and Company Consulting firm concluded that part-time boosts productivity in several ways. Permanent part-time workers tended to perform better. For example, computer operators working reduced hours boosted their productivity by an average of 20 percent without raising their stress levels. Less absenteeism provided yet another source of increased productivity: Absenteeism among part-timers was often half that of full-time workers. Helmut Hageman, the author of the study, further concluded that introducing part-time work can have a tremendous impact on productivity for the many companies suffering from absentee rates of over 10 percent or from "mysterious surges of illness on Fridays and Mondays."

Manager after manager reports the same story: Part-timers work virtually 100 percent of the time on the job. Like members of a relay team who sprint faster for shorter distances than teammates who run the whole distance, part-timers arrive at work to pick up the baton fired up and as one woman put it, "feeling under the gun." The deleterious effects of prolonged full-time work—the fatigue and burn-out—slow down full-time workers. Part-timers can maintain a fiercer pace—often working through breaks and lunch—because they've taken a little time off to recharge.

5. Companies can solve tough staffing problems with part-timers. The use of part-time workers can extend a company's operating hours. For instance, part-time professionals on the West Coast who take on an unusual schedule in exchange for fewer hours can

■ **PART-TIMERS PRODUCE!**

From pharmacy to banking, part-timers are adding to the bottom line:

"It's a simple equation: A satisfied employee equals a productive employee."

—Sandra Sullivan, CEO of Flex-It

"The gain of two hours a day, which have made such a huge difference in my life, have not made a correspondingly huge difference in the amount of work I can do. When I'm at work, I work harder and a lot quicker."

—part-time pharmacist Sarah Sandell

"Some partners are willing to schedule one-hour meetings with everyone who brings in a business plan. I can't use my time like that unless it's a pretty high probability that a proposal will bear fruit."

—part-time venture capitalist M. J. Elmore

"Part-timers may have important relationships at work, but they aren't the ones volunteering for the United Way or mentoring high school students or participating in Friday afternoon beer busts. They don't participate in a lot of extracurricular activities during work hours, because getting the job done during work hours is their top priority."

—Hewlett-Packard manager Nikki Ogden

come in at 6:00 A.M. to handle East Coast customer calls. Second, companies competing in what former *Harvard Business Review* editor Rosabeth Moss Kanter calls the "global corporate Olympics," an environment that often demands a twenty-four-hour workday, can use part-time to boost customer service capabilities. The night banking service introduced by the U.S. securities firm Merrill Lynch, for example, gave it an important competitive advantage in new and tougher international markets that can reach from Canton to Milan.

Also, many CEOs today face the challenge of how to keep staffing costs down while still retaining the ability to innovate, develop new products and businesses, and enter new markets. Sometimes part-time employees can provide a solution. Executives at Whitehall-Robins Healthcare, a division of medical giant American Home Products Corporation, confronted this dilemma when the nonsteroidal antiinflammatory ibuprofen went over-the-counter as Advil® in 1984. The low profit margins on the over-the-counter drugs compared to prescription drugs precluded the expense of expanding the direct sales force. Then president Stan Barshay had a creative solution. Why not start up a part-time sales force? The resulting flextime sales force held 90 percent of the workers to nineteen hours a week. At twenty hours a week, employer benefits kicked in. Barshay's brainchild performed well: Costs stayed down, profits soared, and the part-time sales force, largely comprised of mothers with children and a smattering of retired pharmaceutical managers, was happy.

Does the practice of limiting workers to nineteen hours a week as a way to sidestep benefits payments seem questionable? Yes, in that it extracts an unacceptable price from those workers who desperately need health insurance and other benefits. No, in that such work fills an important need for part-time professionals. Julie Lemke, one of the part-time salespeople with Whitehall, was delighted with the setup. Says Julie, "Most of the people didn't need the benefits. What they really wanted was the flexibility. So the flexibility worked on both sides." (For more on this part-time controversy, see chapter 12.)

6. Your company will spend next to nothing by offering you part-time and will get a lot back. The incremental cost of granting an employee part-time status is quite low. Usually employers prorate their salaries and benefits to reflect the percentage of actual hours worked. If a woman worked twenty hours a week, or 50 percent of a forty-hour workweek, she receives 50 percent of her salary and 50 percent of her benefits. If she shares an office and equipment with coworkers, overhead stays the same.

The cost to administer a part-time program is next to nothing. But what about the big expensive staff of human resource specialists who run these family-friendly programs? Not a problem. Only the largest companies have a specialist devoted solely to administering these programs. Often the people who run the work/life programs juggle their human resources responsibilities with other jobs such as employee training or benefits administration. They struggle to create new family-friendly programs with tiny budgets and little or no staffing. Budgets for work/life programs are so small, says Fran Rodgers, the founder and president of WorkLife Directions in Boston, that they "don't even show up on the pie chart." Therefore, when each employee is viewed as sharing in that cost—because almost all employees use flexible benefits of some sort—the cost per person remains quite low.

If a company doesn't have in-house human resource personnel, they often use what work/family expert Ellen Bravo calls the "Hey, Dolores!" method of winning change. An employee and her manager work out the details between themselves. They then tell "Dolores," the payroll accountant, to adjust the employee's salary and benefits accordingly.

Companies requiring more structure may well need only a written policy. Consulting companies such as Sandra Sullivan's Flex-It specialize in writing flexible policies and training management in how to implement it. All most smaller companies really need, says Sandra Sullivan, is a "global vision statement and a global policy statement that applies to everyone. That's a lay-up. For $3,600 and three days of consulting, and you've got it."

Most companies worry more about the costs of *not* offering the programs. Hewlett-Packard's work/life manager Susan Moriconi speaks for many companies interested in helping employees better balance their lives, "We don't really care whether or not a part-time option results in increased productivity or a dollar savings, although we think it does. As long as the program is cost-neutral, that is, as long as we feel we're getting back as much as we're paying out, HP's happy."

IT CAN WORK FOR YOU
AND YOUR EMPLOYER

The implementation of part-time work arrangements is a step that increasingly spells "winning" in today's competitive markets. For you, the message is clear: Part-time is not about asking for favors. It's about crafting a business deal in which both you and your employer benefit. You offer much-needed expertise and loyalty. In return, your company gives you a reduced schedule that meets your personal needs.

All the research suggests that part-time professionals offer a cheap way to cure turnover-related ills and to ensure long-term company health. However, in spite of mounting evidence that supports a manager saying "yes" to your part-time proposal, sometimes managers' short-term objections will block your way. Read the next chapter about potential objections managers might raise and how to overcome them.

FOUR

How to Beat the Top Fifteen Management Objections

"The safest reaction people can give is, 'No, I don't think it will work.' I cannot think of ever having an idea surface where everyone liked it. It's so much easier, so much safer for people to say, 'No, it won't work.' Then you can't blame them if something doesn't work."

—Congresswoman Pat Schroeder

Ask any work/life expert what the biggest obstacle is to implementing part-time arrangements and most will respond unhesitatingly: middle management. Their objections can crush your request like a truck over an empty soda can, whether those objections are knee-jerk "nos" or carefully considered "what-ifs." Managers make the final decision for or against your part-time request. And well they should. After all, as the people on the frontlines dealing with the logistics of a nonstandard schedule day to day, bosses know that your job performance will have an impact on theirs. That's why your manager will probably have reservations about your working part-time.

However, their objections also create a golden opportunity. An airing of these objections allows you to discuss the nuts-and-bolts of how your part-time job would work and to allay any fears about possible drawbacks. Here are the objections that managers most frequently raise and strategies for overcoming them.

MAJOR OBJECTIONS YOU'LL CONFRONT

1. If I let you work part-time, everybody will want to. The "floodgate effect" objection is based on the fear that once a manager grants one part-time arrangement, the dike will be breached, and a deluge of pent-up additional requests will flood into the manager's office. Granting those requests will inevitably leave the department swimming in unfinished work, missed deadlines, and chaos will follow.

Research, however, clearly sinks this one. None of the many studies has found a single company that has experienced the dread tsunami of requests. Why? Partly for the same reasons that only 2 percent of employees take advantage of flexible work arrangements: most workers can't afford to. Of those that can, many are unwilling to risk steering their careers into untested political waters.

If your manager persists in irrational floodgate fears, suggest a trial period. This accomplishes two things: first, a trial period officially positions your part-time arrangement as a unique pilot program and not as a new policy. This deflects the possibility of coworkers' viewing your special situation as an open door, and in your manager's eyes, open season on him. And second, in the unlikely event that the requests do come rolling in, this strategy gives your manager a way out.

2. How will I explain to others who want to reduce their hours that you can but they can't? I'm safer if nobody works part-time. The equity issue comes up when a manager allows one employee to work part-time and does not accord others the same privilege. Dealing with it can easily become an exercise in diplomacy and semantics. The Chubb Corporation addresses the slippery problem with the concept of "differential equity." Differential equity means there is equity in the process but not in the results. In other words, everybody can ask for part-time, but not everybody gets it. A manager has the irrefutable right to decide that business needs will not be served by granting a part-time request. For example, all employees, regardless of the type of work they do, have the right to write a proposal requesting a part-time telecommuting position, including the part-time security guard who wants to telecommute. But the manager can easily turn it down because it doesn't meet the business needs of the job. Make sure your manager understands the company policy—if there is one—and tell him or her about differential equity if he or she doesn't seem aware of the concept.

3. But what about the Friday meeting? The staff meeting allows managers to update workers on company news, delineate problems, brainstorm solutions, assign project responsibilities, and motivate the troops all in one shot. Quite reasonably, they want to avoid time-consuming individualized debriefings.

Staff meetings also meet your needs. These meetings become a stage where you can visibly demonstrate the ongoing value of your contribution and to counter any notion that you're not a serious player. You want to inject insightful comments and stimulating problem-solving ideas in a meeting, not in an off-line discussion days after the fact.

The solution is clear: If possible, design your schedule to include the standing meeting. If you absolutely must have that day off, offer to attend by teleconference. A client of Sandra Sullivan's took this strategy a step further. She also offered to teleconference for other less regular meetings. "Wouldn't you know," says Sullivan, "there has never been a meeting so urgent that she had to attend over the phone?" Yet it was her willingness to compromise and offer a workable solution that turned the manager's "no" into a "yes."

4. We don't have a part-time policy. This need not be a problem. Formal policies, like jackets and ties in church these days, are not required. Eighty major companies surveyed by Work/Family Directions said they allowed part-time. Yet only 51 percent had formal policies. In many cases, company "policy" is based on what one manager and one employee work out between them. Although an official policy has decided advantages—it sends a signal to managers that part-time requests are legitimate—many part-time employees prefer having no policy. They feel employee and employer can act more nimbly to create a part-time position together whcn no formal policy and bureaucratic process is attached.

If your boss tells you that there is no policy, tell him or her the above information and suggest that the two of you set your own policy. If no one has ever worked part-time in your company and if your manager likes to try new things, sell him on the idea of being innovative and making company history. If this strategy works, make sure to write up a flattering article for the company newsletter. If your boss still doesn't feel comfortable without a policy, check with your human resources department to see about the current status of a part-time policy. Perhaps they would be interested in drawing one up and would help iron out any administrative details.

5. What if customers need to talk to you on your day off? In today's competitive workplace, a lot rides on a company's ability to respond quickly to customers. Managers, therefore, are understandably wary of granting part-time to employees in customer-sensitive jobs. More often than not, nothing short of total transparency to the customer will do. Companies can't afford any glitches in service or any inconvenience to the customer.

There are two approaches to this problem. The first is to make your switch to part-time so invisible that customers never know that you're part-time. When customers call in on Wednesday, your day off, the call is forwarded to your home. Or the voice-mail message simply states: "I'm not in the office today." The listener assumes that you are attending an off-site meeting. The message goes on to refer them to someone else if they need immediate help or it asks them to call you back on Thursday. Interestingly, Karen Stoeller, work/life manager at Harris Bank, observed that the only customer complaint they have ever had in their considerable years of servicing their customers with part-time staff was about one woman who left a voice-mail message on which she said, "I'm at home on Fridays."

The second approach is to make yourself as available to clients from home as you are from the office by using voice mail, e-mail, and call-forwarding and by giving customers your home phone number and the phone numbers of backup staff in case of emergencies.

As an end-run strategy, suggest to your manager that the two of you canvass the customers before drawing the conclusion that a part-time schedule would lead to dissatisfaction. Asking customers directly can yield unexpected responses. Almost without exception, customers prefer to work with people with whom they have formed good working relationships and who understand their account. Almost without exception, what they hate is breaking in a new representative. Their preference for continuity is so strong that as long as customers feel confident their needs will be met, they are often surprisingly open to change.

On a related note, when Ernst & Young customers learned that a service representative who had been working part-time and one day at home, was being forced back to full-time, they called management to complain. They preferred the part-time arrangement: "We liked being able to catch up with her on Fridays when we could count on her being home. When she was at the office, it was impossible. She'd be in meetings or away from her desk, and we'd always end up playing phone tag."

6. It's going to be too much work for me to manage your nonstandard schedule. For each employee, full- or part-time, managers produce annual performance evaluations, personal development plans, and compensation packages. On top of that, for each part-time employee, managers usually must redefine a job to a part-time level, make additional phone calls to set up meetings, and often work around an unusual schedule in order to assign work with customers. To be sure, these additional managerial duties are unlikely to overburden a manager. Nevertheless, do what you can to lighten the load. If nothing else, show sensitivity to and appreciation for the extra work they're taking on. Promise to set a schedule and then stick to it, avoiding erratic schedules that change every week or month. If your boss knows you'll be out on Mondays and Fridays, but can be counted on being there on Tuesday, Wednesday, and Thursday, planning should be fairly straightforward. Second, assure your manager that you will be available in a crunch. If your department is being audited, if you're closing a big deal or working on deadline, your willingness to be flexible is a big point in your favor. Third, take responsibility for keeping others updated on schedule changes. If your company uses computer software scheduling, offer to enter your schedule in the system regularly. All your boss will need to do is push the button to gain access to updated scheduling information.

7. I already have one part-timer on my staff. Another one will mean too much paperwork. Obviously, for every additional part-time person, the extra time spent on additional managerial responsibilities becomes more significant. Hewlett-Packard work/life manager Susan Moriconi advises managers who seek her guidance about granting multiple part-time opportunities that they also have the right to a reasonable working environment just as their employees do. Says Moriconi: "Look, I myself have ten direct reports. If everyone wanted to work part-time, I'd have twenty. In my type of organization, that's too much. Too many part-timers constitutes a legitimate business reason to reject a proposal."

What can you do if the lifeboat's already full and you desperately need to climb aboard? If you accept the premise that part-timers in your manager's group have hit "critical mass," apprise your boss of your interest in going part-time when a part-time position does open up. Consider enlisting your manager's help in spotting other departments where you might find a part-time opportunity. Then redouble your own networking efforts to ferret out areas within the company where you might make a contribution on a part-time basis.

8. If you go part-time, who will pick up the balance of your workload? Good question—and one you need to spend a great deal of time answering before you present your proposal to your manager. Proactively presenting ideas for the workload redistribution before the manager has a chance to start worrying about it is your best defense. The "hire another part-timer to pick up the slack" response is a cop-out and only serves to pile recruiting and hiring work onto the manager who may already feel overburdened.

Look around. Perhaps an ambitious individual in your department would take on chunks of work that would broaden or upgrade her job responsibilities. Assure your manager that while the trainee is learning her job, you'll be right there to make sure the quality of work doesn't deteriorate. When Lynn Tinley, the chief financial officer of VMI, a small software company, decided to reduce her workload, she found the small size of the company disadvantageous because of the correspondingly small pool of potential delegatees. But eventually Tinley found a way to redistribute her excess workload to two employees. She passed off the compilation of statistical reports to a newly hired, full-time marketing person. Next, Tinley taught her assistant to handle some of her accounting functions. Both employees were happy to take on more challenging work and viewed it as a career opportunity.

A word of warning: Don't fall into a trap that trips up part-timers regularly. In your zeal for a reduced schedule, don't promise to achieve your full-time workload on a part-time schedule. Shoehorning your full-time responsibilities into an impossibly cramped period of time is a formula for disaster. You will end up more stressed out than ever and, in the process, you might tarnish your professional reputation.

9. If you work at home, how will I know if you're really working? This is what's called a "line-of-sight-management" problem. An employer believes, if she can't see you working you must not be working. Overturn this objection by converting your part-time request into a productivity issue. Figure out what aspects of your job can be easily measured—writing reports, preparing slide materials, spreadsheets, drawing sketches—and write down what tasks you will accomplish when you work at home. Then commit yourself to delivering these projects on a schedule. Assure your manager that your failure to complete the work as stated constitutes grounds to end the arrangement.

10. Your responsibilities have an impact on too many people in other departments. They'll never go for it. Suddenly it's not just your manager's objections that you must overcome, but objections surfacing at every point of contact outside your own department! A preemptive strike works best here. Call Betty in accounting or John in public relations to see if both would be amenable to contacting you at home on your days off in case of an emergency. To gain their approval, employ the same techniques you used with your direct manager: Promise to publish a clear schedule, make yourself available for meetings, stress how and what work will get done, and suggest a trial period.

If Betty or John resists, take another tack. If your manager or your manager's manager wields sufficient clout in your organization, perhaps he or she could go to bat for you. Pam Craig, a partner in Andersen Consulting's New York office, sometimes lobbies for her part-time employees. When Craig wanted to place one of her part-time employees on a project in another group, the group rejected the plan. Craig then spent a great deal of time on the phone selling them on the merits of the arrangement. Eventually her colleagues agreed to give the woman a chance. Says Craig, "The upshot is that the arrangement has been very successful."

11. I'm afraid of being slapped with a lawsuit. At this writing, we are not aware of any discrimination suits that have been brought against companies for rejecting a part-time proposal. Litigious society that we are, however, such legal actions would surprise no one. In instances where requests for flexibility pile up in one department, a dismayed manager may wonder how he can avoid alienating employees. If he/she prioritizes requests giving greater weight to requests that pertain to family conflicts over other personal requests, this means employees are being treated differently. And once a manager starts to treat people differently, he starts to worry about appearing to discriminate. Again, the best preventative medicine for such a hypothetical suit would be an overriding business need or the differential equity concept.

12. Coworkers will resent it. This resentment could happen. Of 14,000 workers questioned by Hewitt Associates, more than 20 percent responded that they worked longer hours, tackled more difficult assignments, or in other ways covered for full-time coworkers who were parents. It seems only logical that the problem would be worse for part-time working parents. If the work culture demands that full-timers routinely log in ten to twenty overtime hours every week and full-timers observe the twenty-hour-a-week part-timer breezing out the door at three o'clock sharp every day, jealousy and resentment inevitably creep in.

Promise your manager that you will try to manage this negative perception. How? Your willingness to stay late or to take work home when the pressure's on. Poll coworkers yourself to see how they feel about your going part-time, diplomatically reminding them, of course, of the financial hit you will take by doing so. Getting feedback from coworkers and showing them you'll go the extra mile when necessary should take some of the sting out of your enviable schedule. You may also consider purposely taking on the occasional dirty project that no one else wants to do and setting up your child care arrangements so that you don't have to turn into Cinderella at the stroke of 5:00 P.M. Finally, it may help to remind your boss gently of the whines and grumbles heard from coworkers whenever anybody— full-time or not—gets assigned to a special project or team. In general, coworkers resent anybody getting a special privilege. Promise that if coworker resentment reaches the point where it has an impact on group morale, then the arrangement will end.

13. I can't afford a full head count for a part-time position. Concerns about the effect on head count have killed many a part-time request. Understanding the issue will help you understand your own negotiating position, so let's explore it more fully.

Head count simply means the number of employees at a company. Accountants use head count to calculate financial statistics such as revenue per employee or profitability. They also base overhead costs such as rent, utilities, office space, and equipment purchases on head count figures. Division managers may be allocated money to purchase equipment, cover the rent and utilities, and buy supplies based on head count. Accountants also use head count figures when they make reports to stockholders or when they draw up reports to be distributed internally.

But the head count system turns nasty for part-timers because companies that use a head count system count a part-timer as a full head count. Example: A department with fifteen full-time and four part-time (twenty hours) employees would have a head count of nineteen. This penalizes managers for using part-timers in two ways. First of all, it can cost them money because managers pay budget expenses such as benefits, rent, utilities, supplies, and equipment for each head count. Never mind that the head count only uses a portion of the whole amount—the manager foots the bill as if every employee worked full-time. Head count puts the manager in the unenviable position of either having one part-time person who contributes only half to productivity count as one whole person in terms of overhead.

Or, in the case of a job share, two employees do the work of one employee, but are charged the overhead of two people. Often employee bonuses and performance evaluations of the managers are based on revenues per head count figures.

Second, many companies use head count to limit the number of staff members in each department. If the company allows a certain group a head count of twenty and one of those twenty wants to go part-time, the head count will still be twenty even though, accurately speaking, the manager now has nineteen and a half employees. If he or she wants to hire another part-timer to pick up the leftover workload, the manager's got a problem because another part-timer would put the manager over his limit by bringing the head count to twenty-one. The inaccuracies of the head count system may pose a great disincentive for managers to hire part-timers if they are short of open positions.

There is a solution: the full-time equivalency system (FTE). This system doesn't count heads. It counts hours worked. Thus, a part-time employee working half of a forty-hour workweek would be counted as 0.5 FTEs. Example: The same department as above with fifteen full-time and four part-time employees with a nineteen head count would have seventeen full-time equivalencies because each part-time employee would be counted as a half.

Under this system, a manager can readily hire two part-timers to do the work of one. Simple and logical, we thought. Why doesn't everyone do it this way, you ask. On one side of the argument stand those who believe it is too difficult to implement an FTE system for a small percentage of the workforce. In addition, if a company's information systems software is outdated and overloaded with data, the change might require either a major overhaul or a brand-new system. On the other side, representatives from companies who have actually converted from the head count system to FTE, such as Aetna Life and Casualty and Harris Bank, have found the process to be remarkably cheap and easy.

Here are some things you can do:

- Talk to your human resources department for their ideas on ways to circumvent the head count problem. Find out if plans are underway to convert to an FTE system. If not, find out why not. Offer input about why FTE would be a useful improvement.
- Suggest a "de facto" FTE system as described by Susan Moriconi whereby an asterisk appears next to the head count figure indicat-

■ CONVERTING TO AN FTE SYSTEM

How Hard Is It?

Managers, work/life experts, and the accountants who actually converted their own systems tell us:

"It was easy for us to make the switch once we realized our key business measures were off with the old system. Then we were motivated."
—Carol Meyer, managing partner with Andersen Consulting

"It should be a no brainer. It's a stupid accounting thing that's preventing managers from doing the right thing for their employees."
—Hewlett-Packard manager, name withheld by request

"We've been happy with our de facto FTE system. For job-share positions, for example, the management staff just knows that head count is going to be listed as two instead of one, and they adjust the budget accordingly."
—David Kennedy, New England Electric

"Before we went FTE, I used to tell management that it would be easy just to put an asterisk next to a head count number that represents a part-timer. Then we could adjust the numbers."
—Susan Moriconi, HP's work/life manager

"It's a calculation you make once. Then you adjust it annually. Most companies have the software capability to plug in the ratio. If not, it's not a tough computation for accountants to figure out."
—Ellen Bravo, 9to5

"I think the biggest piece of it is from user support, getting the communication out to the company and having them understand what FTE is all about and how it can benefit the managers, supervisors, and employees. Programming it in, well, I hardly remember doing it. It was no big deal."
—Curt Blau, Aetna, Inc., human resources information manager who converted their system to FTE

"Before we had a big system, I used to let people determine the calculations themselves. It was as simple as sticking a paragraph in the budget manual packages explaining how the manager should make the calculation. Then they budget accordingly."
—Tom Nostin, Aetna, Inc., accounting manager

ing that that particular head count be treated at the appropriate percentage rate.

- Research the budgeting system your company uses, and with that information create a detailed cost sheet that shows that your part-time position or your job share does not translate to twice the expenses.

14. Part-time just won't work in this company. Some companies are just plain anti-part-time. In a *Fortune* magazine interview with Microsoft CEO Bill Gates, the conversation turned to Paul Allen, Gates's boyhood friend and the man with whom Gates cofounded the software behemoth. Paul Allen went through a near-fatal bout with cancer, after which he decided to spend more time with his family and on his passion for professional basketball. He proposed working on special projects part-time at Microsoft, more or less in a consultant capacity. Gates responded with all the grace and compassion of Attila the Hun: "It was great that Paul got better. We wanted him back more than anything. But there was just no part-time way to come back to Microsoft. If you were going to be there, you were really going to work hard. We all knew that. It's still the way."

It doesn't have to be "the way," but for some companies, it is. If your company has a "part-time professionals need not apply" culture like Microsoft's, you can choose to leave or you can stay and put up a fight. If you decide to take a stand and fight, make sure you're up to the full-time hours and stress of pioneering a new work option in a hostile culture.

15. I just have a problem with part-timers. Prejudice against part-timers can have many sources. Perhaps your boss's objection stems from a bad experience managing a part-timer. Perhaps your manager thinks and acts more like a cop on the beat, policing more than managing. Perhaps your manager believes that little of substance can be accomplished in a short week. Whatever the reason, such deep-seated biases are often difficult to change. Asking a manager to suspend his or her beliefs during a brief trial period is one possibility, although approval of a test period would appear remote.

You might try probing deeply to find the real objection that is blocking his approval. Then try to break down that objection by asking, "What would it take? What would I have to do to make this work?" Don't allow your boss to sidestep the issue by repeating his initial objection. By pressing for concrete answers, you might hear some objections that you can break down. Listen carefully for any

■ MANAGERS WHO DON'T HAVE A CLUE

Reports of dinosaur-sightings on the part-time front:

"I knew I'd never get part-time from my boss. This was a man who would take an empty briefcase home at night just to give the impression he was going to log more hours that day."
—financial analyst, currently part-time at another firm

"My boss would purposely ask for something on a day he knew I was off."
—former part-time chief financial officer of small company

"When I approached my boss about a job share, he dismissed it out-of-hand: 'Two people managing the same department? You've got to be kidding. That would create unbelievable problems with the people you'd be supervising!' He didn't think about it for more than an instant."
—full-time retail merchandising manager

"I was asked to serve on a committee to review candidates for our group's manager. When I saw that one of the candidates was a working mother of two small children, I took my manager aside and told him I couldn't honestly support her for the position, because in my experience full-time working mothers resent the hell out of part-timers."
—part-time financial analyst with large corporation

"I had been working part-time for three years when I got a new manager. His first comment to me? 'I don't care for part-time people. I don't think it works.' That was the beginning of the end for me."
—former part-time MIS human resources consultant

"Whenever my boss would ask me about my children or make reference to my part-time schedule, he would always say that his cats were his 'kiddies.' As if caring for a cat was the same thing."
—former part-time software writer

hints that your boss thinks you have a performance problem. Often managers hesitate to give this kind of news straight out. However painful to hear, though, now's the time to find out so you can fix any problems before you butt up against any more brick walls.

As a last ditch effort, consider seeking counsel from the human resources department. Proceed carefully and discreetly on this one, however, being careful to deal only with people you can trust to keep your confidence. Your manager would undoubtedly resent your having gone over his head, which could permanently sour your relationship. If you end up leaving the company, let the human resources department know that one of their managers is not practicing what corporate policy is preaching.

■ "The Dinosaur strategy involves ignoring all new directives while lumbering along doing things the way you've always done them."

—Scott Adams, *The Dilbert Principle*, 1996

UNDERSTANDING WHERE THE OBJECTIONS COME FROM

There are the fifteen most common ways managers shoot down part-time proposals. We want to emphasize that we do not mean to imply, nor do we believe, that these anti-part-time managers are malicious. They're just human. And their very human reactions are often rooted in emotion, not logic. First of all, managers worry about anything that might have a negative effect on their own job performance. Second, like most people, they prefer to stay in their own comfort zone, avoiding the risks of trying something different. And third, some managers like to think of themselves as "tough." They think accommodating employees is a kind of weakness and will lead to losing control over them.

Unfortunately, you can rarely address these emotional blind spots head-on any more than you can change people's minds about their children, their pets, or their own talents. Still, it helps to understand where the objections are coming from and realize that it takes people a surprisingly long time to let go of an old pattern and adapt a new one. In the meantime, stick to logical, well-thought-out, business-based points. In sum: Kill 'em with information.

PART THREE

STRATEGIES FOR GETTING IT—FROM THE INSIDE

Alone at Your Level:

An Interview with Chris Schulz

Chris Schulz works four days a week managing clinical information systems at a progressive hospital in the San Francisco Bay area. Schulz manages projects for directors of various departments of the hospital. When we spoke it was 8:30 P.M. on a weeknight and she had just walked in from the video store. She felt so bad about staying up until 2:00 A.M. the night before working on some number crunching and graphs for the hospital's downsizing that she promised her Swedish au pair and her two sons she'd make it up to them with a fun movie night.

Q: *It sounds like you're swamped at work.*

A: Yes, even the directors are calling it the summer from hell. We've got a few months to show that we can balance the budget—or else. All the departments are desperate for data in the panic and they're asking me to provide it.

Q: *So how did you go part-time in this job?*

A: Well, first of all, my job is in project management, which is to say I deal with a lot of people issues. As my boss and I have since found out, it's a hard job to do part-time. At the time we adopted our second son, no one at my level was working part-time. But they had just hired a tremendously talented technical person whom they really wanted for the job. He had the expertise to call his own shots. His stipulation for taking the position was that it would be four-fifths. At first I resented this because I had already made it clear that I wanted to cut back. I reminded my manager that I really wanted part-time and asked him what I could do to get it. Was it something he would consider? I said that I knew I might not get the schedule I wanted right now, but I needed to know for the future. He asked me to write a proposal, and I did for an eight-tenths schedule. He approved it immediately, but I wouldn't actually get the schedule for another eighteen months. I asked him to write that down since nobody else knew he had promised it to me. It was our private agreement, but I was covered if somebody new came along. After eighteen months passed, on July 1, 1993, I got it.

Q: *Why did it take so long?*

A: He anticipated that the workload would go down in about a year. We'd finish a lot of the big projects, and then it would take another six months to stabilize things. It really helped that suddenly I had a role model who set a precedent that allowed me to put together a part-time schedule.

Q: *Did you go public with your private arrangement?*

A: Yes, it's sort of an interesting story how my boss and I ended up broadcasting the new reduced schedule to the rest of the staff. We were just beginning the hospital downsizing in the summer of 1993. My boss ended up using my eight-tenths part-time as an example of what everybody needed to do, that is, to reduce the number of FTEs. The two-tenths of my former full-time schedule was part of what he anted into the downsizing pot. Suddenly, my once-confidential deal got the big public stamp of approval.

Q: *Could you still get promoted working a four-fifths schedule?*

A: No. At least not to a bigger title. But I can increase my expertise. By controlling the projects I design and work on, I increase my marketability outside the hospital. Eventually I'd love to join some small hot consulting group. You can make a ton of money that way and you have a lot of flexibility.

Q: *How have you succeeded in going part-time in a job where very few can?*

A: I think the best piece of advice I've taken is "Manage your manager."

Q: *Meaning?*

A. Well, the most recent example is what I'm doing right now and why I was up until two last night. I'm doing heavy-duty cost analysis. The directors of the various departments in the hospital have a very short time frame in which to come up with large sums of money they're supposed to cut from their operations. One of them asked me to help her find new models of care delivery that would save money. She needed data. I worked day and night, having no idea of exactly what I was supposed to do, but I told her I would give it a shot. I had to learn a new software system. Put everything through the wringer. Create graphics. Then my manager was supposed to take all this stuff on the road. People really liked what I did, so one of the other managers asked my manager, "Can Chris do for us what she did for Margaret?" On my day off, I drove over to the finance department to do a big analysis and had them drag out everything they had.

Q: *Sounds like your part-time schedule is more than full-time.*

A: Yes, but this is a crisis. People who aren't flexible, who won't do anything extra, will find themselves without jobs. With all this stuff under my belt, I'm in a strong position. But it has been the summer from hell. My manager says it can only get better. I choose to look at it as something exciting. We're redesigning the way we give health care.

FIVE

Turning Your Full-time Job into a Part-time One

"Ninety percent of the people that ask for a flexible arrangement do this: They go to their manager and say, 'Gee, I'd love to work a flexible schedule.' And that's it. Period. And they wonder why they don't get it."

—Sandra Sullivan, flexibility consultant

If you're on the inside, you have the most power of all part-time professional wannabes. In fact, a 1993 Catalyst survey of employees with part-time arrangements indicated that most of them had been insiders with *seven years* of company experience before switching to part-time. As an insider, you've already established yourself as reliable, your talents as invaluable, your loyalty unswerving, your track record impeccable. You know the people, the management philosophy, the corporate perks and quirks. Your coworkers trust you. Perhaps your boss has occasionally—or even just once—muttered the word *indispensable* and your name in the same sentence. You couldn't ask for more leverage when it comes to negotiating a reduced schedule.

Your company wants you to stay. As we saw in chapter 3, replacing a highly skilled employee is expensive and time-consuming. Hiring and training a new person is potentially unpleasant. According to a 1989 Catalyst report, "the single greatest motivator for companies to explore the use of flexible work arrangements . . . is the retention of high-performing, valued employees." So, if your boss knows she can count on you to get the work done well and on time, chances are she won't reject your proposal—at least not immediately—if only because she'll recognize that you aren't happy with the arrangement you have.

Still, it won't be easy.

First of all, the opportunity is not going to come knocking for you. It's rare for a boss to walk in one Monday, even after you've won the company a multimillion-dollar contract, and say, "I think I'll cut back Jamison's hours so she can spend more time with her first-grader, that cute little son-of-a-gun." You'll need to raise the issue yourself.

Facing the emotional and managerial objections discussed in chapter 4 might throw you on the defensive. Don't let yourself be thrown. Instead, be prepared. Shelly Smith, a mangement-level job-share partner at Hewlett-Packard, recommends that you approach your part-time proposal as if it were a marketing project:

1. *Overresearch.* Ask around. Assess the corporate culture to find out how open your company is to part-time. Who else is doing it? Who would go for it and why? What are the benefits to everyone involved? Where could you be most useful to the company? To your manager? To coworkers? To the customer?

2. *Design and focus.* Pinpoint exactly where the part-time opportunity is and visualize how it will fit the schedules of your full-time colleagues. Design the "product" according to the "marketing" needs. Troubleshoot with a confidante and spot weaknesses to which your boss may object.

3. *Write the killer proposal.* Be explicit. Write down hours, days, special meeting arrangements, new home-office equipment you'll purchase, etc. Cover it all. Use calendars if you feel they will demonstrate your actual time in the office better, because managers love visual aids. Feel free to give your manager several options—she'll appreciate the choice.

4. *Make the showstopping presentation.* Be confident. Use the right language. It's always best to frame your words through the company's words and not your own. Initiate the discussion as a blueprint for a solution, not as a problem for your manager to solve. And most of all, don't position the arrangement as a favor. You're not asking for any favors. Your personal reasons are not the issue here, only the business matters.

5. *Negotiate the arrangement you want.* Agree to stay until 8:00 P.M. on Tuesdays in exchange for the Friday at home. Take a minor salary cut if they'll pay for all your home-office technology needs.

Perhaps we should add a sixth step: Persist. Above, Sandy Sullivan, the flexibility consultant, says that 90 percent of people who request a flexible schedule ask and don't follow up. Her model of persistence is to kill them with information. "Ask them what their major objection is, then break down that objection. The more prepared you are, the more likely they are to turn a no into a yes. Managers are just scared—they're just afraid of change."

This chapter will help you to do just that. It will help you do the research, put together a complete proposal, and, finally, negotiate your way to your desired part-time position.

OVERRESEARCH

Planning and preparation represent 80 percent of success in any negotiation. At this point in the book, you're probably already 40 percent of the way there. Chapter 1 evaluated which part-time work option is best for you and introduced some scheduling issues. Chapter 4 looked at potential objections your manager might raise and how to overcome them. But you're not done preparing yet. You must look closely at your negotiating partner: Size up the boss and the company culture so that you can plan your pitch accordingly. And size up your own motivations and leverage, too. What is your clout with the company? The more research you do the easier it will be to focus on the exact position you want.

Sizing up the Decision Maker

It is not always clear who the major players in the decision are. Will your boss have the final say-so? Does the department head's opinion factor in? Perhaps the ultimate decision is made by the company's number-two vice president with whom you've never talked one-on-one. If possible, try to make sure that your direct supervisor takes part in the negotiations as his or her backing is critical. Figuring out who the players are determines the voice and strategy of the proposal. Lynn Tinley, a former part-time CFO of a Silicon Valley software company, went through lengthy negotiations with someone other than her boss. Missing that critical link caused problems down the line. Her direct boss didn't buy into her new schedule totally. Even though her schedule was legitimate, he continued to send the hidden message that he really wanted her and expected her to be at the office every day. For instance, he would frequently call for work to be turned in on days when she was off.

Often the boss takes the issue to higher-ups and will also need the nod from the human resources department. Do these people know you and your work? If not, you'll need to document more of your successes. What other key people or departments will be affected by your going part-time? Maybe you'll need to make several copies of your proposal.

Once you've got the players (and decided who will be receptive to the idea and who will cause problems), track down others within your company who have won or lost the game already and ask about their experiences. Start a list of success stories, complete with manager's names and phone numbers, so that you can provide these references during negotiations, if necessary. If your company doesn't have a part-time track record, go outside the company and seek out successful parallel situations that you can add to your proposal.

Remember, the human resources department is your ally, too, especially in a large corporation where you may not know of others in your situation. Find out the policies and guidelines concerning proposals, and compensation and benefits. Ask human resources if they have a sample proposal for you to look at or if they can suggest any contacts that would help you build your case.

How well a flexible job option works depends on the person as well as the job. You've already decided you want to simplify your life by working part-time. Here are some questions to help you zero in on the option that will work best for you and will help you capitalize on your experience, abilities, and interests. Tom Peters calls the contemporary business world the Age of Homework. No one is going to hand you a job; you are going to have to coach yourself through the process. It's your responsibility to size up your needs, design an option that will fit in your workplace, and then pursue that option for all you're worth. Many people want to jump ahead, opting for action over reflection, but most of the happy endings we've heard about resulted from a thorough front-end self-assessment process.

What's Your Leverage?

"The problem with Hollywood," says Kathryn Linehan, part-time media consultant, "is that everything's about who you know and what you've done lately.'' But we all know it's not just Hollywood. It's no surprise that negotiating a part-time professional position is also about what you've done lately. The more impressive your contributions, the stronger your track record, the greater your clout. The more recent, the better. Clearly, the best time to ask for part-time is when you're riding the crest of a professional wave, not when you're in the trough. What do your past performance reviews look like? How long have you been there? What accomplishments illustrate your particular skills or strengths that you could include in a proposal. What aspects of your job require your unique experience?

We recommend spending some time digging up evidence that can prove your value to the organization. Congratulatory letters, memos or performance reviews are all possibilities. Career guru Richard Bolles writes in *What Color Is Your Parachute?* that ''the more time you spend on figuring out what makes you stand out from nineteen other people who can do what you do, the better your chances.''

We want to emphasize that this doesn't mean you have to be a superstar. Although most companies we talked to look on part-time as a privilege awarded to top performers, that usually means the top 50 percent. Most employers put it like CFO Tinley: ''I just have a bias for competence. Your professional credibility and reputation for excellent work will go a long way toward silencing critics of your plan.'' Conversely, if you're viewed as a marginal performer or have been on probation at any time, it's going to be a much tougher sell.

For example, Lori Johnson's track record at Shell Oil may have done all the selling for her. She was moving up the Houston organization, and had already paid her dues the old-fashioned way, in middle management. As one of the few female department managers working long hours in their research-and-development facility, she knew she could talk openly with her boss. Johnson told him she couldn't continue to work at that pace now that she had children and suggested that he start looking around for a replacement. At that time in 1989, no one in her large division at Shell worked part-time. Oddly enough, he was the one who suggested a part-time schedule. He helped place her in her current position as an in-house business trainer. ''It seemed like such a leap for Shell that I said, okay I'll try it. It was still off the track in a group that someone once referred to as 'that funky little group called training,' but it has allowed me to achieve my objectives,'' says Johnson. ''What really helped me was that they looked around and said, 'Who else can do this?' And when there's not anybody apparent, you've got it made.'' And it doesn't hurt to be a veteran. "I spent nine years at Shell creating a name for myself and now I don't really have to sell myself that hard anymore."

DESIGN AND FOCUS

Traditionally when we want a better situation, we want to be promoted or hired into an already existing position. But most part-time professional positions do not already exist. Top Fortune 1000 clothing designer Donna Karan loves to say, "If it's not in my closet, I design it." And so can you. When preparing for part-time negotiations, *haute couture* means creating a blend of responsibilities that you excel at, enjoy doing, and that are also valuable to your employer. The following three exercises will help you to design that job.

Break Down Your Job

Using your job description as a guide, break your current job down into modules and rank them according to their importance to you and to your employer. In their book on flexible work arrangements, Maria Laqueur and Donna Dickinson suggest keeping a log of daily activities, keeping track of the amount of time you spend on each, and ranking them according to importance. Make sure to include breakfast meetings, work-related social obligations, and time you spend working at night and on weekends.

Analyze the Breakdown

Look at your job breakdown and designate which parts you want and can keep and which you would be happy to lose. When making your list of responsibilities you want to keep, consider (1) what pieces of the job you enjoy and excel at (and are highly valued by your company); (2) when each task can be accomplished (before or after office hours); (3) where it must be done (over the phone from home or only at the office); and (4) who else could either share or take over a portion of your current workload (the time-wasters could be delegated or eliminated).

Find a Niche

Look around your department and see if you can identify a weakness and then design a part-time job to fill in the gap. That way you're not just serving yourself—you're filling a need. Take Amy Rothwell's experience at an executive search firm in Philadelphia where her job placing high-level executives at the CEO and VP level required travel at a moment's notice. After the birth of her first child, Rothwell cut her work week down to four days a week, and stayed on call on the fifth. Says Rothwell, "After my second child, I took a hard look at the two-hour-and-twenty-minute commute and at the fact that my four-year-old was starting a school with morning-only hours. On top of that, I was pregnant." Knowing the industry and being realistic, Rothwell left the firm to focus on midlevel recruiting, work that she can mostly do from home. "I may have left some prestige behind," says Rothwell, "but that's okay. I'm now managing my own business and am enjoying the career satisfaction that working on your own brings." The lesson is that it's sometimes easier to create your perfect opportunity than it is to garner support for a scaled-back version of your current job.

Write the Killer Proposal

There is no avoiding it—you've got to write it down. And it's up to you whether the words are written in brick, wood, or straw. The killer proposal, a comprehensive and well-defined part-time job proposal, should be built to provide a clear picture of what job you want to perform, why it's needed, and *how* you are going to perform it. After reading this section, you should be able to write your own killer proposal in just a few hours—especially if you've done your research.

Caroline Albright, a full-time public-relations manager with For-asa, Inc., a medium-size San Francisco company that sells educational products and services, went through the process of designing a document that would help her negotiate a part-time position. The former University of Texas cheerleader is thirty-two and has been a public relations manager for five years, enjoying a reputation for solid contribution and being easy to work with. After Albright and her husband had done all the "number crunching and out-of-the box thinking we could stand," they finally concluded there was no way she could continue working full-time and take care of two little girls eighteen months apart in age. Full-time was definitely too much but she didn't want to surrender her job completely.

She calculated that twenty-four hours a week would allow her to get some "real work" done. Albright began by determining which three-fifths of her job she wanted to retain. Her responsibilities included handling all communication with the media, designing com-

■ **FIVE REASONS TO PUT IT IN WRITING**

Even if it's not required these explanations might even convince you to go to your keyboard right now.

1. "How do I know what I think until I write it down?" This quote by novelist E. M. Forster illustrates the chief virtue of putting it in writing: It helps you clarify your thinking on the subject. The writing process forces you to analyze all aspects of your proposed job, from workload to scheduling, and then evaluate its workability. An added bonus: In the process of persuading yourself of the merits of your concept, you gain the confidence to sell it to someone else.

2. "A written proposal tells the employer how serious you are," says Nancie Tatum, a human resources consultant with a software company. Writing it down elevates your proposal from the status of a friendly understanding to a formal business agreement.

3. A killer proposal makes it difficult for managers, especially those who know you, to turn you down. A killer proposal that anticipates and surmounts their objections bulletproofs your case against a manager's potential concerns.

4. A written proposal serves as "workquake" insurance. Today's constantly changing business environment often leads to games of managerial musical chairs. Chances are, after one manager agrees to your proposal, another manager—this one in the dark about your flexible arrangement—will replace her. A verbal agreement becomes a matter of "he said, she said," and you don't want to risk hearing a "that was then, this is now."

5. In companies where no flexible work arrangements exist, a killer proposal can actually increase your power within the organization, even though you're part-time. Your innovative request to do a professional job part-time shows unusual initiative. A smart manager might well consider your risk-taking attitude to be advantageous for her and the company. Innovators with follow-through are a company asset, no matter how you look at it.

pany brochures and other marketing materials, and managing several out-of-town trade shows every year. She examined her own strengths and interests, what parts would best fit into a reduced schedule, and which parts of her work were most important to her boss. She concluded that the straight PR segment offered her the best opportunity. As you read through this section, you will see how Caroline distilled her part-time concept into a well-thought-out proposal that eventually landed her the job she wanted.

Getting Started: Anatomy of the Killer Proposal

Although the most common variety is a two- or three-pager, killer proposals come in all shapes and sizes. Memorandums of understanding, cover letters, and ten-page documents in legalese have garnered professional-level part-time jobs as well. You must judge for yourself what type of document would be most appropriate for your situation.

In general, if you have obtained a verbal go-ahead from your employer or if your employer frequently works with part-time professionals, a memo or one-page document will suffice. However, more complex job arrangements, as well as employers uncertain or skeptical about initiating part-time arrangements, warrant longer, more formal proposals.

Although every killer proposal is unique in its content and style, most include these sections:

- The *job summary* outlines the basic components of the job you want and how it meets a business need for the employer. It appears first, but is frequently the last item to be completed.
- The *qualifications* section tells the employer why she should rely on *you* to do the job in this alternative arrangement instead of any of ten or more candidates who will work full-time.
- The *job description* details the scope of your job, including the breakdown of responsibilities we did in the focus stage and a plan for meeting them.
- The *logistics* section addresses scheduling and communication issues; offers solutions for getting the work done, including those pieces that you no longer have time to do; provides a few specific examples through common scenarios and a plan for a performance evaluation; and outlines any new equipment that may be needed.
- The *employer benefits* section shows the employer what advantages your flexible part-time arrangement offers the company, your manager, coworkers, customers, and subordinates.
- The *compensation* section proposes a salary and benefits package. You might find it advantageous to hold off on filling this section out until you succeed in selling the first part of your plan to your manager.

- The *appendixes* (optional) contain supplemental articles, case studies or anecdotal evidence that support part-time work of the type you are proposing.

The Job Summary—What *You* will do for *Them!*

In two or three succinct, strong paragraphs the job summary does the heavy lifting for your whole proposal. Often the only section a manager will read carefully, it must be intriguing and viable enough to keep your boss reading.

The basic components are the title of the job, a list of responsibilities, the business need your job addresses, and what uniquely qualifies you for the position and the type of work arrangement you propose. Including a sentence indicating the reason you want the part-time job is optional. Keep this part brief and clear, you'll elaborate later.

TIPS WHEN WRITING THE SUMMARY

1. *Ask yourself what you can do for your company—not what your company can do for you.* The secret of a winning job summary is to position yourself up-front as having the ability to satisfy a pressing business need or solve a particular problem. A "look what I'm gonna do for you" proposal is much more effective than the proposal that seems to beg for a favor, a common flaw of flexible-work proposals.

2. *Think in terms of benefits to your company, not just jobs performed.* Citing real benefits instead of listing responsibilities or accomplishments can be difficult, but it pays off. Independent contractor Elaine Kearney started her job proposal with "I will set up four user forums" as a benefit. Then she went a step further and added, "Four new user forums (network) would mean almost 1,000 more attendees at the company's annual conference." That's when the employer will really take notice.

3. *Assume that your employer will only read the summary.* Write it to stand alone, keeping it brief but compelling enough to invite further reading. Don't use references to other sections— a busy decision maker who only intends to glance at the rest of the document will get annoyed at complicated cross-references.

4. *Revise the job summary when you're done with the rest of the proposal.* Make sure it captures any important points that were added when you fleshed out the rest of the proposal.

Caroline Albright used her five-year history with Forasa and her extensive knowledge of the company's dependence on public relations efforts to boost sales and to keep customers. She exploits this business need to her advantage in her summary on page 93.

Qualifications—Position Yourself as Different and Better

The Qualifications section is your opportunity to highlight what skills or experience make you indispensable to the employer. Here is your chance to go beyond the standard résumé. Your qualifications section is an opportunity to give you an edge over your competition by positioning yourself as the logical, and possibly the *only,* choice. If you're a long-time company veteran or a heavy-hitter, this is your chance to show in a nonthreatening way that you deserve the opportunity.

TIPS WHEN WRITING THE QUALIFICATIONS SECTION

1. *Don't just be different, be important.* For example, Elaine Kearney wrote her own part-time ticket because she was the only one in her firm with the knowledge to write the highly technical contracts and bylaws for organizing a user group. Similarly, a sales representative we spoke with held a lucrative part-time position because of her fluency in Mandarin and her familiarity with Asian markets. Maybe you specialize in a particular kind of law or medicine or focus on a particular industry.

2. *Perform an informal market survey to figure out what specialized skills your company needs.* Listen for people in your company or industry saying, "Gosh, if we could only find someone who did *Web site design,*" or "No one has been able to do *diversity training* for us effectively." Or, ask respected co-workers where the biggest needs are in the company. These statements are invitations to the savvy part-time professional ready to carve out her niche. If your set of skills doesn't fit, think about how you can gain the skills or experience you need to fill the niche.

3. *Quantify your accomplishments when possible.* Hard facts, such as "Generated $1 million in client billings" or "Contributed 20 percent of the company's sales last year" demonstrate competence and reliability, the two qualities most essential for part-time success.

4. *Concentrate on your merits, not your reasons for wanting part-*

time employment. Tell the employer what you bring to the table. You wouldn't argue for a raise because you wanted a bigger house. Similarly, whether your reason is to be with your family more, to care for an aging parent, or simply to pursue a personal interest, *it is irrelevant to the employer.* Your employer is interested in your merits only.

Early in her career, Albright learned the value of what management guru Tom Peters calls the "how fat is your Rolodex?" factor. Her networking efforts resulted in personal contacts that are vital to Forasa's public relations efforts. In her qualifications section, she emphasized her long-term relationships with editors and analysts in the news media and highlighted her most measurable public relations accomplishments (see pages 95–96).

Job Description: The Substance

The Job Description section lists your responsibilities in detail and outlines anything concrete you will produce. You should be painstakingly inclusive here—don't leave any job out, even one as menial as filing.

TIPS WHEN WRITING THE JOB DESCRIPTION

1. *List responsibilities in terms of tasks, projects, clients, customers, patients, volumes written—whatever is relevant to your business.* Breaking your job into discrete parts helps you spot potential problems you need to plan for.
2. *Summarize the responsibilities into a list of what you promise to deliver.* State precisely what you will complete or milestones you will reach.
3. *Avoid vague promises.* For example, write "I will place fifty ads per quarter in trade journals," not "I will make Forasa a household word."

Albright divided her job into discrete projects and tasks. She would be responsible for developing the overall press strategy every quarter and continue to write and edit press releases and other press briefing materials. In addition, she would manage the activities of the public relations firm, brief editors and analysts when making important announcements, and help executives prepare for interviews. She promised to deliver exposure in trade magazines, newspapers, and analysts' reports.

The Logistics—the Nuts and Bolts

How exactly is all of this going to work? The Logistics section gives the blueprint. What is your back-up plan if you're sick? How will you communicate with coworkers and managers? Who will evaluate the quality of your work and when? How will you handle meetings that occur on your day off? Who will do the parts of your job that you're jettisoning? What equipment will you have at home, if any, and who will pay for it?

Albright proposed a twenty-four hour workweek during which she would work from 8:00 to 3:00 Monday through Thursday, with a break for lunch. This schedule allows her to spend some time with her children in the afternoon and allows her to participate in lunch meetings with analysts and editors. Her contingency plan relied on her availability via phone, e-mail, and fax machine in her off hours. Luckily, she had a flexible child-care arrangement to accommodate interruptions when she's working at home. Albright has already found another employee to write marketing materials and will start training a new employee to manage trade shows. Albright also proposed that the company split the expense of the home-office equipment she must purchase.

Last, Albright proposed a three-month trial period. At the end of that time, she and her boss will decide whether the plan worked.

TIPS WHEN WRITING THE LOGISTICS SECTION

1. *Be clear about your schedule.* "I will work from 8:00 to 12:00, Monday through Friday," is better than "I will work twenty hours per week."

2. *Explain your reasons for the schedule you propose if they are relevent to your employer.* A Hewlett-Packard saleswoman proposed working from 2:00 to 7:00, Monday through Thursday, so she could telephone the distributors in Asia during business hours. Without the explanation, the schedule would definitely have raised an eyebrow—did she just want to sleep late?

3. *Identify potential scheduling conflicts.* By presenting a plan for overcoming potential problems, you can preempt objections from your manager.

4. *Do not underestimate the hours necessary to complete your proposed workload.* Part-time professionals cite self-inflicted overscheduling as the number-one pitfall of the arrangement. Estimate the number of hours you will need to carry out each task to verify your proposed schedule. Make certain that you

■ SOME THINGS TO THINK ABOUT WHEN DEVISING A SCHEDULE

"With a Tuesday/Thursday schedule, it seemed like both days were Mondays. It would take me two hours each day to get back in the swing of things."

—physical therapist

"Working five short four-hour days didn't give me time to concentrate deeply enough to accomplish anything substantial. I needed at least five hours at a clip."

—radar engineer

"Coming in for partial days every day of the week work out better for client contact."

—CPA

"I scheduled for visibility. Most of the law partners were always there in the afternoons. So I worked in the afternoons from 1:00 to 5:00 so that it looked like I was always there at their disposal."

—tax attorney

"Personally and professionally I needed time around the coffee machine and also lunches with colleagues."

—marketing manager

"My forty-minute-each-way commute meant that it was terribly inefficient to work a short day five days a week."

—marketing researcher

really can do everything in the time allotted. Otherwise, you may find yourself getting part-time pay for full-time work— not the bargain you were looking for.

5. *Help your manager find an owner for the parts of your job you're relinquishing.* Suggesting alternatives not only solves the problem for your manager, it also removes a possible objection to your plan. But be careful not to slough off too much grunt work on peers.

6. *Establish checkpoints in the performance evaluation part.* Be specific when describing what performance is to be measured. Managers are understandably reluctant to agree to a "trust me" approach. For example, instead of saying you will compile

sales statistics, say you will report the customer sales statistics by industry and by region for the quarterly board meeting.

7. *Think about offering a trial period.* A trial period, typically three to six months, gives the employer a chance to back out if it's not working. And it gives you a chance to adjust your workload if necessary.

8. *Don't be afraid to ask for something that will help make you successful.* Many part-time professionals are afraid of jeopardizing an already precarious situation. If an allowance for a cellular phone or a separate phone line would make the difference, go for it.

Employer Benefits—What's in It for Them?

Ideally, everyone who will be affected by your part-time switch needs to win here. What possible value will the company and other coworkers, departments, and customers derive from the new arrangement?

Albright focused on the continuity of her working relationships with the firm and continued access to her media contacts. She also mentioned the opportunity for cross training that would result from the redistribution of parts of her work. At this point, she decided to keep the discussion focused on her immediate coworkers and didn't load the proposal with stats and anecdotes about the general and long-term gains derived from working flexibly described in chapter 2.

Compensation: Don't Give Away Too Much

Your company may have very clear guidelines for compensation and benefits for part-time employees. If so, just plug in the prorated

---

■ **TWO THINGS NOT TO DO IN THE BENEFITS SECTION**

1. *Avoid thinly veiled threats.* "If this proposal is rejected, the company will lose a valuable employee"—even if it's true—is *not* a company benefit, and it will only call your loyalty and judgment into question.

2. *Don't dump a ton of documentation on managers right off the bat.* Save the documentation of articles and anecdotes about other companies that have implemented part-time work arrangements successfully for later. Nancy Austin suggests that your documentation be available "on request." If you make something new seem so academic that there are references, they might not want to touch it.

version. For example, Caroline Albright knew that Forasa prorated everything, including benefits for employees who worked twenty hours or more. Since she wanted to work a three-fifths schedule, she simply suggested that the company prorate her salary and benefits at that rate. She secured health and dental insurance from her husband's company, so she passed on those. Keep in mind that while Albright's firm prorates salaries based on a forty-hour week, some professional firms use a base of fifty hours a week. If you're concerned about being paid for overtime, then an hourly wage would cover it.

If there are no guidelines, write "to be determined" in the compensation section and start networking. Contact professional organizations such as the Association of Part-Time Professionals or your industry's trade association to get some comparables. Network with counterparts in other organizations to find out how they are compensated.

According to a recent article by Kirsten Schabacher in *Executive Female* magazine, employers generally use three criteria for determining salaries: the job's impact on the company's bottom line; the amount of technical skill or knowledge required to do the job well; and accountability, how much the company's success rides on the independent judgments of the person holding the job.

Appendixes—Supporting Documents

Your appendixes include articles and studies to buttress your case, plus a short bibliography of information on related topics. We've already located much of the research, which can be found in the Endnotes. Remember that this section is optional and you may not want to overwhelm your boss with reams of reading. The most important part of your proposal is the proposal itself.

■ TWO MORE FINISHING TOUCHES—GIVE YOUR PROPOSAL THE WINNING EDGE

1. *Make sure your proposal makes a good first impression.* Your document should look clean and professional. It must be typed and free of spelling and grammatical errors. It should be businesslike and to the point. Concise sentences and paragraphs make your document easy to understand. The use of bullets, businesslike fonts and formats, and a lot of white space make your document visually appealing.

2. *Get a second opinion.* Even professional writers need an editor! Ask the best writer you know to review it for you before you present it.

SAMPLE PROPOSAL: Caroline Albright

JOB SUMMARY

Public relations is critical to Forasa's business strategy of growing to $100 million annual revenue by 1999. Since I took over the public relations function three years ago, Forasa has received substantially increased media coverage resulting in a positive public image. This work has helped generate new business and keep existing customers.

In addition to public relations, I have been responsible for various marketing writing projects and trade shows. In the future, I believe I can continue to make a significant contribution by focusing my efforts on public relations. I am confident that I can accomplish the quarterly goals outlined in the FY 1995 Marketing Strategic Plan in a twenty-hour-per-week schedule.

If my proposal is accepted, Forasa will receive continued improvement in coverage and placement of articles through my unique access to key analysts and editors in our industry.

JOB DESCRIPTION
Responsibilities

As public relations manager at Forasa, I will be responsible for the following tasks:

- Develop the overall press strategy on a quarterly basis.
- Write/edit press releases as needed.
- Write/edit press briefing materials for major announcements.
- Manage activities of the retained outside public relations firm, including editing their work, negotiating new rates, and discussing announcement strategies.
- Brief editors and analysts about important announcements to ensure good press coverage for the company.
- Brief executives about announcement details so they can prepare for interviews.
- Travel to major press announcements (one per quarter).

Deliverables

- Three minor announcements per quarter.
- One or two major announcements per quarter.
- Positive exposure in trade magazines, newspapers, and analyst reports about the announcements.

Schedule

I propose a twenty-hour-per-week schedule in which I will work from 8:00 until 3:30, Tuesday through Thursday, with a break for lunch. This schedule allows me the flexibility to call all time zones effectively and participate in lunch meetings with key editors and analysts.

Contingency Plan

Past experience suggests that there will be unscheduled events that require my immediate attention and extra hours. The following plan accommodates these situations:

- I will set up a home office with a personal computer, printer, fax machine, and a separate phone line for business-related calls.
- I will use my home office to supplement my writing and project management time when required for major or emergency events.
- I will accept work-related phone calls at home, even on my off days.
- I will schedule the quarterly strategy development meeting between major announcements.

Other

If I devote my full attention to public relations, as I am suggesting in this proposal, there remains the issue of what to do with my other responsibilities of writing marketing materials and managing trade shows. Janet Devine assumed the writing task during my maternity leave. She has indicated to me and to her manager that she enjoyed and would like to keep this extra responsibility as a way of broadening her skill set. In addition, Forasa is not scheduled to participate in another trade show for another quarter, and by that time, one of the new staff members can take over this more junior-level task.

RESOURCES NEEDED

I anticipate occasions that will require my off-hours attention. I propose setting up a home office with a personal computer, printer, fax machine, and a separate phone line for business-related calls. I suggest splitting the cost in the following manner:

Home Office Summary

Item	C. Albright portion	Forasa portion	
Fax machine	$600		
Printer	$300		
Install separate telephone line	$30		
Telephone service (annual charge)	$240	$300	(estimated usage)
Portable computer		$1,000	(net amount— see * below)
TOTAL	$1,170	$1,300	

*Forasa will be hiring two new marketing staff members next month, both of whom will need desktop personal computers. I propose giving my existing PC to one of the new hires and purchasing a portable computer for me that I can use at the office, at home, and on business trips. The net difference would be $1,000 if purchased under the company-wide discount agreement. Plus, if Forasa purchases the portable, it can be placed on the company-wide service plan and be counted as a depreciable asset.

PERFORMANCE EVALUATION

Because a part-time arrangement is new for both of us, I propose a three-month examination period, during which I agree to deliver the following:

- New product announcement, code-named "Rainbow"
- New London office announcement
- Announcement about the new VP of Sales
- Second quarter earnings announcement
- Same, or increased coverage in trade publications (per CLN Research)
- Public relations strategy for next quarter

Should we both agree to continue the part-time arrangement after the examination period, I will receive my regular annual performance and salary reviews every June.

QUALIFICATIONS

In my three years as public relations manager, I cultivated strong, professional relationships with the editors and analysts in our industry. Consequently, Forasa increased its coverage in trade magazines and newspapers by 150 percent and increased marketplace awareness from 33 percent two years ago to 59 percent today. (*Source:* CLN Research) Also, public relations activities generated 300 new leads in 1994 compared to 120 in 1993. Plus, I negotiated a new contract with the public relations agency, saving Forasa $110,000 over the last two years.

BENEFITS

The strong working relationships Forasa enjoys with Guggenheim Public Relations continues uninterrupted.

Long-standing contacts with the media people continue to develop, not subjected to a ramp-up period with someone new.

New career development and training opportunities open up for several Forasa employees. Janet Devine looks upon her new marketing function as a career opportunity and has also expressed an interest in being trained to write and edit press releases. An additional staff member trained in trade show management skills is a positive for both the staff member in terms of development and for Forasa in terms of cross training.

The schedule allows me to participate in lunch meetings with key editors and analysts and to call in all time zones. Because I have child care on my day off and have made myself available for phone calls on that day, clients get full-time coverage of major clients.

COMPENSATION

Proposed salary: $25,000 per year based on my previous full-time rate of $50,000 per year.

Proposed benefits: Benefits will be allocated according to Forasa's written policy on part-time work. In summary:

Benefit	Eligible at twenty hours per week?
Health insurance	no
Dental insurance	no
401(k)	yes
Disability insurance	yes
Unemployment insurance	yes
Vacation	yes (prorated)
Stock purchase plan	yes (prorated)

MAKE THE SHOWSTOPPING PRESENTATION

Now that you've written the masterpiece, you must find the right time to make your case. As usual, timing is everything. If you time your killer proposal in conjunction with a desperate baby-sitter situation or when you're feeling panicky because your work-family balance is out of control, your boss won't be receptive, he'll just think it's a bad week, not a professional issue. Nor is your ninth month of pregnancy a time to make such a huge decision. Chances are you've already waited a significant amount of time to bring this up in the first place, another few days won't make a difference. Other times to avoid are when your division is short-handed, on deadline, or being taken over.

Don't leave your proposal in your boss's in-box—even if you've already discussed what's in it. Make an appointment to talk some scheduling things over and be very careful about how you word your initial request for part-time arrangement. If you really startle the manager, she may jump to the "this is a problem" stance from the beginning. Try to keep the meeting and the discussion on your terms as much as possible. Maybe write down a loose script to prep yourself before you go in. It's important to keep the dialogue professional; this is no time to share war stories about juggling work and family. Keep the tone and language on business terms.

Once your completed killer proposal is in your boss's hands, the defining moment has come. Like the entrepreneur anticipating her first bank loan, you will soon learn if your proposal is truly a killer— that is, if it garners you the job you want—or if it has at least opened the door to negotiate. Often, you will not hear back for a while as the proposal gets sent up the ranks for consideration. Waiting is always the hardest part.

If your manager finds your proposal worth trying out but isn't quite sold, begin preparations for negotiating your final deal.

NEGOTIATE THE ARRANGEMENT YOU WANT

The best description of a successful negotiation is where the parties walk away after a deal is struck, each believing he got what was important to him. In the end the terms will be a compromise. Now is the time to stand up for yourself and your need for balance. Know which things you will not sacrifice, which you could give up, and which can be traded in the negotiating process. Again, do enough homework so you have a good idea what your negotiating partner's priorities are. Questions to ask yourself before the meeting:

- Do I have a fallback position?
- Am I prepared to compromise if my pitch for the perfect work arrangement is not accepted?
- Where is the middle ground?
- If I am forced to remain with the status quo, have I won or lost anything?
- Am I prepared to accept that nothing may change?

Now, remind yourself not to get defensive and take a deep cleansing breath . . . and go on in.

Don't forget you've got options to give your manager if necessary. One would allow you to maintain your relationships with customers; this other one would allow you to cross-train several employees; this other one would extend office hours, etc. Listen very carefully to your boss. Don't be so preoccupied that you miss a good offer or don't refute the right point. Also listen for the objections your boss *isn't* bringing up. Your boss probably has silent objections that he doesn't feel comfortable broaching, like a history of day-care troubles or some very recent missed deadlines. It's better if you deal with these hidden troubles up front by raising them yourself with this approach, "I've wondered why you haven't asked me about that late quarterly report. Are you afraid that may happen again?"

When money comes up women tend to fidget. Our only advice here is to get over it. Negotiations are about money and if you give in, it is you who loses.

Discuss and elaborate every point. You can't negotiate too much. If you leave that meeting without fighting for more insurance, chances are you won't be able to bring it up later. Use your proposal as a cue to go over each point.

Stand firm on keeping the tasks that make the best use of your talents and that you enjoy doing the most. Just because you are getting the schedule you want doesn't mean you have to forfeit the job you love. If the negotiations hit a low point, look for areas of mutual interest, things you can agree on to get through the stalemate.

Here's one last checklist to run through before you tie the bow around your new flexible package:

- Have you discussed your current and future expectations for the job?
- Have you discussed how special aspects of the job will be handled, such as travel, overtime, and bonuses?
- Did you discuss promotability?
- Did you come up with an acceptable temporary trial period?
- Have you set a date for the next review?

Now, don't kick yourself if after you meet with your boss you realize you gave in to something you really didn't want to and now it's making you unhappy. You can ask to meet again and explain that you were going over the agreement and you wanted to revisit an issue or two that don't really work out after all. And next time, if you're not sure of how you feel, instead of settling, try to buy yourself some time to think about it. For example, "I'm not sure if I would be willing to come in on alternating Fridays. I hadn't considered that option. I see now how important it is to you because of the meetings, though. I'd like to think about that one and see if we can find a better solution. Maybe we could address this part again tomorrow?"

If Someone Closes a Door, Then Open a Window

If your proposal is rejected, try to find out why by asking nonthreatening, open-ended questions such as, "Could you tell me more about why this plan didn't fit the needs of the company?" or "What problems did you see with the proposal?" or "Are there alternative arrangements that would be more workable?" If your proposal is shot down, it may not be because of your qualifications, or because of holes in the plan. The problem might be an employer who is hostile to part-time work arrangements or any other of the chapter 7 objections. Keep plugging. If this company is really not open to flexible employment practices, find one that is.

We've covered how to do everything possible to make this part-time work arrangement earn approval from your boss and peers. Now all that's left is making it work for you, which we cover in Part Five.

■ THE SEVEN BIGGEST NEGOTIATING MISTAKES

"Don't go into negotiations with the attitude that you're asking for a favor. What happens when you ask for a favor? You owe them something. And that's not a strong negotiating position."
—Sandra Sullivan

"Don't whine. Base your case on business needs. If you spend too much time on personal reasons for needing part-time, your manager will think you're overly focused on baby-sitters and pediatricians and not enough on profit margins and customer service."
—Nikki Ogden, HP manager

"Don't let your boss pressure you into agreeing to do a job in twenty hours that will take thirty or forty. And don't fool yourself into setting yourself up for doing a full-time job for part-time pay."
—Cindy Bitner, former part-time banker

"Approaching a manager in a defensive, aggressive manner in public is a bad tactic and I've seen that done. An employee actually approached her manager at a social activity and caught him off-guard, and when his first response was negative—he was worrying about how to phrase it so people around wouldn't misinterpret his answer . . ."
—Susan Moriconi, HP work/life manager

"Don't assume your manager understands all aspects of your job. You've got to make your boss understand them. Your boss needs to understand the elements of your job that won't be done when you're not there and think through how that piece of it is going to get done."
—David Kennedy, Vice President, Human Resources, New England Electric

"Avoid an attitude of entitlement. Most managers favor people who appear willing to carry a heavy load and don't give the impression they're going to strictly interpret all their rights as part-timers and turn into clockwatchers."
—Cheryl LaFleur, Vice President and General Counsel, New England Electric

"If your part-time schedule is going to create problems, you've gotta fix it before you go into negotiations."
—part-time CEO Nancy Anderson

SIX
Job Sharing

"People at companies might think it will be too confusing to work with both Janine and Ruth. But what they don't consider is that people like Janine and Ruth want a flexible work arrangement so much that they will do whatever it takes to make it work."

—Diane Harris, work/family expert

Job sharing is largely unpioneered territory with, as yet, untapped potential. How far it will develop nobody really knows at this point. Even avid supporters are surprised at how well job sharing can work and at the high level at which job sharers can perform.

When we started researching the book, we asked a middle management job-share pair from Hewlett-Packard if they thought there was a ceiling within their company beyond which job sharing could not work. They both agreed that, yes, once you reach the functional manager level, job sharing caps out. "Too many people issues, the travel, the egos. Executives at that level don't want to share the decision making with anyone else," they said. Within the year, an article in the *San Jose Mercury News* appeared featuring Janice Chaffin, a woman who had been promoted to general manager of Hewlett-Packard's 600-person, $4.35 billion General Systems Division. She would be job sharing the position with another woman.

Job sharing, a flexible work arrangement that allows two people to share the work of one full-time job, increasingly involves high-level, high-pressure jobs. Whether it's office manager, sales associate, or CFO, women who want to job share probably are already juggling a full load of work responsibilities. Adding yet another person to the act adds a high potential for mixed signals and confusion. This chapter offers guidelines for finding the right partner, structuring your job share, determining your schedule, and managing communication issues. Once your two-person band is ready for prime time, we will offer tips for working smoothly together and avoiding common pitfalls, and even for advancing your career as a team.

THE DATING GAME: FINDING THE RIGHT PARTNER

Job-share relationships can become as intense as marriages, so it pays to look carefully before you leap. This is no time for impulsive decisions just because you are desperate to cut back your hours. The safest place to find a partner is within your own workplace. Although finding a job-share partner at any level is tough, the higher up the success ladder you go, the fewer the suitable partners. You've got to be highly selective when searching for your co-you: objective, practical, and uncompromising.

With so much on the line you'll need to ask a lot of serious questions: How will she act under stress? Can I trust her judgment? Can I trust *her?* Are we both committed enough to the relationship to invest the time and effort in building a solid partnership? Will she treat me as an equal? Will she tend to act independently without consulting me? Will I end up doing all of the routine work while she hogs more of the glamour jobs? Trust your intuition. If anything makes you uneasy or strong negative emotions start to surface, even if you can't put your finger on it, perhaps you're not done looking.

Here's a list of the important compatibility issues to consider according to those who have chosen wisely and not-so-wisely: philosophy, approach, similar or complementary strengths, and personality.

Philosophy

Ideally, you and your partners will have the same work ethic and moral ethics. But the philosophy of how you work is much more comprehensive than this. Veterinarian Julie Berman credits the success of her job share to the fact that she and her partner share the same philosophy of taking care of their patients. In a mixed practice this means dogs, cats, and snakes as well as pigs and horses—and their owners. Her first job share was with a male veterinarian with whom she didn't share the same philosophical foundation. Said Berman of her former partner, "A classic scene was that he would head home for the day leaving sixteen phone messages that hadn't been returned. When I arrived in the afternoon, I'd spend an hour and a half on the phone returning his phone calls. His level of communicating with the pet owners was not nearly what mine was."

Approach

The way you approach work need not be exactly the same, but it needs to be compatible. Perhaps your gusto and her ingenuity or, alternatively, her ambition and your shortcuts make for a dynamic work team. Shelly Smith and Patty O'Brien, job-sharing managers at Hewlett-Packard, think a similar approach to work is necessary. O'Brien illustrates her point using the decision-making process: "Suppose one of us made decisions based on gut feeling while the other only felt comfortable with a decision backed up by tons of numbers. When the time came to make an important call, the gut-feeling person might well think that her partner's analysis was completely irrelevent to the final decision. That wouldn't work." Another Hewlett-Packard job-share pair, Susan Lovegren and Nancy Kelly, concur. For example, says Kelly, both she and Lovegren opt for quick and dirty when it comes to preparing slides for staff meetings. "Our priority is content. We save the sexy color graphics and fonts for major presentations." If one of the pair felt that polishing slides to perfection was necessary, she would end up spending long hours doing this, and it could become a sore point. Setting up hypothetical situations that cover such issues will help you identify potential problems.

Similar or Complementary Strengths

Most job-share partners agree that duplicate backgrounds and skills are unnecessary. But they should be complementary. Combine your creativity with her finesse and acuity for deadlines and you've got a part-time dream team. Or, just add your cool logic with her fire and burn through every sales goal on your coast. Susan Lovegren and Nancy Kelly, staffing and diversity program managers at Hewlett-Packard, have been job sharing since 1989. This is the third job they've shared. They credit their success to shared values and complementary skills. The extrovert Lovegren tends to be in a "selling mode'' a lot of the time. Nancy, more reserved and analytical, asks a lot of questions and is an excellent listener. The combination of skills make them superb at handling both internal concerns and external customers.

Personality

It shouldn't matter but it does. And unfortunately most of these intangible qualities won't show up on a Myers-Briggs personality test. If you're planning on trusting and respecting this alter ego, it will be a lot easier if you genuinely like her. Susan Davis, an Indianapolis pediatrician, job shares her pediatric practice with another woman. The fact that neither of them is overly competitive plus their genuine liking for each other makes job sharing a viable long-term solution for them.

WHAT MANAGERS THINK

The managers of job sharers we interviewed almost all enthusiastically gave gold stars to the "two heads are better than one" experience. Besides the coverage during absences, one partner can cross-train the other. Job sharers can both work on a project during peak periods or when the job calls for one employee to be in two places at the same time. A job share can also feature a junior/senior team where the senior member trains the junior member. Managers enjoy the benefits of the greater range of skills, experiences, and viewpoints job sharers bring to the table. Contrary to expectations that job sharers will suck up management time, managers find they save time with job shares. Job-share partners bounce problems and potential solutions off each other and make decisions with confidence—without asking for input from their manager.

Other managers—especially those that have never tried it—remain skeptical. They point out that job sharing, unlike pizza specials, is not quite the "two-for-one deal" it's advertised to be. Because most job sharers each work three days a week with one day of overlap, this means a company pays for six days and gets five days of work. Other managers worry that they and customers will invest twice as much time dealing with job sharers. They wonder, will I have to train two people at twice the cost? Will the coworkers and I have to repeat everything? Will I have to write two performance evaluations? Still other managers at companies using the head count system don't want to get saddled with two heads on their budget instead of one.

Many of you, especially where job sharing is a new idea, will have to sell your manager on the concept. Here are some strategies.

1. *Prepare a killer proposal.* While it's not necessary to recreate the Magna Carta, your proposal should spell out the details of your plan. Include a "co-résumé" with five to ten bullets of your separate achievements. (See two sample proposals at the end of the chapter.)

2. *Hone your presentation.* Plan ahead and practice so that your presentation is clear and shows your potential boss how well you can work together.

3. *Show the benefits.* Look at all the people your job share will affect. List those people and organizations in a special section in which you outline how your job share will benefit them.

4. *Suggest a trial period.* The trial period is your and your co-workers' safety net. If the job share doesn't work for either of you or for your boss or coworkers, the trial period gives you an out.

SETTING IT UP—SOME THINGS TO THINK ABOUT

This is where the rubber meets the road. How will you split up the job? How will you handle communication with each other? With managers? With customers and coworkers? How will you set it up so that people you work with don't have to start over with a problem or idea when they're working with the other partner? How will you decide who does what? If Monday is always the staff meeting, will the person who works on Mondays always gets the exposure of making the presentation? If you manage people, will you divide performance evaluations or do them together? Will you ask people to direct their questions to one of you as their primary manager? Or will you both act as if you were just one person so that when an employee comes to one of you with a problem, you must be sure to pass the info on? Who will attend which meeting? Who gets managed by whom? The following sections address these questions.

STRUCTURING THE JOB SHARE

Job shares can be structured three ways. First of all, partners may *job split*, that is, they divide responsiblities into two part-time jobs. Job splitters don't worry much about being seamless. They generally work on separate projects or different aspects of a project while still providing backup coverage. For example, Susan Burke currently job splits a research and development marketing position at Norwest Financial Corporation. Burke, the banker, handles the analytical and financial aspects, while her partner, the marketing whiz, handles the creative and writing end. Sometimes they work independently. At other times they come together to collaborate.

The second approach is the true *job share,* in which two people work together as one individual. Partners jointly share the full range of tasks. Both work on the same projects, with either partner able to pick up where the other left off; they keep each other updated on every meeting, on every project. For example, one job-share team of social workers has become so blended in the minds of the staff at a hospital cancer ward in San Francisco that colleagues address their memos to "Blanne," a blend of their names, Bill and Anne.

A third approach *divides work by clients or subject.* For example, when nurse practitioner Michele Helmuth worked with a partner running a health clinic for employees at Palo Alto biotechnology firm Syntex Corporation, her partner's area of expertise was skeletal and Michele's was cardiovascular. They decided who took which client by matching client needs to their special areas of expertise. Similarly, the Indianapolis pediatricians each took separate patients, but backed each other up.

Scheduling

Job sharers can design schedules in a number of ways depending on the type of work the partners do, the needs of the coworkers and managers, and the personal needs of the team members. Job sharers can work three to four full days a week with one day a week overlapping. Or they can work partial days every week. Others work one week on and one week off. A job-share team of elementary schoolteachers, for example, organizes their schedule so that one partner teaches the first semester, while the other picks up the second semester.

A common problem is that partners feel obligated to work full-time while one partner is on vacation or taking a sick day. Lovegren and Kelly suggest that you use a full-time employee as your bench-mark. If the full-timers are taking off July 5, you should, too. When one of you needs a week in the mountains, there's no reason to feel like the other partner has to offer full-time coverage. After all, there's not complete coverage when a full-time employee is on vacation.

Communicating with Each Other

Recently a news show reported that in an average day men speak about 5,000 words. And women 9,000. It's good to know that women are already good communicators because in a job-share arrangement, they need to be, especially if they work in the true job-share arrangement described above.

Nothing is as important in your job-share relationship as communicating effectively with each other. Some positions will be so straightforward they lend themselves to leaving a quick memo or voice mail at the end of each day. Other responsibilities may call for something more intricate.

Still, the need for abundant communication doesn't mean there shouldn't be times you won't or can't be reached. Otherwise, what's the point of job sharing? The only way to stay informed (and still part-time) is to develop an efficient communication pattern.

Here are some ideas that work.

1. *Dump it all on hump day*. Use one day a week, usually your overlap day, to brief each other. Changeover Wednesday is most frequently used for mutual debriefing.
2. *Be a reporter on the recorder*. If your partner lives near you, you can relay the day's activities and problems into a minirec-order while driving to her home, then drop it off. The next morning, she could listen to the log on her way to work.
3. *Log it*. Keep an ongoing activities log, similar to a tickler file. Or try what Smith and O'Brien have done to upgrade their system. Says O'Brien, "We list actions we need to take in a book. On the days that we're in the office, we work off that list to get things done. What I don't do will carry over to Smith's day, and so forth. When items stay on the list for too long, that means neither of us thought whatever it was rated a high enough priority to spend time on it. Having two people agree it wasn't worth the time validates letting it go."
4. *Divide and conquer*. Smith and O'Brien also leave a daily voice-mail update. Leaving and listening to messages from

each other takes up about eight hours a week total, but the time is worth it. Lovegren and Kelly have refined this method. They cluster their messages by projects. Then they forward the messages to the appropriate person, attaching memos to the voice mails like "taken care of" or "referred to so-and-so." They also established a second dummy line that stores messages for future attention. This clears their main mailbox, but keeps the message accessible.

5. *Tap in to the office data bank.* Susan Davis, the Indianapolis pediatrician, can gain access to patient files through her home computer.

6. *Use a* nom de job share. Some writers use a *nom de plume* to create a certain effect. Likewise, job sharers can simplify internal office communications by using a pseudonym that is a combination of both names.

Communicating with Your Boss

A policy for returning phone calls, responding to emergencies, and documenting how you and your partner communicate should satisfy your boss. For example, you might tell your boss you'll return e-mail messages twice daily and voice-mail messages within two hours. Weekly updates are a good idea, too. The goal of communicating with your boss is to never allow her to feel that she doesn't know what is going on, and to avoid putting her in a situation where she appears uninformed. Janice Chaffin, who manages a job-share pair at HP says, "I don't want to have to explain to my manager that this is a job share and that's why we've dropped the ball."

Whichever method of communication you choose, you'll know you're doing it right if you get the same reaction the Bockus/Olson team got from their boss: "Before we walk out of staff meetings, the other job sharer already knows—and she's at home today!"

Communicating with Your Coworkers

Start communicating openly right after the initial announcement. Sit down with your staff and share the news and the logistics. Let it be known that you expect feedback and welcome suggestions. Tell everyone how and when each of you is available. Take questions and take your time. Resistance is likely, but you may be pleasantly surprised. Most coworkers prefer to deal with the slight inconveniences of a job-share situation than with breaking in a new person.

Handling the Media

As a result of their cutting-edge work arrangement, job sharers often find themselves in the limelight. Coworkers as well as reporters get curious about job sharers. Don't feel obligated to assume the role of the job-sharing expert, especially during the early weeks. Focus on your job and getting it done effectively. Also, make sure that you check with your employer before you agree to an interview with a reporter.

■ A CAUTIONARY TALE FOR JOB SHARERS

When management guru and speaker Nancy Austin signed up to do a big project for a client, she needed a job-share pair within a Silicon Valley corporation to provide her with critical information. As an outspoken advocate of women in the workplace, Austin wanted and fully expected a "wow" experience from the job-share pair—"the added flexibility, the quicker response time, the focus on producing results, the synergy of half plus half equals two."

Instead, Austin says, it turned out to be "double the lackluster performance." Usually in a situation like this, says Austin, "I can work around one person to get the information I need. But in this case, I had to work around two, so I ended up feeling ganged up on. Everybody else in the company was evidently afraid of criticizing the pair because it was not corporately correct to say, 'Wait a minute, this job share isn't working.' " Meanwhile, the job sharers had no idea they were a problem. Austin notes wryly, they thought their innovative arrangement was "the coolest thing going."

The moral to the story: Initially you may enjoy a honeymoon period, but not for long. In the end, it's getting the work done that makes your manager want to keep you around.

HAVE REGULAR "HOW'S IT GOING?" MEETINGS

Beginning a few weeks after the job starts, schedule regular meetings to look at the logistics of the job share and to figure out what's working, what's not, and to adjust accordingly. Every job-share pair we talked to mentioned the necessity of making alterations in the plan and adjustments in the schedule.

Two common problems are described following:

- *The honeymooner syndrome.* Like honeymooners who often seemed attached at the hip, both job-share partners show up at the same meetings and the same functions. Duplicating efforts in this way limits the amount of time you have to accomplish other work.
- *The job share is not the job.* Don't spend so much time working on the logistics of job sharing that you neglect the work. Working on streamlining your communication systems, using the prioritizing systems described earlier, can go a long way toward cutting back the time required to exchange information.

PERFORMANCE EVALUATIONS

How you handle the performance evaluation will depend on your company and your arrangement. Often managers prefer to deal with job-share team members as "one job, one evaluation." But if your partner was on a different pay scale or if you use the "job-split" tactic to divide the work, you may want to be evaluated separately so you'll get proper, honest feedback about the quality of your work. Still, even if your reviews will occur individually, you may wish to prepare for it together so you can refresh each other on the year's accomplishments and make sure you're on the same wavelength when interpreting those accomplishments.

ADVANCING YOUR CAREER AS A POWER COUPLE

Advancing as a job-share team can be tougher. When Bockus and Olson first made their job-share proposal, they specifically said they didn't want the new arrangement to defer advancement or affect salary raises or ranking. But, Bockus says, "I think people thought, 'Well, Carol and Susan are happy now because they're in a job-sharing situation so we don't have to worry about satisfying any more career requirements for them.' As a result, we gained responsibility and experience—but we didn't move forward." Job-share manager Janice Chaffin agrees: "People mistakenly think that part-timers have decided to park in their jobs and not develop. But the job sharers I manage are committed to advancing. Managers should realize it's unrealistic to expect these individuals to content themselves with the job share and not think about the next step in their careers."

Lovegren and Kelly feel it's up to the team to find the opportunity to get promoted, but they also think management should lend a hand in coaching and grooming. If your boss won't budge on the issue of promotions, you may ultimately decide to look for a new job-share position at a new company or to go out on your own as independent contracting partners as Carol Olson and Susan Bockus did.

Hewlett-Packard job sharers Susan Lovegren and Nancy Kelly recommend a strategy for job sharers looking for a new position. "The basic plan we suggest is to have one person go in and establish a relationship and sell the organization on that person's skills. Then and only then do you say, 'Oh, by the way, I have a job-share partner with so-and-so complementary skills who can bring x, y, and z to the table.' "

Lovegren advocates holding back the part-time data until later in the interview process: "I would never start out by disclosing that I'm in a part-time situation or that I'm interested in part-time. Why throw up roadblocks? By doing that you're biasing your interviewer before you've even had a chance to get on the dance floor." Lovegren and Kelly also recommend extensive role playing in advance of the interview. They even suggest coordinating outfits to avoid looking like twins in dress-alike blue pinstripe suits.

Managing as a Job-Share Team

Job sharing offers a leading solution for retaining hard-won management responsibilities as a part-timer. Through sharing a management job, the job sharers get what they want most—high-powered responsibilities and part-time—and employers get full-time coverage of a job. Beyond the traditional "two halves equal more than one" benefit, however, Shelly Smith and Patty O'Brien, contend that job sharing offers organizations other unique advantages. First of all, they feel that as a team they can more easily focus their group on the highest priority work. Says O'Brien, "A manager who works alone might not have that same confidence and may waste company resources on projects with little value." Second, the pair feels that by working together, they can more quickly identify and deal with poor performers. Both Smith and O'Brien were experienced managers before they started job sharing. They recall how one problem employee could monopolize their time. As individual managers, they tended to procrastinate, bending over backward to give the employee the benefit of the doubt, first trying one coaching approach, then another. As a team, however, much like parents, Smith and O'Brien feel confident that if they both notice a performance problem, it's real and not a result of their own coaching style. Says Smith, "We can isolate a problem with an employee and deal with that directly. This allows us to spend more time with the good employees in the group, keeping them productive and moving forward professionally."

Smith and O'Brien's manager, Janice Chaffin, also buys into the theory that two managers can be better than one. Says Chaffin of the pair she manages, "Their business planning job requires a high degree of strategic thinking. Together, they develop very creative solutions to complex business problems. One person working in their job might have a harder time." However, Chaffin quickly cautions that while job sharing works for Smith and O'Brien's position, she would not necessarily offer it as an option to other members of her group. Chaffin points out, "A business planning job like theirs is not so reactive to the field or to customers. In jobs with more customer interaction, I couldn't afford any hiccups in communication."

The fact that job sharing provides continuity for maternity leaves, vacations, and other absences takes on particular importance at the management level. When O'Brien went on maternity leave to have her second baby, for example, Smith volunteered to jump in full-time. According to manager Chaffin, "Shelly coming back full-time was wonderful. Otherwise, *I* would have had to cover on the days with no manager." Even if Smith didn't agree to go full-time during her partner's leave, they all agree that even a *part-time* manager would have been better than *no* manager.

What Happens If One Member Leaves

Job sharing is not forever. Change is inevitable. Eventually one of you will relocate, have another baby and take an extended leave, decide to work full-time, or accept a promotion. For this reason, the smart job-sharer who wants to continue job sharing is always on the lookout for new potential partners both within and outside of the company. The end of a job-share relationship provides a chance for you to review your own situation. Whatever happens, the most important thing is not to let the breakup of the partnership between you and your ex-job-share partner burn any bridges between the two of you or to your employer.

SOME FLASH CARDS ON MAKING IT WORK

- Keep your partner up to speed so no one is blindsided by unexpected developments.
- Limit the number of changes you take on all at once. If you're starting a job share, don't upgrade the level of your work immediately, too.
- Never question your partner's decision in front of your staff.
- Make your business relationship—not your friendship—the top priority.
- Be sensitive to your staff's morale and take occasional, informal polls on your performance.
- Remember not to second-guess your partner repeatedly.
- Share the credit.
- Keep an overly competitive spirit in check.
- Always give your partner the benefit of the doubt.

Could the Marriage Have Been Saved?

We don't want to minimize the potential downside of job sharing. For this reason, we think it's instructive to learn from job shares that didn't work as well as from those that were successful. When a job share fails, each team member risks her professional reputation, the good opinion of her boss and coworkers, and her ability to continue to work part-time within that same organization. The dissolution of a job-share team gets sticky for all concerned. Who will continue in the job, if anyone? How will others perceive the breakup? Where will both of you work? Can you still work in the same department? Who will do the work while you figure things out?

Women willing to talk about a job share that failed were as rare as a cab on a rainy day. Ex-job-share partners are understandably hesitant to bad-mouth their former partners. But we impressed on our interviewees how important it was that readers be able to recognize when a problem is on the horizon. Our sources shared some of their stories but insisted on anonymity. Here are some typical problems and some possible solutions.

IRRECONCILIABLE SKILLS

"We did great in the early phases of projects—planning, gathering data. But as soon as we had to produce press releases or brochures, something concrete, it turned into a train wreck. She was more experienced than I was and she held that over my head like a club, making me feel like I was incompetent."

Solution: If you're lacking computer skills or are twice as slow at analysis, find out how to get your skills up to speed. If you don't have a performance problem, perhaps your partner is too territorial to ever allow you to succeed in her areas of expertise. If you want to stick with the job share because you need the flexibility, think about redesigning it and playing to your partner's strengths as well as to yours. Offer to do more research and support while she sticks with the writing and design. If your work is stellar, you can't be lost in a shadow.

THE BUSINESS WASN'T FIRST

"She was experiencing a lot of personal problems, all of which she would share with me on Wednesdays or at night on the phone. I worried that at any moment she would break down, quit, and leave me high and dry. If we had the opportunity to take on an interesting project, I knew before even asking her, she wouldn't want to do it if it meant any extra work. You know that team-building exercise they do in a lot of seminars where you stand with a partner behind you and fall back? Well, I always kept thinking that if I fell back, I could never trust her to catch me."

Solution: People's personal problems do affect their work performance. When this happens, the impact can have a devastating effect on a partnership. Share your concerns with your partner. Acknowledge the seriousness of her personal situation but let her know that you consider getting the work done a top priority. Also tell her that you are interested in advancing your career; therefore, if the situation doesn't improve, you will be forced to start looking around for another work situation.

THE TWO-TO-ONE RATIO

"It really bugged me that I was doing most of the heavy lifting. She didn't really have the experience or the skill level for the work we were doing, but she didn't seem to realize it. One time we had to prepare a big report for a quarterly meeting. I suggested that she call several people for input that I thought was critical. She blew it off saying she thought that it was overkill. Because I thought it was important, and it was my reputation on the line, I did it anyway but I had to tiptoe around her while I was doing it, making twice as much work for me. I was always having to play the Big Bad Boss, a role that I didn't want."

Solution: Interview each other extensively beforehand to avoid this clash of work standards. If you've never worked with her, go through a dry run of typical projects you'll be working on such as writing reports to see just how she approaches the task. If you're already knee-deep in this situation, explain that while you understand that sometimes the extra work isn't necessary, in this case, you feel your client responds to thoroughness. Or simply say that if the work secures your team's reputation, it's worth the overkill.

IF YOU DON'T MEET HALFWAY

"She had this 'you can't tell me anything' attitude kids right out of college often have. I think she and her husband weren't planning on staying in Chicago for long anyway, so she didn't care that much about the job, but I did."

Solution: A "you can't tell me anything" attitude is exactly the wrong attitude for a job-share situation. If you end up with someone with an uneven level of ambition or commitment, get out as soon as you can—enlist your bosses' help if you have to.

SECOND FIDDLE SYNDROME

"She was so good at impressing our managers, and I wasn't. Somehow I got the feeling I was viewed as being the weak link in the team."

Solution: You might be overreacting. If your job-share partner has a warmer personality than yours, then naturally people are going to feel more comfortable talking to her. You may have problem-solving skills or analytical abilities that people value just as much. On the other hand, perhaps your partner is, in fact, undercutting you by insinuating that she's doing all the work. Tactfully broach the subject with your partner and discuss tactics for promoting yourselves as a team.

COMMITMENT MAKES THE DIFFERENCE

At its best, a job-sharing arrangement can reduce the risk of being mommy-tracked as well as cut down on burnout and overload. Job sharing isn't easy. Neither is marriage. But like a marriage, if both partners and their skills are basically compatible, the job share will probably work if both partners are willing to work at the relationship. And for most of the happy job sharers we talked to, the flexibility and opportunity to compete in the workplace at a high professional level was well worth the effort of overcoming the difficulties.

SAMPLE PROPOSALS

Here are two examples of what a job-share proposal might look like. The first is adapted from a proposal kindly loaned to us by a highly placed job-share team in a high-tech corporation. The second is a more general version of what a proposal in the health-care industry might look like.

PROPOSAL 1

Marketing Programs Manager
Job Share Proposal

Proposal

Margie Welsch and Elaine Brown to share the position of market-ing manager within the General Solutions Group.

Objectives

Successfully roll out marketing programs.

and

Successfully demonstrate that a job-share team has significant advantages to Techcorp and to the employees.

Benefits

To Hewlett-Packard: The company retains and motivates two proven managers with a combination of over fifteen years of Techcorp experience at a reasonable cost, while positioning Techcorp as a leader in the industry and an excellent place for parents to work.

To Techcorp:

Experience: This job share offers GSG two proven managers with solutions/programs marketing experience, applied to strate-gically important marketing programs. The individuals have complementary skills and experience with GSG's business and partner divisions. This experience will be key in maintaining the strong momentum of existing marketing programs and more ef-fectively adding new programs.

Flexibility: Because the proposed job-share managers are will-ing to assist the organization beyond their job-share hours when business necessitates and circumstances allow, GSG gains the flexibility for additional assistance during peak times in the department.

Creativity: This combination will be valuable in providing a forum for brainstorming. Creative ideas and breakthrough thinking will be critical to marketing, which is increasingly recognized as requiring a different approach.

Quality: In a fast-paced organization, the ability to have two sets of eyes review critical documents, presentations, and marketing plans and activities offers the opportunity for more thorough and accurate work.

To marketing staff: Provides two proven managers to learn from, seek advice and feedback from, and receive support from, in ranking and promotion opportunities.

To job-share managers: The employees are able to maintain career continuity and a high level of contribution while gaining time for parenting and community involvement.

Job Share Specifics: A True Sharing of the Position

The job-share team will share the role of marketing programs manager rather than dividing the job into two halves. Overall group responsibilities will be shared. Some individual responsibilities may be decided upon by the job-share managers to promote productivity and effectiveness but will be handled so that the individual ownership is transparent or has minimal impact on the overall functioning of the position. A common outlook regarding the position and excellent communication and trust between the job-share managers is essential. The following list outlines some methods used by job-share teams that we believe will contribute to our success.

1. The staff meeting will be held on the overlap day.
2. Each job-share manager will check her fax, voice mail, etc., routinely, even on "off" days. Both managers will have equipped home offices.
3. Each job-share manager will maintain a common notebook and filing system for all projects that will provide a central resource for sharing information firsthand. The status of every project will be readily available.
4. Recruiting efforts and all personnel matters will be shared and jointly administered.
5. The job-share manager in the office has full decision-making power and responsibility for resolving issues for the entire group.

6. The job share will be reviewed every six months with the reporting manager to ensure that the team is meeting its objectives.

Concern for the People Issues Within the Group

The productivity and morale of our people are our top concern, and as managers, we believe they will benefit from the job share.

Having varied perspectives and experiences to draw from can be extremely helpful to an individual as she develops and grows in her job, both personally and professionally. In order to make each individual feel positive about the job-share management team, we plan to manage as follows:

1. Each individual will have equal access to each job-share manager.
2. Regular one-on-one meetings between the job-share managers and marketing engineers will be arranged to best meet the needs of the individual, whether this is a joint meeting, an alternating meeting, or a regular meeting with only one of the job-share managers.
3. Job-share managers will do joint performance evaluations for each individual in the group.
4. Salary will be administered jointly.
5. Both managers will be familiar with the issues and content of all areas of the group.
6. Open-door policy will exist for the marketing engineers to go to either job-share manager, both of them, or to the job-share managers' manager for issue resolution.

Ranking, Evaluations, and Pay

It is important for the job-share team to be evaluated jointly but for each job-share manager to understand her respective areas for improvements.

It is important to put first priority on getting the entire job done in a seamless and consistent manner that makes the team transparent to internal and external customers. It is also important to continue to grow and develop and be compensated for overall contributions to HP.

1. Review of job-share program every six months to ensure that the job-share team is working.

2. Ranking, pay, and evaluations of job-share managers will be jointly based on the accomplishments of the group.
3. Individual development plans and strengths/weaknesses assessments will be created for each job-share manager.

Flexible Time Off and Business Need on "Off" Days

It is in the best interest of the job-share team to maximize coverage of the job at all times and be flexible about changing business needs. As a result, vacation time will be scheduled to maximize coverage. Each job-share manager will strive to be available for responding to business needs that require her presence. Travel will be shared by both job-share managers according to business need.

Work Schedule: Margie and Elaine will each work thirty hours per week for a total of sixty hours and a full-time equivalency (FTE) head count of 1.5. We will work three consecutive ten-hour days a week in the office with an overlap day on Wednesday. Margie will be in the office on Monday, Tuesday, and Wednesday and Elaine on Wednesday, Thursday, and Friday. Holidays will be handled according to Techcorp's policy for regular part-time employees. All efforts will be made by the team to minimize overlap of vacation time to maximize coverage of the job. Extra days worked by either team member will be compensated by alternate time off at a time consistent with the needs of the job.

PROPOSAL 2
Proposal for Job Share of the Clinical Research Associate Position

NEED FOR JOB-SHARE POSITION

The full-time clinical research associate (CRA) position is necessary in order to provide support and resource information for the research team. Activities will include initial review and management of all safety data for all U.S. studies and will include data collection and processing of all serious events as specified in the current standard operating procedure. Other projects may be assigned to this position on an as-needed basis.

The two full-time clinical research associates who would share this position are currently on maternity leave of absence. Both CRAs have extensive clinical research experience in the area and have recently been working on two large, complex studies. Both

CRAs have a history of excellent performance reviews and have the ability and drive necessary to maintain a high standard of excellence of this shared position.

PERCENTAGE OF TIME WORKED

Each employee will work 50 percent of the time and both will report to the same team member, forty hours in two weeks. The schedule will be determined as needed when projects and training require. If a job-share partner requests extended time off, i.e., medical disability, extended vacation, etc., the other partner agrees to cover the workload of the missing partner as needed.

COMMUNICATION

In order to allow the partners to communicate about specific job needs or current job events, they will plan to talk over the phone every workday as well as make use of voice mail when necessary. Both partners will share appropriate master files and workspace as needed. Each employee will be flexible regarding her work schedule to meet in person with each other or members of the research team.

RESIGNATION OR TERMINATION OF A PARTNER

If one partner resigns or is terminated from the position, the other partner may choose to continue full-time. If she decides to continue the job-share position, she agrees to cover the workload until a new employee is hired. At this time, the company may choose to reevaluate the effectiveness of the share.

SALARY

The total salary for the partners will not exceed the salary for one person in that position.

BENEFITS

Each employee will qualify as a regular part-time employee and receive prorated vacation based on the number of hours she is regularly scheduled to work.

Signed _____ (employee 1)
Signed _____ (employee 2)
Signed _____ (manager)

PART FOUR

STRATEGIES FOR GETTING IT—FROM THE OUTSIDE

Playing Up Your Strengths:

An Interview with Judy Chang

"You can see that luck pervades my professional life," says engineer Judy Chang who holds what she calls "the perfect part-time job" as the alumni coordinator for the computer science department at the University of Illinois in Champaign-Urbana. Besides developing relationships with U. of I. alums—work that in the gray Midwest winter "forces" her to travel to sunny California—the thirty-eight-year-old mother of a first-grader also edits an alumni magazine, maintains alumni databases, and organizes fund-raising events.

Q: *How'd you get started on the part-time track at the University of Illinois?*

A: I started with their temp agency, Extra Help. Temping was great because it allowed me to float from department to department getting a bird's-eye view of things. That way, I didn't plug into a permanent job I knew nothing about. You can be the person who takes care of the sheep in animal sciences, you can set up parties for visitors, or you can do clerical stuff. Eventually I settled down in a part-time job in the Afro-American studies department for a few years—interesting work, interesting people—until I heard about my current job.

Q: *How did you hear about it?*

A: An acquaintance happened to be on the search committee for this job. She sent me the job description with a note that said, "This job is tailor-made for you. You'd be nuts not to go after it." So I had one day to prepare my résumé. I got help from my next-door neighbor sprucing it up, updating my references. I played up my computer skills so that even if I only had a working knowledge of a software program, my résumé made me out to be an expert in it. And it worked.

Q: *Did you have any trouble negotiating your part-time deal?*

A: It was always a part-time job—20 hours a week. I think I beat out the other fifteen people who applied for the job though because I impressed them with the work samples I brought in to the interview—past issues of newsletters, some disks showing the type of little computerized office systems I'd set up in my previous job. I put the disk into their computer and said, "Here's how you use the database I wrote. If you have a student you're looking for, you press this button and it zaps you to this. Then you press this button and it zaps that to you." They liked the razzle-dazzle. I think it was the slickness of the presentation that won me the job.

Q: *Could someone just walk in from the outside and land a development job with the University of Illinois?*

A: Sure. They frequently hire from the outside. They want fresh ideas, new blood. But all these jobs require a high level of computer skills. They want you to be able to turn out a newsletter. They want you to be able to handle the databases.

Q: *So how should a person from the outside, or someone who has been at home for a while, market herself for such a job?*

A: If you could walk in and tell the department head that you could cut the workload by half by computerizing things, you'd have it made. You see, a lot of the administrative people who do the nitty-gritty work, the data entry, are intimidated by technology so there's a lot of resistance to computerizing offices. So along with having the computer skills, you need to be able to teach them. It's amazing how many departments at the University of Illinois still do things on index cards, on Rolodex cross-reference systems that you could do on a computer in a snap. The skills it takes aren't rocket science. They just take time to learn. They're perfect to learn at home, in fact.

Q: *So, getting up to speed on computers is key to getting a good job?*

A: Absolutely. You can get a low-level part-time job with people skills alone. But if you can use a computer like you use a calculator as a way to cut down work in an office, then you're truly marketable. These days, too, I think you have to be Internet literate because that's the whole wave of the future. If you can walk in and say, "I can use the Internet, I can put things on the World Wide Web, I can write a Web page," that's going to pay off big.

SEVEN
Coming in from the Outside

"As a rule, the best jobs do not go to the most qualified individuals; they generally go to the best job hunters. Even though you may compete with people who have stronger credentials, you can still get the job you want if you're willing to put in the extra effort to outstrip the competition."

—Laura Morin, *Everywoman's Jobsearch Guide*

If conducting a regular job search is like playing a tough game of tennis, then searching for part-time work raises the net a few inches. Why? Most companies offer part-time as a way to retain valued employees, and they expect new hires to work full-time. This chapter tells you how to compensate for that extra high net. It details the trickier shots you must take and the fancier footwork you need to outplay the competition.

FINDING YOUR FOCUS

Spend some time thinking about the industry or field you want, the job you would enjoy doing and could do well, and the market for that job. For example, do you want to keep doing the same kind of work but do it in a smaller company more open to part-time? Do

■ **WRITING YOUR OBJECTIVE**

It may be helpful to set up a job objective. A job objective helps you focus your job search. It tells you what kind of job you're looking for in what industry, located where, and using what skills. Once you have completed the following statement, it can become the job objective in a résumé.

Think about how you might complete the following statement:

A position as a _____ in the _____ field or industry that will allow me to use my _____ skills in a company that will offer me part-time challenging work located in _____.

you want to change areas within the same field? Do you want something totally new?

Once you find your focus, sharpen it. If your training or expertise falls short of what your desired job requires, think about how you could acquire the needed expertise. Sometimes stacking a new subspecialty onto an existing one or adding a new skill or two that gives a twist to existing professional skills can catapult you to a much higher level of employability. And according to Harvard professor of economics Rosabeth Moss Kanter, in today's marketplace, employability is the only job security.

Once you have focused on your job objective, you can begin to target companies that can offer you the kind of position you are seeking.

FINDING PART-TIME JOB LEADS: OLD WAYS ARE WORST

You won't find many ads for good part-time work in the local paper, although you'll see plenty of opportunities to flip burgers and do telemarketing. The handful that do appear in the classifieds often turn out to be dead ends, either undesirable jobs that nobody internal wanted or so old they've already been snapped up.

Does this mean reading the classifieds is a waste of time? Absolutely not.

• **Read ads for information.** For instance, if a company is hiring engineers this month, chances are they'll be hiring support personnel next month. By reading ads in trade journals targeted to your industry or field, you can learn what companies are looking for as well as pick up valuable vocabulary and "buzzwords" to use in your résumé. You'll get a feel for the national job market by reading the ads in the big papers such as *The New York Times* and *The Los Angeles Times*. Try the *Wall Street Journal's National Business Employment Weekly,* a compilation of job listings pulled from its four regional editions.

• **Don't rule out following up on a full-time lead.** This strategy works best when (1) your skills or area of expertise is in great demand, (2) you're willing to work in the thirty-hour-per-week range, (3) you don't need benefits because your spouse's plan already covers you, or (4) you already have a job-share partner in mind.

• **Check government listings.** At the federal level, check with the Office of Personnel Management. A program called the OPM Connection is designed to match federal employees who want to work part-time with federal agencies seeking to fill vacancies suitable for either part-time or job-sharing arrangements. Programs are available in Boston, Chicago, Los Angeles, and Washington, D.C. In addition, most state and local governments have agencies that offer part-time.

• **Follow a professional "job line," electronic job listings published by professional associations.** When Henci Goer, freelance writer and author of *Obstetric Myths Versus Research Realities,* decided she needed a regular paycheck to help fund her son's private university tuition, she joined the American Medical Writer's Association for the networking possibilities and to follow their jobline. The next month she noticed a company advertising a position writing abstracts for a health electronic database, a perfect fit for the skills she had honed when researching her book. Although the job was advertised as a full-time job that would be done at the company, she pursued it and eventually managed to negotiate for a part-time position working out of her home.

FOUR WAYS TO TAP INTO THE MOST PROMISING JOB MARKET— UNPUBLISHED OPPORTUNITIES

1. Don't look where all the other job hunters look. Over 70 percent of job openings are not advertised. And much of that hidden job market can be found in small companies. Since 1970 two out of every three new jobs have been created by organizations with 100 or fewer employees. The profile of the "perfect" part-time company is small, fast-growing, and upsizing. Reading the business section of the paper and trade journals and networking are good places to start the research process. Experts suggest researching two or three at a time to keep the process manageable. According to Jackie Larson and Cheri Comstock, authors of *The New Rules of the Job Search Game,* job hunters who focus on three great companies at a time not only keep the process manageable, but also generate the most interviews in the shortest time.

2. Once you've got a good prospect in sight, research the heck out of the company. Reading the annual report is only the beginning. Visit the local library and find as many articles on the company or comparable companies as you can. Concentrate on computer databases such as InfoTrak, Lexis-Nexis, and CompuServ. These will be more up-to-date than the books in the reference section. InfoTrak, for example, allows you to pull up a printout on a company replete with names of divisions, a description of their products and services, and relevant statistics as well as the latest articles that have appeared about it. Another useful resource is *Peterson's Hidden Job Market,* a publication describing the 2,000 fastest-growing companies in various fields that are hiring now. Some experts recommend that you stick with companies that have at least 20 percent sales growth to avoid signing on with a company on the verge of a downsizing cycle. Many larger cities also have publications that list the names of key managers within certain businesses. Once you've done the library research, try to contact an employee of the company or somebody who has done business with them to learn more. Up close and personal knowledge is always the most valuable.

3. Once you've done your due diligence, figure out where you could fit in. Is the company growing so quickly it needs help with recruiting and interviews? Can you do something that would help a small company make the transition to a larger size? The trick is to spot the problems for which you can provide the solution.

4. Network, network, network. Networking is the primary way to generate good leads. If 80 percent of all new jobs come from personal contacts, that figure probably exceeds 90 percent for part-time jobs.

• **Anyone could be your connection to a good lead.** Tell everyone you're interested in part-time work and the type of work you're looking for. Network at professional organizations, mixed industry trade associations, seminars, and conferences. Talk to former colleagues and employers. Pay the $30 for the monthly dinner for your professional organization and put the word out. Don't forget anyone. Review your Christmas card list, your doctors and veterinarians, sports contacts, your baby-sitter, church and club members, salespeople, and the guy sitting next to you on the ski lift. While you might not want to advertise that you're looking for a job to vendors, clients, and customers, chitchatting with them about job opportunities could lead you to a gold mine of information.

• **General and vague won't win you leads.** Practice stating your qualifications and the type of job you're looking for. When part-time computer marketing specialist Sharlene Low was looking for a job, she couldn't understand why the process wasn't working. She kept letting people know she was looking for a part-time job; the people she told always offered to show her résumé around. Off went the résumé and then *nada*. She finally realized she wasn't giving enough information. When she began adding a little three-sentence statement telling the contact about her qualifications (often even close friends have no idea!) and the specific type of job she was looking for, her efforts started to pay off.

• **Prime the pump.** Find out how you can best make contact with this person. What would be the best approach to take? Can you use his/her name? What is the lead's area of expertise?

• **Tit for tat.** According to employment consultant Richard Van Doren, the key to networking is giving something back—or offering to give back. Says Van Doren, ask yourself, "What can I give this person in exchange for his/her time?" It could be as trivial as copying articles of interest or as significant as giving them a lead on a job that isn't right for you but might be right for them.

• **Part-time professionals together.** Networking associations targeted for professionals seeking flexible work arrangements are springing up across the country. The National Association of Part-Time Professionals located in Falls Church, Virginia (703-734-7975), is a good resource and can provide information about local chapters. It also offers a newsletter, *Working Options*, that highlights companies implementing flexible policies as well as a short listing of part-time job leads. In addition, a Job Referral Service provides access to job vacancies as soon as they come into the data bank.

• **Go professional**. Most executive recruiters limit their services to people looking for full-time work. However, a new breed of executive recruitment agency now targets women who want flexible work, including part-time. A few reputable firms include *Part-Time Resources* in Cos Cob, Connecticut, *Professional Alternatives* in Minnetonka, Minnesota, *Executive Options, Ltd.*, in Northbrook, Illinois, and Chicago, *Part-Time Professional Placements, Inc.* in Potomac, Maryland, *Professional Balance, LC* in Dallas, Texas, and *Alterna Track* in New York. Most of these agencies charge the future employer a percentage of your first annual salary

Five years ago Andrea Meltzer co-founded Executive Options in Northbrook, Ilinois, a firm placing executives in part-time projects, temporary projects, and permanent part-time positions. Her clients range from small firms to Fortune 500 companies. Business has grown by 50 percent, says Meltzer, herself a part-time entrepreneur. "Of the 6,000 names or so we have in the database, approximately 60 percent are people who have been burned by downsizings and elect to go into consulting." But the firm also deals with a large number of "professional moms" who want to balance work and family for a limited period of time and for many women who have full-time jobs and are very discreetly looking around for part-time. Meltzer adds, "Of course, we never divulge any information about a client or company without the permission of both parties."

Meltzer says it's not just the superstars who get the good part-time professional work, although she concedes that "there's a lot of mediocrity out there and they don't usually get the great placements." Still, it's not difficult to find someone with the qualifications a company is looking for, says Meltzer, "What is difficult is finding someone with the right personality fit. Ninety percent of it is chemistry."

• **Check out local career counseling centers.** A counseling center for women or senior citizens is most likely to have part-time leads. At Radcliffe Career Services in Cambridge, Massachusetts, for example, most of the staff members work part-time. The Career Action Center in Palo Alto, California, offers counseling services to the community for $45 an hour as well as offering a well-stocked resource library, job-hunting support groups, and access to many Bay Area companies.

TARGETING YOUR RÉSUMÉ FOR PART-TIME: QUESTIONS AND ANSWERS

Q: *Is a résumé for part-time different from a full-time one?*

A: The purpose of any résumé, full-time or part-time, is to keep you in the screening process. The résumé should highlight your marketable talents and skills so that you get the chance to discuss them with an interviewer.

Q: *So should I put "part-time" in the job objective?*

A: Perhaps. If the job you're applying for is part-time, feel free. But best not if you're applying for a full-time position because a preference for part-time may eliminate you from consideration before the screener even reads your qualifications. This issue places you squarely on the horns of an ethical dilemma. Does concealing your interest in part-time constitute bait and switch? There are three schools of thought on this one:

   1. **Include "part-time" in your job objective and hope for the best.** This is known as the Gallipoli approach. Gallipoli was the site of an ill-fated World War I British campaign in which thousands of Australian-New Zealand troops were sent out against impossible odds. Gunned down by entrenched, determined, and prepared enemy ranks, the few survivors are still celebrated today as great war heroes. Similarly, the chances are intimidatingly high that your résumé will be gunned down before you take two steps out of the trenches. The argument *for* this approach, of course, is that it weeds out employers who are dead set against part-time, thus saving you time in the end.

   2. **Hedge your bets by leaving out "part-time" in the résumé.** Instead mention in your cover letter that you "have a preference for working thirty hours a week." This softer approach indicates you're willing to work full-time if the job is right, thereby increasing the odds that your résumé won't be set aside. And, after all, everything is negotiable! You have a strong preference for part-time, but maybe a job offer at twice the expected pay, a company car, and benefits and stock options that will allow your husband to stay home with the kids *might* cause you to rethink your position. This way the door is open for you to negotiate for part-time, and you can't be accused of misleading your potential employer.

   3. **Don't mention "part-time" on any piece of paper or in conversation.** After all, tough times call for tough measures. This approach definitely keeps you moving along in the screening process and gives you a chance to sell yourself in the interview. If you have the derring-do for this "Oh, by-the-way" approach, you had better be prepared with a sales pitch sharp enough to overcome the interviewer's annoyance when you reveal your agenda. You can pull this off if you can persuade the interviewer you can add big value to the

company, solve huge problems, cut costs dramatically, and bring in major clients.

Caution: Whichever strategy you choose, avoid the words *part-time* unless you mean twenty hours a week or less. Employers will tend to assume this is what "part-time" means and dismiss you out of hand.

Q: *How much do you disclose in the cover letter?*

A: Some experts suggest addressing the objection to part-time hours head-on. Your cover letter would say something like: "You probably don't think in terms of having anyone do this job part-time, but here's my proposal . . . I think it would be worthwhile for both of us to sit down and talk . . . There's no question in my mind that I can do an outstanding job for you. I realize that there may be others who apply for this job as full-time, but I feel the quality of my experience is key. Because of the variety of things I've done and the level of responsibility, I think I can do in thirty hours what most candidates will do in forty." You might also suggest a trial period right in the cover letter.

Q: *If my experience has been part-time, should I put that in my résumé?*

A: Not necessarily. Experience is experience. If you ran a diagnostic system for an HMO, you ran a diagnostic system for an HMO. It shouldn't really matter how many hours you spent doing it. However, if it helps you persuade the employer that you can get the job done in twenty-five hours a week, bring it up during the interview. Otherwise, don't give potential employers any reason to set your résumé aside. On a related note, Arlene Rossen Cardozo, author of *Sequencing*, notes that it should be discriminatory for companies to advertise that full-time experience is required.

Q: *If I have a job-share partner in mind, should I send the employer two résumés?*

A: Probably not, unless you have a reason to believe the employer prefers a job-share team. If employers get two résumés and one cover letter that says you want to job share, the reaction will probably be to set it aside because it's too complicated. Probably both you and your job-share partner should each conduct your own search. When either of you gets a call for an interview, deal with the job-share issue then.

PART-TIME INTERVIEW TACTICS

If the job you're interviewing for was advertised as part-time, proceed to knock them dead in the usual fashion.

But if you've gotten in the door via the "Oh, by the way" route, prepare for the tour de force of the part-time interview game. First, you must persuade the employer that you're hands-down the best person for the job. *Then* you persuade her that you can do the job part-time. The real trick is to do all this without looking like you just committed a crime.

Here are some tips to guide you through the part-time interview process:

• **Make sure you're pitching to the right batter.** If the person who needs to get the work done—your manager—can see the quality of your work and your qualifications, that person will be more willing to be flexible than a personnel representative who only knows the company policy and may not understand the needs of the job. Henci Goer experienced this firsthand when she interviewed for her job as a medical abstractor. She made the mistake of telling personnel that she wasn't interested in full-time in-house employment, "I proposed part-time hours and I also proposed a telecommuting arrangement that would save me a forty-five-minute drive each way up and down the peninsula," at which point the interviewer shut down the interview and showed Goer the door.

That evening as she and her husband rehashed the failed interview, she realized her tactical error. Goer got lucky, though. The company didn't fill the position and a few weeks later she got a call from the department manager offering her part-time work at home. Still, Goer learned her lesson and would never make that mistake again.

• **Anticipate nosiness.** Face it, potential employers poke around. They'll find a way to ask everything they want to know. You just need the right answers. If an employer asks, "Why would you want to leave an established career at an employment agency for an essentially entry-level position in marketing?" don't come back with, "Because I need the flexibility more than I need exciting work" (even though it may be true). Instead, say something to the effect that you feel you've stopped growing in your current position, you want to expand your skills, how and why you got interested in this new area, and, of course, why your former work makes you even more valuable as an employee.

• **Sense what they're not saying.** Bring up objections the employer probably has but is hesitant to verbalize. For example, "It would be understandable if you were concerned that as a part-timer I might not be available to help out in crunch times or that I might be less committed than a full-time employee. I can assure you that the reason I am looking for part-time work is because I want to be able to be 100 percent committed to my job. I have never experienced any problems separating my family life from my work life. I want you to know that I'm very flexible and more than willing to put in extra time when necessary."

• **Decide what is nonnegotiable.** Know before you walk in if you absolutely must have full health coverage and disability. Know what salary range you will accept as well as the hours and schedule you insist on.

• **Practice answering tough questions on videotape.** People who haven't practiced handling tough questions come off badly when an interviewer probes. So if there are any questions likely to make you look like you're hiding something, don't even think about an interview until you've practiced on videotape.

• **Don't ask about company part-time or work/life policies in the interview.** You should already know from your research. And if you don't, now isn't the time.

• **Don't give the employer the impression that you'll take anything as long as it's part-time.** Employers like employees with clear direction and focused job interests. And you won't like "anything as long as it's part-time" for very long.

• **Don't give up half your salary for no reason.** Part-time expert Maria Laqueur advises that you protect yourself against an employer who's trying for too good a deal, i.e., a full-time employee with part-time hours and no benefits. Is the boss trying to save a few bucks or does she really just need someone three days a week? Questions to ask: Is this a new or existing position? If new, who created it and why? If it's an existing one, how many hours a week did the last person work and was she successful in meeting the goals of the job? Are there other part-time employees on staff, and if so, in what position?

• **Understand your package.** Find out if you will be compensated with extra pay or comp time if you work extra hours. Also ask if you will be able to make a transition from part-time to full-time in the future. Don't underestimate the importance of paid leaves. The income you stand to lose by not being paid for vacations, sick leave, and holidays can amount to a sizable chunk of cash. If you suspect the number of hours you work will fluctuate radically and will include a lot of overtime, you may want to negotiate an hourly rate instead of a salary.

IF YOU'RE USING THE "OH, BY-THE-WAY" APPROACH . . .

• **Timing is everything.** Wait until you feel the employer is sold on you before you broach the subject. Only until you feel the employer is sold do you say: "I would actually prefer to do this job in four days a week." Then jump in with some eye-opening statistics on increased productivity and some examples of others in parallel situations who are doing it part-time and the names and phone numbers of their managers if necessary.

• **Use a proposal approach to sell your part-time job.** You should have a tentative idea of what parts of the job you want to do and the logistics of doing it before you walk in to the interview. As you find out more about the job in the interview process, adjust your proposal accordingly. You could also suggest a trial period just as you would if you were converting your full-time job.

ALL YOU NEED IS SALESMANSHIP AND A LITTLE LUCK

Coming in from the outside and getting a good part-time job isn't easy, but it can be done. People do it all the time. But you won't usually get one using traditional methods. You're going to do a lot of thinking and conceptualizing work before you even step out to talk to a new employer. The trick is, you've got to seek the job and, at the same time, educate the employer. Read the next chapter if you're trying to pull this off after having been home with the kids for a few years.

EIGHT

Sequencers Reenter the Workforce After Staying Home

"I think if a woman cannot go back to a productive and satisfying career after staying home for three years, then the problem is in the workplace and not with the woman. You do not lose your capacity for thinking or whatever else is required as a result of staying home to raise children. "

—Karen Nussbaum, Director of Working Women's
    Department, AFL-CIO

If you are a professional woman trying to reenter the workplace part-time after at-home motherhood, you face some unique challenges. The difficulty of your reentry depends on the length of time you've been out of the job market and on your competence level when you left. If you rocketed home trailing clouds of acclaim for your last project or deal and if you've kept up in your field, the aura may still be there. It may be a simple matter of calling your former employer and letting him or her know you're available. On the other hand, if the last time you held a job, voice mail was when someone yelled over from the next cubicle and you vaguely remember placing the cover over your IBM Selectric, you'll need more time and effort to scrape the rust off your résumé.

Most women who have achieved a high level of success feel that up to two or three years is a manageable absence. Reentry is tougher after five years. According to *Newsweek* writer Barbara Kantowitz,

"Once you pass that crucial half decade mark, you're basically starting from scratch." Whatever your situation, there's no need to sit at home full of self-doubt and semipanic about your dismal job prospects. It may be harder to come back after being home over five years, but it can be done, as such luminaries as Sandra Day O'Connor, Geraldine Ferraro, and Jeanne Kirkpatrick have proved.

REMEMBER THE BICYCLE: SOME THINGS YOU NEVER FORGET

Keeping up your confidence is key for sequencing women. Job rejection can be especially tough on sequencing women who already doubt their abilities to return to the business world. But minds do not turn to mush at home. You are the same person you always were with the same intellectual talents. It's like riding a bicycle: Once you climb onto the seat and start peddling, you'll remember everything you learned earlier.

After her first child was born, software writer Karen Gage went back part-time with a software company in Cupertino, California. She took a job because she worried that she was getting stale and that "No one would hire me, so I would be forever without work." After two years of "total craziness," Gage decided to stay home full-time until her children were older. Says Gage, "I realized that I could always pick up the latest information on the latest system when I wanted to get back in. And the qualities that make you a good engineer don't decay—clarity and care and attention to detail. There's very little at this point that's going to make me forget how to be a good engineer." Ditto New Yorker Vivian Droszdoff, an at-home mom who is planning to switch from executive recruiting to professional fund-raising. Says Droszdoff, "I've been in sales so long. If you can sell a product or a service, you can sell anything. Whether you're selling attorneys or you're selling a charity, you never lose that."

PRACTICE SAFE SEQUENCING

There are three things you can do to ensure reentry: (1) Keep a toe in with freelance work, (2) keep an ear out for today's skills, and (3) use volunteer work as a springboard.

Stay Visible and Connected
• **Act as if you're employed because you are.** Do a little freelancing in your field. Start a consulting business, teach some classes, or write an article or two for your favorite trade journal. Keep up with your field, too. Read trade journals carefully. Experts note that reading trade journals regularly and carefully is the equivalent of taking two years' worth of college courses in your field.
• **Maintain contacts with former colleagues.** Schedule lunches regularly with your former boss or colleagues. Drop in from time to time at the office and see what's going on.

Stay in Touch with the World of Functional Skills
• **It's no longer wpm, it's http://.** Take classes to learn new software or seminars to keep your certification current in nursing, teaching, or accounting. You may not think you have time to squeeze continuing education in between rounds of carpooling, but it's easier than starting completely over in five years.
• **Learn a new skill.** Skill building is what starts to put muscle on a résumé that has become atrophied by years of disuse and by changes in the workplace. Smaller companies—just where you are mostly likely to find the part-time hours you want—are looking for employees who can do a little of everything from sales and marketing to answering the phone.
• **Develop a portable skill.** Use your time at home to learn a new technology or other skill requiring a high degree of expertise such as designing Web sites on the Internet or technical writing. A portable skill is one that you can do anywhere—an employment guarantee in any city.
• **Strengthen your weak spots.** If you have a love-hate relationship with computers, take some courses at your community college and practice at night after the kids are in bed. Make friends with electronic spreadsheets if you need to. Take calculus or statistics if math has always been a weakness. If you're like most people, you're mortified of speaking to a group. Join Toastmasters to get comfortable making presentations, a skill that employers always find useful.

Volunteer to Stay Employable
Forget the old Army adage "Volunteer for nothing." Patricia Lindh, vice president of the Bank of America and former assistant to Betty Ford, observes, "Women's experience in volunteerism is invaluable. You learn how to move people along, how to lead them.

You do not order, fire, or pay them. You have to *persuade* them to your way of thinking. Well-chosen nonprofit work is not idle time. It can really be superior on-the-job training for your next career.''

Here are some ideas for using volunteer work as a way to keep up and to build marketable skills:

• **Forget stuffing envelopes or bringing the soft drinks.** Choose volunteer work that gives you solid work experience. Be the treasurer of the Sports Boosters Club and make sure you put the $150,000 budget data on Excel or Intuit. Become an officer or a committee member of your professional association. Write educational grants. If you're a pharmacist, dispense prescriptions at a free clinic. If you're a lawyer, do some pro bono work at the legal clinic.

• **Look at a volunteer organization as a potential first client**. Laurel Prokop, an independent contractor who does graphic design and desktop publishing, did volunteer graphics work for the Multiple Sclerosis Foundation in Fort Collins, Colorado. Says Prokop, ''I didn't get any money, but I still consider them to be my first client. That volunteer job gave me something to put in my portfolio.''

• **Volunteer for visibility.** It's not really who you know—it's who knows you. By making yourself visible in the PTA, city government, and other civic organizations, you become a known quantity. Your good reputation will transfer over when you begin your job search.

• **Look for internship opportunities.** Internships are an excellent way to gain on-the-job experience. Usually interns receive a legal contract in which the supervisor carefully spells out the required work and training. At the end of the internship, interns receive a transcript showing what work was completed and what skills were used, a document that can be invaluable in landing a paid job.

■ ''SITCOMS: Single Income, Two Children, Oppressive Mortgage.''

—Faith Popcorn, *Clicking*

IF IT'S BEEN A WHILE

While most mothering skills aren't technical, raising children does involve such business management skills as managing a large facility, scheduling and supervising daily activities, and budgeting. Unfortunately, personnel managers today aren't always as generous in their recognition of the skills involved as they should be.

What to do?

• **Be realistic about your marketability.** How you performed at home or how you dealt with friends over the years may not be relevant to your performance on the job. Be realistic about the marketability of your "people" skills and the need to acquire new hard skills. Usually it is the person with the most skills who survives— or at least gets the job. Friends or relatives employed in the field that interests you can help you assess your current skills and tell you what more you need.

• **Approach looking for a job as a job in itself.** Set manageable goals—composing a cover letter, making ten phone calls, updating a résumé—and define success as completing those goals.

• **Book it.** If you don't know what you want to do, buy a book on recareering. Books such as Richard Bolles's *What Color Is Your Parachute?* can help you make a full-scale assessment of your passions, priorities, and aptitudes.

• **Get assessed.** Career counselors, women's centers, or testing and assessment firms all offer testing and counseling services that produce highly sophisticated career feedback. Because such individualized testing is quite expensive, try to get a personal recommendation before you sign up.

• **Check out government programs for dislocated workers.** By the time Sharlene Low had been at home with her children for over eight years, her prior nine years as a computer sales manager with Hewlett-Packard had become a distant memory. Interested in returning to the workforce, she heard about a federal program called NOVA Private Industry Council, a program that provides outplacement services for individuals found eligible for Dislocated Worker Status under the federal Job Training Partnership Act (JTPA). She found that her time out of the workplace and the obsolesence of her skills qualified her for the program.

She began a round of workshops, including "Assessment of Personality/Management Types," "Transferable Skills," "Vocational Aptitudes," "Interests and Values," "Clarifying Your Job Objective," and "Defining Yourself as a Product." NOVA counselors not only coached her on résumé writing and interviewing skills, but also helped her to research companies that might fit her needs and skills and placed her in temporary assignments there. Says Low, "I went from believing that nobody would ever hire me—I had been away so long the only thing I understood about a fax machine was my ability to recognize the funny ringing sound—to believing that I had a lot to offer.''

The training paid off in dollars and cents as well. When an employer offered Low a salary well below what she had earned before staying home, she politely but firmly refused to settle. Says Low, ''The words came rolling out of my mouth—I shocked myself. I said very calmly just as if I had practiced, 'Although I haven't worked outside the home for over eight years and may have lost some of my technical knowledge, I believe my experience and skillset are worth more than that.' '' She then named the salary she wanted and she got it. Says Low, ''Had I not gone through the NOVA program, I would have just said, okay, I'll take it.''

TIPS TO HELP SEQUENCERS FIND JOB LEADS (ON TOP OF THE REGULAR STUFF!)

• **Let a temp agency find leads for you.** Over 38 percent of temp jobs become regular positions. Not surprisingly then, temping is a leading way for sequencers to get back in the workforce. Besides providing skills training and the opportunity to test out various companies, temping lets you get a foot in the door, the most difficult step for most sequencers. The downside here is that most—not all— temp agencies require employees to work the business hours of the clients. So while you can usually manage to get summers off, you'll probably have to commit to regular business hours when you take on a project.

• **Use your neighborhood network.** Make a list of everybody you know, leaving no stone unturned. Talk about your job goal at the school, church or synagogue, hospital, and the organization where you've volunteered. Don't forget to share your qualifications and the type of work you're looking for so they have something concrete to work with. Make sure they understand your work experience and educational background, specific skills, and the personal qualities that will make you a valuable asset.

• **Join a job search support organization for sequencers.** FE- MALE (Formerly Employed Mothers at the Leading Edge), a national support network for at-home mothers who plan to return to the workforce, is a good place to start. This organization with local chapters all over the United States, based in Elmhurst, Illinois (708-941-3553), helps women make the transition from the workplace to home but also has groups for ''seasoned'' at-home mothers who are trying to go back to work. If there's no job-hunting group in your area, start your own. Meet every week with women who are also gearing up for reentry to set goals, share leads, swap job-hunting tips, and offer support.

UNMOTHBALLING YOUR RÉSUMÉ

A Ziggy cartoon depicts him seated opposite a stern personnel official behind a desk. Says the personnel official sardonically: ''Any honors and awards since the third grade spelling bee?''

Sequencing can create an occupational hazard on your résumé. To fill in the blanks, a well-crafted résumé dresses up your special skills and qualifications while downplaying the gap between paid job experiences. Here's how:

- **Acknowledge the gap either in the résumé or cover letter.** Tell what you were doing during the gap that makes you a valuable employee. If you taught yourself to do computer graphics or honed your sales and presentation skills by chairing a local speaker series, say so.

> ''Make sure there's something there that speaks to the gap. Absent that information, you wonder what happened. Did they get fired? Haven't they been able to find work for ten years? Did they join the KGB for four years? Today we receive so many résumés that if one brings up any question at all, it goes to the side.''
>
> —David Kennedy, human resources vice president of New England Electric

- **Use volunteer experience but call it pro bono work.** Remember that it isn't necessary to indicate that you weren't paid for this work experience. Experience is experience. Packaging your work as *pro bono* rather than volunteer sounds more professional.
- **Quantify work you've done.** For example: I edited a newsletter for the Northern California Track and Field Association with readership increasing 28 percent in one year. I organized an educational

task force that successfully wrote a statewide education initiative that was adopted with a 73 percent favorable vote. I trained and supervised a staff of eight. I implemented a new computer system at the school resulting in a 30 percent increase in efficiency.

• **Organize your résumé to present you in the strongest light.** First of all, if you haven't attended school recently, move your personal and educational info to the end. Second, some experts recomend a functional résumé format that presents skills and accomplishments under broad skill areas or functions instead of as part of work experience. This allows you to highlight your qualifications while minimizing your lack of recent work experience. The actual dates of your job experiences and education come later.

• **Avoid corny pseudo titles.** "Home CEO" or "Home Engineer" sound silly. Besides, at-home motherhood doesn't need disguising.

• **Don't give personal information unless it's relevant to the job.** No one cares that you garden, play bridge, collect rocks, or that you're a quick learner. Some experts recommend that you mention athletic abilities such as golf, tennis, marathon racing—but only if you're serious. Do not include your age, weight, height, marital status, race, religion, or other personal information unless you feel it's pertinent to the job you're seeking.

• **Make sure your résumé reaches human hands.** As many as three-quarters of the Fortune 500 companies use electronic résumé scanning to eliminate candidates without the necessary skills. Therefore, be specific about your skills. If you can use Power Point and Excel, make sure to include that. Don't staple your résumé, and don't use super-small type or decorative fonts that won't be recognized by a scanner.

INTERVIEWING FOR SEQUENCERS: BASIC BLOCKING AND TACKLING

Most of us lack the magic wit and style of Bombeck, the late humorist and prolific writer of columns and books on housewives. We must instead depend on basic blocking and tackling to get through the interview process.

• **Find your best profile.** Reframe your time out of the workforce as adding value to the company. Not only have you put in time getting your kids off to a good start, freeing you now to commit yourself 100 percent to a part-time job, but you've gained valuable

■ "During a job interview Erma Bombeck told the personnel manager that she had been a wife and mother for all those years and
needed extra sheets over and above those on the application to
list her background and skills. Needless to say, she got the job."

—Charles Logue, Ph.D., *Outplace
Yourself* and *Secrets of an Executive Outplacement Counselor*

skills that take a long time to learn. If an employer is suspicious of
the credibility of your consulting work, briefly explain and show a
list of the companies and projects you worked on as well as showing
work samples.

• **You don't have a lot of experience and that's okay.** Don't
argue when the inteviewer says you don't really have enough experience in this field. Instead, acknowledge the concern and then overcome the objection. You say, "I realize there may be others with
more years of experience, but I feel the quality of my experience is
the key. Because of the variety of things I've done and the level of
responsibility I've had, I think my five years are equal to what most
people accomplish in ten. There's no question in my mind that I can
do an outstanding job for you."

• **Take samples of your work.** An impressive portfolio of draw-
ings, published articles, a book, slides, ad copy, a database on disk,
or letters of recommendation speak louder than words to back up
your statements about your accomplishments and productivity.

• **If they lowball, play hardball.** You might feel so grateful to
have a job that you'll be tempted to accept a low starting salary.
You might have the mistaken impression that you can increase your
salary substantially within the first year once you demonstrate your
value to the boss. The reality is that your starting salary will probably
not increase substantially because most employers are not interested
in renegotiating a salary once you have accepted. This is your best
shot at a good salary—take it.

NO APOLOGIES NECESSARY

Whatever you do, don't apologize for your time at home. In fact, at-
home motherhood is similar to part-time professional work in that
the negative stigma associated with it is diminishing. Both jobs require skills, daring, commitment, creativity, and tenacity.

NINE
You, Inc.

"The small business entrepreneur is the new hero (and often heroine) of the economy."

—Faith Popcorn, *Clicking*

If you're setting up shop as an independent contractor, consultant, or freelancer, your product is yourself—your knowledge, skills, experience, and contacts. Whether your business is giving time-management seminars, programming computers, designing diets, or writing technical manuals, the issues are the same—organizing, marketing, bidding, billing, and keeping clients happy. Oh yes, and finding the time in between to do the work! On the following pages you'll find strategies successful part-time entrepreneurs use and tips from the experts to help you plan, start the business, keep it going, and, if you want, keep it growing.

THE PART-TIME ENTREPRENEUR: DOES $30,000 SPELL SUCCESS?

A survey by Paul and Sarah Edwards, authors of *Working From Home,* found that the home businesspersons who consider themselves *successful* make an average of $61,000 annually. Successful part-time

145

pros would probably bring in half or more of that, approximately $30,000. Is that close to what you had in mind?

Your income depends largely on how much time and energy you want to dedicate to working and on the type of work you do. You may not even think of yourself as starting a business—you just want to do a little freelancing until the kids are in college. Or you may plan to launch your business in a dramatic way. Either way, if you approach independent contracting as the viable business that it is, not just as a professional hobby in which you're going to dabble, you can significantly increase the dollar returns for whatever investment of time you make.

GETTING STARTED

A quick reality check: If you thought your cubicle was small, wait until you try to fit a professional office into your personal mess. You'll become arch enemies with your library (it's never open when you need it, and overdue fines stack up fast). You'll become good friends with the cashier at Kinko's, Office Depot, and your local Barnes and Noble (a library substitute). You may feel you're married to the refrigerator you'll be so attracted. Dressing for success may become clean jeans and combing your hair when the FedEx truck arrives for a signature. Power lunches these days are PB&Js and Oreo cookies. You'll need a two-line phone, especially if you have teenagers, and a "Not now—I'm working" sign handy. The point is that running a business from home will bring new challenges—and distractions—that are vastly different from corporate-business-as-usual.

While You're Still Employed . . .

In general, experts recommend not quitting your old job until you set up your home office, you save six months salary, and you line up at least one project. Here's how you can begin to prepare before you resign.

DEVELOP YOUR PRODUCT—DEVELOP YOURSELF

The most important prep work you can do is to hone your marketable skills and establish relationships that can help you when you're on your own. Learn from the corporation what skills you need to brush up on. Do you know how to write a press release? What computer software is best for your home-billing system? Get ready for self-reliance. Hang a few safety nets. Become multiskilled and an expert at multitasking. Learn the Web, know the Net. Become one with your computer. Through power lunches, cocktail hours, and trade events you've met hundreds of people who can become your bank of potential clients. Nurture these relationships as you test your networking skills—you'll need these contacts to be your word-of-mouth when you branch out solo.

DEFINE YOUR MARKET NICHE

Defining your unique talents and matching those talents to a narrow niche of the market greatly enhances your chances of success. Joan Silver, for example, fills a specialized niche of the employment recruiting industry. The Connecticut-based Silver owns and operates BioTech, a provider of technical support personnel to government research facilities. Her biggest customer, Ames Research, the research arm of NASA, hires Silver to supply people to carry out short-term life science research projects for researchers, usually professors. Scientists call her and say, "I've got so-and-so research going on. I need people to help me, and I need help with all the paperwork."

LINE UP YOUR FIRST CLIENT BEFORE YOU LEAVE

Susan Bockus and Carol Olson, the former Hewlett-Packard job-share team, eventually started their own consulting business and had a client ready to go. Says Bockus, "Having the client made it easier to leave—it gave us that little shot of confidence we needed to make our move." The trend toward downsizing and outsourcing supports this "one-for-the-road" strategy. As companies slough off whole departments such as human resources and information systems to outside consultants, it's not uncommon to be let go one week, and be rehired in the same capacity the following week—as a contractor.

MAKE SURE YOUR HEALTH IS COVERED

You might be able to take advantage of your husband's group medical. If not, then try COBRA or a similar interim insurance as backup. The labor laws are changing, but currently the law entitles you to extend your insurance coverage for up to eighteen months after leaving a company. You pay the full amount of the premium your employer would normally pay, plus another 2% for overhead. Needless to say, you should start shopping around for other coverage well before the eighteen-month window closes. For insurance help, call the National Insurance Consumer Help Line at 800-942-4242.

CHECK INTO DISABILITY INSURANCE

According to Joseph Anthony in *Kiplinger's Revised and Updated Working for Yourself*, disability insurance is more critical for ICs than life insurance. The odds are better than 50-50 that a 35-year-old will at some point before reaching age 65 be disabled for 90 days or more. Unlike medical insurance, employees cannot retain disability coverage from their previous job. A group disability policy cannot be transferred when you leave the company to start your own business nor can you purchase a new individual policy. Why? Because you don't have a track record of earnings and profits in your new business that an insurance provider could review to see what level of benefits you would qualify for. This catch-22 often puts entrepreneurs in a coverage bind.

The solution: Get an individual policy while you're employed. If you purchase it while employed, you can keep it once you're on your own.

MAKE SURE YOU'RE LEGAL

• **The noncompete clause.** As more and more high-level professionals take the consulting plunge, the "noncompete clause" has become a sensitive issue. Check the contract you signed with your employer to see if you signed a noncompete clause when you started working. It may prohibit you from competing with your employer for a specific period of time. In other words, if you're setting up shop in the same business as your employer, it may be illegal for you to leave your old company one day and start your new venture the next.

In practice, what constitutes the "competition" in the noncompete clause is a matter of legal opinion. Usually, walking away with the knowledge that you hold in your own head does not violate such agreements. Taking real work with you like a client or the design of a product you were developing at the time might.

Check around to find out how your company handles such issues and how your contract is interpreted. If there's any question about restrictions, see an attorney for advice. Usually the best referrals for attorneys are obtained by asking others in similar businesses.

• **Zoning, business permits, and licenses.** In addition to corporate legalities, you should check out the neighborhood rules. Every community is different, but there may be zoning regulations at the city or county level that restrict home businesses. Usually, this is no problem unless customers visit your home regularly, your business requires frequent truck deliveries, or you operate a hard rock recording studio. You can sidestep the issue by meeting with clients at their offices, in a hotel conference room, or over breakfast. Start by checking around with other home businesspeople for input. Then call your city/county zoning commission and make discreet inquiries.

Chances are good you'll need some official pieces of paper to get started. Find out what trademarks, licenses, business permits, or trade name registrations are required. Check with your city and county governments first by asking for the zoning or planning commission. Then contact your state government to make sure you're in compliance. If you're selling a product, for example, you will be required to pay sales tax on products sold at retail.

• **As a contractor, you'll need a contract.** An airtight contract that covers your agreement with clients can be your best friend in the sometimes cruel world of being out there without a company—and their legal department—to back you up. Seattle contractor Laurel Prokop took ideas that she liked from others' contracts, then had a lawyer draw one up for her. She considers the lawyer's fee money well spent. Without a contract, you'll have weak grounds on which to resolve any questions concerning the scope of work, schedule, terms of payment, or collection of an outstanding account.

Home Sweet Home Office

THE SETUP

The dream setup is a separate home office with a separate entrance far away from *Barney* and unmade beds. Far more often, part-time professionals settle for the guest bedroom, den, or the basement. But you don't have to dedicate a separate room—dressing screens can section off your apartment. The dining room table that's only used for holidays could be pressed into service. Furniture costs for your *sanctum sanctorum* can be kept low. You don't need leather couches and Oriental rugs. Instead shop garage sales for shelves and a desk or call retail office furniture stores to see if they warehouse damaged goods. My own tip: Splurge on a good ergonomic chair. The kitchen chair I sat on for two years nearly put me and my back out of business. You don't have to spend $500 on a Steelcase swivel—I bought my life-changing chair at a yard sale for $15.

■ A survey published by *Home Run,* a magazine for home workers, revealed that 50 percent of people working from home use uncomfortable chairs that they would refuse at work. Incidentally, a final "terrifying" statistic was that more than a third allowed their children to play unchecked on their computer. The authors asked, "How would the clients feel if they knew?"

EQUIPMENT

Start-up costs can be kept reasonable, especially if you don't need a copier. My office cost me less than $4,000 including a computer, printer, modem, fax machine, new bookshelves, computer stand, filing cabinet, and voice mail service.

If you can't afford any glitches in your system, consider working with a computer consultant who can help you add to your system, streamline the system you've already got, develop security measures if you need them, and help you deal with a system meltdown or other disaster. Get a referral from friends to help you locate a free-lance systems manager. According to Ellen Parlapiano and Patricia Cobe, authors of *Mompreneurs*, IBM and AT&T are among the big companies that have special small business divisions that for a nominal fee will work with you and offer an estimate. Some people also purchase service contracts or extended service plans to protect themselves from technological breakdown.

PICKUP LINES

Three phone lines might get you up and running: one line for your computer, one for your fax, and one line for yourself. Also consider a two-line telephone. The purchase of the phones ($100) and the monthly services makes this a more expensive option, but probably well worth it. Because two-line phones have two distinctly different rings for each line, you know in advance whether it's a business call or your neighbor so you can adjust your demeanor accordingly. Decide on your phone setup before you have your business cards printed. An answering machine with call waiting is a popular option but many callers dislike being put on hold while you handle another call. We recommend a voice mail service that allows a caller to leave a message while you're talking.

Contact your phone company and ask for business service if you feel you need a consultation. Be aware that many phone companies charge businesses significantly higher rates than they charge individuals for basic services.

■ GADGETS, STRATEGIES, AND A LIBRARY

These add-ons and bonus baubles will ease your day-to-day communications and errands:

- A "fax board" added to a computer's hard drive allows you to send files from your computer to someone else's fax machine and to receive faxed transmissions. You'll save time because you won't have to print your document first. One drawback: You can't use it to send materials that aren't already in your computer's memory.
- Don't sell your old typewriter. It will come in handy for filling out forms and addressing envelopes.
- If you really want to free your hands to type on the keyboard or to move around while talking, invest in a headset ($75 for a plug-in and $150 for a cordless).
- Invest $15 in a postage scale. This will save extra trips to the post office and the waste of putting extra stamps on a letter that weighs less than you think.
- Don't forget to budget monthly on-line research and e-mail fees. If you're a telecommuter, you'll love this high-tech freedom.
- Budget $150 a year for subscriptions to magazines that will keep you in touch and make a useful library. Some suggestions: *Home Office Computing,* the American Management Association's *Review, Inc.,* your industry's best trade magazine, and a hardware and software review like *Macworld* or *PC.*

LIABILITY INSURANCE

Consider buying liability insurance. If a neighborhood boy comes in to help you stuff envelopes and falls down the stairs or a UPS employee slips on some ice leaving a package on your stoop, the accident may not be automatically covered under your regular homeowner's insurance. Ask your insurance agent for advice.

Getting a rider to your homeowner's policy to protect against theft, fire, vandalism, and other disasters to your home office is just plain smart. Most homeowners don't discover the fine print excluding business losses until they fill out claims.

Creating a Professional Image

WHAT'S IN A NAME?

First decide on your job title and description. Are you a contractor or consultant? Principal or president? The difference between an independent contractor and a consultant, says one executive, is that "a consultant comes in and dispenses advice and makes recommendations on how to solve a problem. A contractor comes in and does the work. They're the arms and legs; the consultant is the brains." But that's a matter of opinion. Technically, the terms *consultant*, *independent contractor*, and *freelancer* are interchangeable. Sometimes the person who recommends solutions for a problem is the same person who actually does the work in carrying out the recommendations because the client doesn't have anyone in-house with the skills to complete the work. Find out what the buzzword is in your industry and go with it.

Next, decide on a name. Before you settle on something cute like Fifi's Fonts or Research First, remember that your name is the first thing potential clients see and will adorn every card, envelope, and piece of stationery you hand or send out. So yes, be clever, but first be professional.

When naming your company, think long-term. A personal name announces that you work alone. If your part-time professional business is strictly a bridge until the kids get older, then probably just using a name such as Jane Bittner, Instructional Designer, is a good choice. However, if you plan on growing your business into a company, consider a name that will accommodate expansion. For example, Nancy's Newsdesk is limiting whereas Chambers Publishing could stand for a multiemployee operation.

Also, think strategically. Where will the name appear? What will make it stand out? An interesting spelling or logo? Does alphabetical order make a difference? For example, when my friend was starting her home appraisal business, she knew that picking an *A* word would put her first when people let their fingers do the walking. She christened her venture Accurate Appraisals, and, in fact, most Yellow Pages referrals do call her first because *A* is first on the list.

PERCEPTION, PERCEPTION, PERCEPTION

When you set up your enterprise, don't let your image slip through the cracks. Like the Groucho Marx line, "I wouldn't want to belong to any club that would have me as a member," ask yourself, "Would

I hire me?'' Clients like to deal with people who are going to be around for a while, so don't let your presence seem temporary. A common criticism of home-based businesspeople is that they have the look and feel of an amateur outfit, reinforcing the impression that a home business is not a real business.

Some simple solutions:

1. **Invest in basic paper goods.** You don't need to go overboard and rent a cushy downtown office with a view and a showroom, but you do need a professional-looking business card and good stationery. As a finishing touch you might add a classy brochure describing your services, picturing your work or listing your biggest accomplishments and clients (with their permission, of course).

2. **Define your expertise within your field.** If you don't do this, you won't stand out from the pack in the clients' minds. Unless they are convinced that you are the current leader, the client will have only price to go by. The more tangible your products the easier it is to sell and the higher you can set your fees. Generalists may have a bigger market of available business, but specialists can command a higher price.

According to consulting expert Lynne Hobbs, the most common mistake she sees independent contractors making today is failing to define themselves and their service adequately. In an interview with the Association of Part-Time Professionals, Hobbs said she meets many ''communications consultants,'' a description that indicates very little. Is this communication consultant's expertise in the area of public relations or advertising? Does she serve the technical or scientific fields, the public or private sector? If you target your corner of the market, you'll turn away fewer clients. Besides, you can always say yes when a client requests something outside your area if you feel competent to handle it.

SOLITARY CONFINEMENT

Isolation can give even the most enthusiastic entrepreneur a case of the post-hanging-the-shingle blues. According to a Roper poll, a third of home workers worry about isolation, yet home business experts Sarah and Paul Edwards point out that only 10 to 12 percent of those in other surveys actually reported feeling isolated and lonely. According to the Edwards, the negative feeling is most acute at the

■ GOING FOR THE GIMMICK—GOING FOR THE GRANDEUR

Here are eleven promotional ideas:

1. Tap into the local press; see if anyone needs a columnist or bi-weekly Q&A column. Fax monthly press releases to them with seminar dates or other announcements.
2. Use direct mail that you create with desktop publishing as a marketing tool. You can write a newsletter that offers service and information or just a flier with a coupon for 10 percent off an initial consultation.
3. Network to establish yourself as an opinion leader in your trade. Brush up on presentation skills and volunteer to offer a seminar or keynote address at the next trade conference.
4. Establish a weekly Internet chat session.
5. Offer seminars.
6. When appropriate, send a letter to the editor of the local paper. Anything that is run is a free advertisement.
7. Approach your local cable TV or radio broadcasters to make a special guest appearance.
8. Give to local charities because it is the right thing to do. But know that your logo on Little League tee-shirts or religious bulletins helps you, too. Local endorsements help you stand out as a community leader.
9. Become a featured or occasional contributor to trade and consumer media. Study the publications carefully before submitting your idea so that you understand the audience and what type of material the publication needs. Once you get an article in, send reprints to past, present, and future clients. If you can't write, retain another independent contractor to ghostwrite it for you.
10. Start your own personal World Wide Web site.
11. Don't turn your nose up to such time-honored gimmicks as offering coupons, passing out matchbooks or key chains, coffee cups, calendars, notepads, and other novelties made up for your business. If your business grows, consider what the blimp did for Goodyear.

beginning. Once business routines become established and clients are on the line, the problem fades.

"Although I'm the type of person who likes alone time, I felt very isolated," says Los Gatos, California, speechwriter Kathleen

Dixon. "I quickly found out that alone time and isolation are two different things. Overnight I lost the social structure that comes from an office environment—seeing people in the hall, the flurry of communication. Then suddenly it stops. It's gone. It's just you and your computer sitting in your bedroom. Yes, you can go out to lunch, and yes, you can plan to see people, but it's not the same. I think it's important for anybody going into the consulting business to expect an adjustment period." Dixon's home-alone syndrome let up as her business grew and she could rent office space in a nearby bustling downtown where she would have colleagues.

Some independent contractors have a delayed reaction to the isolation. Karin Abarbanel, author of *Overcoming the Emotional Roadblocks of Starting a Homebased Business,* estimates isolation begins four to six months *after* starting a business. Once the excitement and novelty have worn off, reality begins to sink in. The prospect of doing your own booking, billing, and bookkeeping can in itself be depressing and accentuates the scary feeling of being totally on your own. You quickly gain a new appreciation of the infrastructure of a big company and what it does for its employees.

Recovery ideas:

* Schedule regular people breaks. If face-to-face contact isn't possible, use the phone just to hear the sound of another adult human voice.
* Play soft music in the background to break the silence.
* Volunteer on an advisory board, take seminars at entrepreneurial associations.
* Get on-line. The chat lines, job lines, and bulletin boards offer the chance to connect with other people doing exactly what you're doing. A small warning though, don't give out too much information over the Internet, you never know exactly whom you're chatting with.
* Form a "virtual office" for some cyberspace office colleagues. If you're a writer, meet regularly with another group of writers to edit each other's work every week or two. Teaming up with another contractor, even if it's very casual, will help reduce your isolation and will give you a chance to exchange leads, develop potential partnerships or subcontractors, share mailing lists, and run group specials.

What If They Find Out I'm a Frog?

Most people going out on their own have what Kathleen Dixon calls the Frog Syndrome. Says Dixon, "The fear is that after seventeen years of writing in the news industry, they'll discover I'm *not* royalty, but just a frog who doesn't have any capabilities. The fear is that somehow I managed to get along by the skin of my teeth up till now, and now that I'm on my own, I'm going to be exposed as the frog I really am.'' This fear of being revealed as an imposter is natural but completely irrational. As you begin to establish yourself, you will learn your market value and you'll learn to know you're worth it.

Cynthia McCulley, a part-time marketing consultant for high-tech companies including Toshiba, was worried the first time a client offered her $120 an hour. "I said to myself, 'Who am I kidding? I don't know if I'm that good! I hope they feel like they're getting their money's worth.' " McCulley says her professional acting training helped her overcome the frog feeling. She would get up in the morning and say to herself, "Okay, I'm going to be a consultant today!" You can do the same: Pretend the part, and soon it won't be an act anymore.

Setting Fees

Everyone devises her own formula. Some use target earnings; some change their rate depending on the client; others go strictly by the going rate. Many double what they would earn as an employee.

The salient point in any fee-setting formula is this: You *must* know the real cost of doing business and build that into your fee. Remember, you can only bill the client for actual time spent working on the project. This seems fairly fundamental, but too many contractors fall into the trap of doing sixty hours of work and getting paid for forty. If you expect to stay in business, in addition to labor and job expenses, your fee must account for nonbillable time:

1. Marketing time (paperwork, phone calls, invoicing, driving time, and travel)
2. The benefits accorded a "fully-loaded" employee such as health insurance, taxes, sick leave, vacations, retirement funds, etc.

It is hard to keep track of the number of hours you spend on a project. Says Dixon, "As a writer, how do you measure time in the shower for mentally outlining a speech or when you're watering the plants and you're thinking about the speech? The work requires more than the time spent sitting at the computer. It takes time to process the material mentally.'' Try to figure some of that in. In addition, even if you know how long it will take to do a job, build in extra time to account for the meetings and conferences with executives, decision makers, and other employees. On top of all that, the job will always take longer than you estimate.

Although common wisdom says "double your employee rate," some experts think doubling is not enough. Seann Maxwell, author of the manual, *Consult and Grow Rich*, believes the contractor must charge two and a half to three times what she would be earning as an employee! Just charge double, which is the standard rule of thumb, and you will barely break even.

Know the Going Rate and Don't Lowball

While clients might wonder whether they are being overcharged by consultants, most of the independent contractors we interviewed took a conservative approach to setting their fees. Speech writer Kathleen Dixon explains: "The going rate for speech-writers in my line of work is between $75 and $125. I charge competitive rates, but I don't inflate my prices just because I can. In the beginning I felt uncomfortable charging these rates. I'd think, after all, I'm not a neurosurgeon. But there's no need to feel that way." Dixon is fair, but she isn't foolish, either. She doubled the rate she was earning at Apple Computer, Inc., when she was one of CEO John Sculley's main wordsmiths. "If you're too low-priced, people don't think you're any good." She adds, "Plus it's much harder to raise your prices once they've been established, so if I don't go out of the starting gate at a reasonable price for both me and the client, I may not be in the race for long."

Another Apple employee, attorney Cynthia Cannady, advises looking beyond the going rate of other contractors: "Be aware of what your direct competition is doing. But also keep in mind that your competition may also be a big firm whose price you can usually beat." For example, a private practice lawyer working from home can probably get away with charging $90, whereas a large firm with its steep overhead would have to charge $240.

LINING UP WORK

Setting up your home shop is nothing compared with lining up clients—and there are more potential sinkholes along the way than books to help you avoid them. These guidelines will help.

■ **DOING THE MATH: MORE CALCULATING IDEAS**

- Make sure to figure your bonuses (which you won't get now) into the equation.

- Consider keeping your rate lower and adding a 10 percent surcharge for phone charges and other expenses. This way your rate looks more competitive.

- If you're going to bid on a project in a line of work that is new to you, leave room to revise your final fee as you go along by giving a high and low estimate. Without experience estimating the time necessary to complete the work, you could easily end up with a check for $3,000 when you deserve $7,000.

- Some contractors charge clients for phone consultations if they exceed five minutes. This helps clients focus their questions and become aware of the ticking clock.

- Do not undersell your efforts or give the client the impression that a job is going to be a piece of cake. Most jobs turn out to be more difficult than they look in the beginning.

- Some fees are based on a market average. Survey comparable service providers and pick a number in the middle.

- Consider charging a good-faith deposit or advance. This helps your cash flow and will protect you from customers who are just shopping around but demand you pencil them in all the same. A serious client shouldn't object.

- Loosely estimate with a "not to exceed" price cap. It gives you both flexibility.

Concentrate on Building Relationships

Make building relationships your top priority, says Seann Maxwell, president of Maxwell Consultants International, which provides advice to consultants. According to Maxwell, you should spend your time establishing positive relationships so that clients recommend you to other clients, rather than "wasting time and money writing up beautiful proposals." Maxwell observes that often this relationship approach allows you to skip the proposal stage so you can take over the reins of a project immediately. Says Maxwell, "This allows you to spend your time more productively. You become intimately familiar with the goals and attitudes of the client and can focus on defining a project from beginning to end. That done, contractors simply write a brief letter of agreement reiterating what was discussed and agreed upon."

Laurel Prokop works this way. Her clients depend on her and vice versa. Says the forty-five-year-old mother of two, ''We build a rapport so strong that it's as if I'm in their company. I understand their goals, their methods, and they value that understanding. And none of this proposal and bidding stuff. I trust them. They trust me to deliver quality works. I keep a time log and then I bill them.''

When and How to Submit a Bid

1. Be selective about bids and proposals. You don't get paid for those glamorous color presentations unless you win. Unfortunately, clients sometimes ask for proposals even though they have no intention of giving the business to the bidders. Says Maxwell, ''I see this all the time . . . consultants wasting time and money writing proposals just so the client can keep other consultants honest.'' For example, when a client asks ten consultants to make a proposal on a $20,000 job, each consultant spends between $500 and $1,000 preparing a proposal. In many cases the client already has selected the winner but simply wants to scan the playing field or is required to hear a certain number of bids before he contracts with his standby anyway.

2. Define the assignment's scope of work precisely. The biggest mistake consultants make is bidding on a poorly defined project. You need to know *exactly* what your client expects from the beginning to end. If you don't, you won't get paid enough and most likely the customer won't be satisfied either. Defining the project ensures that enough time is built in to do the work and to be fairly compensated.

3. Spell out your fees and services. Make sure to include the cost of your labor and any supplies or expenses that you will pass on to your clients so they know what dollar total will appear on the bill. Spell out your services exactly—what you will be doing for them at every point—and explicitly point out what your bid does *not* include. Important: State explicitly here what you will be willing to do in terms of revision or follow-up work.

4. Avoid firm bids. Firm bids can wipe out your profit, so be as specific as possible and leave room for adjusting your fees to accommodate additional requirements. For example, Laurel Prokop is working with a book publisher who always demands a firm bid, but Prokop has resolved to skip that in the future. Says Prokop, ''They insist on a firm bid from me, then they end up giving me twice as much work as they proposed. The stuff they give me to work with isn't anything like it should be—pretty raw—and requires a lot of extra editing. They think they're going to get the extra work for nothing. I'm sorry, that's not the way I work.''

5. Pay attention to your instincts when selecting clients. Maxwell has found intuition to be the best judge of client relationships. ''Whenever I override my gut feeling about the clients and move ahead with a project, I invariably end up with problems completing the job or collecting my fees, and feeling bad about the clients. Then they have bad feelings toward me, too. No one benefits from this kind of lose-lose situation. I no longer take assignments unless I like the client. Having the flexibility to select your clients is one of the great benefits of being a consultant.'' Incidentally, if there's any question about a client's ability to pay, order a credit report from Equifax or another credit-checking agency.

Write Winning Proposals

Sometimes a formal proposal is absolutely necessary. Larger companies often expect a formal proposal. For example, the year biotech services contractor Joan Silver had her first child, NASA put a project out to bid, which meant Silver had to work up a fifty-page proposal. Although most of you won't have to strut your stuff for fifty pages, quite a few consultants believe their best business resulted from creative, drop-dead proposals.

The standard proposal includes a written summary that outlines the problem, steps, timetable, and solution. It should also give background and qualifications of the consultants involved. Make sure you study the project and know the problems that the client expects you to solve. The element that separates one independent contractor from another is the quality of her ideas, so make sure the content is top drawer. Practice your presentation of the proposal. Experts agree that clinching the deal depends more on what you *tell* them you will do than on the written proposal.

SELL THE SIZZLE

Your proposal is the most obvious marketing tool you've got, says proposal guru Don Krache. Use a marketing approach that is innovative, an approach Krache calls ''selling the sizzle.'' Don't be afraid to put a ''little language'' in your proposal, Krache advises, so that readers will feel they're talking to a real, live human being.

HOW FAR DO YOU TAKE A PROPOSAL?

This is tricky. Your proposal must be compelling enough to persuade the client you've got a solution to their problem while, at the same time, retaining enough mystery that they can't steal your ideas and assign someone in-house to execute your plan. Consultants tell us that giving the farm away is a legitimate concern. What to do? First, concentrate on relationship building. You know the clients well enough to know if they're going to pull a stunt like that, you know the budget, and the clients know you can deliver. Second, when you present your proposal, verbally or written, do it in broad, general terms. For example, give them the big concepts, but no details on how to implement them.

DON'T DELAY BILLING AND WORK ON THE CLIENT'S NICKEL

Decide when you will bill your clients—when the project is completely done or when a portion of it is completed. Most contractors ask for payment within thirty days, but some run a tighter schedule, asking for the first payment within two weeks.

Work on the clients' money whenever possible. Many top consultants collect the first month's fees to be held as a retainer. You submit invoices every two weeks or at the end of the month. Then the retainer is credited to the clients' account and accounted for at the end of the project. The challenge here is to make sure your clients feel like they're getting their money's worth and also to make sure that your retainer is adequate.

■ PART-TIME PROFESSIONAL FACT

According to *Consultants Times,* a New Hampshire industry organization, only one in ten solo *management* consultants is still around after two years.

MANAGING THE BUSINESS

As your own boss you will be free to decide when you do what, a luxury nine-to-fivers are denied. But successful part-time contractors will also tell you that this work style, far from allowing a free spirit to develop unfettered, demands a great deal of attention to client management and a healthy dose of what Paul and Sarah Edwards aptly call "self-management muscle."

Managing Clients—Seven Tips

1. CONCENTRATE ON TWO OR THREE GOOD CLIENTS

Some part-time independent contractors prefer to screen their business opportunities carefully, limiting themselves to one or two good clients. They are willing (and can afford) to run the risk of long dry periods in order to control their own time and avoid overcommitment. In fact, the dry periods are the reason they're independent contracting. Telecommunications specialist Laurie Garda, for example, thrives on the feast-or-famine philosophy: "I take the work as I can get it. My personal situation is flexible so I can easily go two to twelve weeks without working."

2. GIVE SPECIAL TREATMENT TO OLD CUSTOMERS

Appreciate your old customers. Treat all your customers like kings, no matter how many assignments you've done for them. Getting into bad habits, such as not returning phone calls immediately or ignoring a casual promise (like faxing an article or loaning a reference manual), can cause resentment to build up and may lead to their giving your assignments to someone else.

3. OFFER VALUE-ADDED SERVICE

Individual business owners can often offer a client a lot more extra service than a large outside firm can. According to graphic designer/writer Laurel Prokop, sometimes companies make the mistake of hiring a larger graphics design firm over her because they think the twenty-seven designers that work at the firm will be able to give their account a lot more attention. Not so, says Prokop. "There's one person assigned to them and when that one person is sick or takes a vacation, the work stops. But from me they would get a phone call the day before I'm supposed to go in. They get someone to deliver it overnight if that's what they need. They get real personal attention."

4. KEEP MARKETING YOURSELF EVEN WHEN YOU'RE BOOKED

This is especially true if you're spending almost all your time with just one client. If you lose that client, you risk your business. When your last project is finished, it may be a long time before you find another. If you don't have time, find some other consultants to act as subcontractors. According to Seann Maxwell, successful consultants devote at least 15 percent of their time to marketing, even when they are at their busiest.

5. DON'T FALL ON YOUR SWORD TRYING TO MAKE AN UNHAPPY CLIENT HAPPY

It happens. If one of your clients is unhappy with the work you did, don't spend open-ended periods of time mending it. Chances are, they're going to stay that way. Do your best to engineer a graceful parting and then move on.

6. CONDUCT YOUR BUSINESS WITH THE HIGHEST OF ETHICAL STANDARDS

A short list of the basics: Be accurate in representing yourself in all your activities; only sign up for work for which you are qualified and can provide within the time agreed; let clients know immediately if you're going to be late; honor client confidentiality; never be one of those consultants who pad their invoices or who charge the client the full freight when an assistant is doing most of the work.

7. DON'T FEEL OBLIGATED TO LET CLIENTS KNOW YOU WORK PART-TIME

The dictum "Don't ask, don't tell," doesn't just apply to homosexuals in the army. Most independent contractors feel it's unwise to let clients know about their part-time status. If they have to attend to family matters, the client just assumes you can't be there because of other business. Says software marketer Betsy Mace, "I never give clients the impression that they have me exclusively. It's a wonderful way to control your time on-site without being perceived as a slacker."

On the other hand, Susan Davis, the Indianapolis pediatrician, tells her patients right upfront about her part-time status. Does that cause a problem for patients? Davis says no. "Sometimes that leads them to pick one doctor over the other. But we provide other services many full-timers don't, like our morning phone hours, where we reserve an hour each morning just for updates and questions. We've only had one or two complaints through the years. Most are very happy with it."

Managing Your Time—Eight Ways to Work Smarter

1. SPEND YOUR TIME DOING WORK THAT WILL PAY THE BILLS

Don't spend too much time on administrative details—answering the phone, writing down messages, typing letters, and bookkeeping—and too little time getting work done that someone will pay you for.

Tricks to manage this problem: Pick one day to process bills. Restrict your phone time to certain parts of the day, one or two hours in the morning, for example. Let your answering machine handle the rest of the load. Strictly limit the amount of time you spend doing e-mail, and definitely discipline yourself to surf the net only when you're taking a break. Write letters every Friday, but not the same day you do bills. Do several errands at the same time instead of shopping in the morning, hitting the copy shop in the afternoon, and the library at night. Make calls that are billable from your carphone en route to appointments.

2. KEEP YOUR CLIENTS SEPARATE AND CARRY A BIG BRIEFCASE—OR TWO

Cynthia McCulley, a high-tech marketing consultant, points out that it can be tough to stay organized and efficient with multiple clients. Says McCulley, ''I have folders for each company with all the phone numbers and notes related to the project, but if for some reason I'm working at one company and I need to call people for the other company and I don't have the folder, it gets ugly.'' Her advice: Keep to-do lists for each company with you wherever you go, put phone numbers on the to-do list so you have them handy. She also finds it helpful to have a briefcase or canvas bag for each company in her car. Besides keeping your paperwork separate, Betsy Mace recommends disciplining yourself to work on one project at a time for several hours at a clip. Then put that all away before you begin Client Two.

3. DEVELOP A SYSTEM FOR LOGGING YOUR TIME

Some clients want a strict accounting of how you spent your time, your exact phone calls, conversations with whom, much like lawyers log billable time. Most of the independent contractors we talked to, however, used a more casual system. Betsy Mace, for example, uses the daily schedule in her Daytimer as a reference point. At lunchtime, she notes starting/stopping times from that morning and does the same thing that evening. Don't put this off. One contractor especially cautions against letting this go over a weekend: By Monday it'll be like Watergate—you'll have no recollection.

4. TRACK YOUR BUSINESS

Seann Maxwell recommends investing in a software program that tracks prospects. A tickler file function that will tell you when to call people back is particularly useful. The system also acts as a snooze alarm, to let you know when the next client (and the next check) are no longer in sight. Filemaker Pro and Contact Management Programs are both good and offer ''Print Label'' and ''Mail Merge'' capabilities with a word processor.

5. USE GOALS TO HELP YOU MANAGE YOUR TIME MORE EFFECTIVELY

First of all, make your goals specific. For example, instead of saying you want to get more clients, say you want to have ten new clients by this time next year. Instead of saying you want to appear more professional, say you will produce a professional brochure within six months. Second, if an opportunity comes along that has nothing to do with your general goals, say no. For example, if you're a technical writer who wants two or three good clients, turn down offers to do newsletters for a bunch of small customers. If you only want to work twenty-five hours a week, don't feel like you must say yes to every job offer that comes along. Wendy Gibson, a public relations and marketing consultant, fell into this trap and was soon working full-time. She soon learned to say, ''I'm really busy right now and can't take on another project, but let me recommend some people who might be able to help you.''

6. DON'T LET MONEY BECOME THE GOAL, IF IT ISN'T

Set financial goals and stick to them even though the income may be tempting. ''The money becomes an addiction. You think, if I do this one project, I can do the addition on the house,'' says Wendy Gibson, whose viewpoint was reiterated by many people we interviewed. Telecommunications specialist Laurie Garda describes how she started thinking of every hour of every day as billable time: ''Every time a nonwork-related activity comes up, you equate it with how much money you could be (but won't be) earning while you're doing other things.'' Several women observed that their husbands seemed to get hooked on the income, too, and had a hard time helping them refuse additional work.

7. TAKE A TIME MANAGEMENT SEMINAR

The easiest way to learn good time-management skills is to invest $200 in a seminar such as Franklin Quest. These programs help with big-picture goal planning and daily micromanagement. As you gain control of your time, you'll learn to build in the two-for-one rule: For every ten hours of work for a client, you'll more likely spend twenty hours working. This kind of planning and time allotting can prove to be the independent contractor's biggest challenge.

8. EXPECT EXTRA-TIGHT DEADLINES

As a self-employed business consultant, Suzanne Ely cringes every time she's asked to set a deadline because this forces her to face her professional and personal choices head-on. For example, if she contracts to complete some data collection, analysis, and forecasting and to draft a summary report late on a Tuesday afternoon, as a full-timer she might be able to complete the work by the end of the day this Friday. However, because she officially works only on Tuesdays and Thursdays, a comfortable deadline would be *next* Friday. "But," says Ely, "to be competitive with full-timers and so as not to impose my work/life choices on my clients, I have to commit to *this* Friday, which means working the ten-to-three night shift three nights in a row with no relief from waking the children at seven-thirty."

BOOKKEEPING

Why It's Important

Unless the type of independent contractor you are is an independent bookkeeper, read this section very carefully. First of all, as a business owner, you need to track your profits and control your expenses. Second, as a business owner, you will find yourself having a more intimate relationship with the IRS than you had as an employee. Bookkeeping is key to keeping your relationship with the IRS clean. If you're going to take business deductions, *you must keep accurate records.*

The Basic Books

You will need a journal or a computer program in which you can record your daily receipts and expenses. Include everything: postage, lunches with clients, fax paper purchases, office supplies, telephone bills, professional dues, gasoline mileage, new equipment. The easiest method is to do it by hand in a ledger. On the left page record your income; on the right page, business expenses. Then at the end of the

TIPS FROM SUCCESSFUL PART-TIME INDEPENDENT CONTRACTORS

"I treat everybody like a potential customer because in truth everybody is a potential client or someone who can lead you to a client. Maybe they have a spouse, colleague, or an acquaintance who has a job. After all, everybody knows somebody."

—Laurel Prokop, corporate communications consultant

"I've learned to prioritize. I do less critical work during nap times because it's too frustrating to get involved in serious work only to have her wake up. The hard-core work waits until I have child care."

—Suzanne Ely, management consultant specializing in voice technologies

"I spend a significant amount of time reading and researching and talking to people about developments in my industry, things I need to know at some level. If you don't do that, you're dead in the water. You're not marketable. Period."

—Elaine Kearney, business development consultant

"You need to make sure you understand where you are on the learning curve. The first time you do a certain type of project, you may not make a lot of money, but as you do more work in the area, you can increase your profit as your expertise grows.

—Cynthia McCulley, high-tech marketing consultant

"You always do your best. You've got to look over your work and make sure it's good. There are a lot of contractors who talk a lot and charge a lot, but never really deliver anything. I think there are a lot of contractors who don't care about the quality of their work. I know because I've hired contractors who don't care as much if what they deliver is top notch. You've got more freedom, so the temptation is always there with independent contracting to just go skiing when you've got a deadline."

—Betsy Mace, software marketing consultant

"I've got two faxes, I'm on-line, I've got an 800 number. My idea is to make it as easy as possible for these people."

—Joan Silver, biotech support contractor

month or quarter, add up figures and net out the difference to see if you're in the black or in the red.

Keep a paper trail. Keep all receipts, preferably filed by expense category (we throw all our receipts in a big box, one more instance of not leading by example). Remember to save all tax records, payroll and personnel records, shipping records, and contracts for seven years.

YOU AND THE IRS

To an independent contractor, the IRS is the FBI. The threat of hefty penalties, time in the slammer, and other imagined horrors has given millions of entrepreneurs gray hair, sleepless nights, and anxiety attacks. Is this because all independent contractors cheat? No. It's because IRS guidelines are murky and the laws change frequently. Many part-time contractors are so busy getting their work done and taking care of their families, they have little time to keep up with changes and sweat the paperwork details. But ignoring the paperwork will only increase the intensity of your anxiety and will make it more difficult to file correctly.

> ■ "I said to my mom, I feel like the government's trying to run us out of business before we even start. In a country built on entrepreneurs, it seems like a funny way to operate, to penalize people who build small businesses. The tax penalties were shocking."
>
> —Kathleen Dixon

Seek Professional Help

Consult an accountant or financial planner, preferably one that is familiar with the type of business you run. The $200 you spend on a consultation can save you thousands in terms of taxes and additional time freed up from tax work. Besides filling out your tax returns, an accountant can file your quarterly estimated taxes, evaluate whether you qualify for the home office deduction, keep you updated on changes in the tax laws, explain your tax liabilities when you hire people, and help prepare you for an audit.

Sometimes you can get free advice. Accountants and lawyers often offer free twenty-minute initial consultations. Associations also offer free advice to women starting businesses. Try the National Association for Women's Business Owners (NAWBO) and the Women's Network for Entrepreneurial Training (WNET). For federal programs that offer training call the Small Business Administration (SBA) at 800-827-5722. The Office of Women's Business Ownership, an arm of the SBA, is a good place to start.

The Self-Employment Tax and the Joy of Deductions

When you're employed by someone else, your employer foots the bill for half of your Social Security and Medicare taxes, a benefit you probably took for granted. But when you're self-employed, you will pay the self-employment tax, which goes for Social Security and Medicare, all by yourself. More specifically, if you net $400 or more from your business, you will pay 15.3 percent of your net income in self-employment taxes. Most independent contractors estimate their incomes and pay these taxes four times a year.

The self-employment tax is the bad news. The good news is that you'll be able to deduct half of it. Say your self-employment tax is $1,000. You could put $500 of that on your detailed deductions, reducing your taxable income by $500. This is $500 you don't have to pay your tax rate on.

More Joy of Tax Deductions

That's just the beginning of potential business tax deductions you can enjoy as an independent contractor. You qualify as a business if you realize a profit at least three years out of five. As a business you are then entitled to reduce your taxable income by making the same kind of business deductions that IBM or General Motors takes—deductions for advertising, business-related education seminars and classes, mailings, stationery, supplies, and equipment. You can even deduct your home office as long as the portion of your home you wish to claim as a business is used exclusively and regularly for business. But be careful. The IRS is meaner than a junkyard dog guarding this deduction. If you have a sofabed for Grandma or a television that the family watches occasionally, your office doesn't qualify. It must also be the principal place of business or a place where you meet with customers or clients. For more on tax deductions, see Paul and Sarah Edwards's, *Working From Home*, or Ellen Parlapiano and Patricia Cobe's, *Mompreneurs*.

Be careful to follow the IRS rules. Bookkeeping and careful adherence to the rules are absolutely necessary because many of your major deductions will send up a red flag to the IRS. The home office definitely falls in this category. In fact, many new independent contractors are so afraid of an audit, they don't claim the home office deduction, the biggest tax break of all. Discuss this situation with your accountant or lawyer or call the IRS office listed under United States Government in your phone book if you have any question at all about the legitimacy of your deductions.

The IRS Controversy with Independent Contractors: IC or EE?

Because of the rapid growth of independent contractors, the IRS wants to make sure that employees and employers do not abuse the arrangement as a way to avoid paying taxes. The IRS has strict guidelines to classify your business and it regularly reclassifies people from independent contractors to employees. It's important to your pocketbook to safeguard your independent contractor classification: If you're classified as an employee, you give up the opportunity to claim deductions and your employer has to pick up half of your Social Security taxes.

If the IRS decrees that you're an employee, not an independent contractor, you could be in deep yogurt. The penalties for misclassifying are fairly steep. Fortunately, companies are now tuned in to the issue and often have contractors fill out their own questionnaires to make sure everything's on the up and up. If a company miscategorizes a person as a contractor rather than an employee, then the employer must pay back withholding taxes and FICA taxes and is subject to a 100 percent fine. You must pay back any taxes and are also subject to a fine.

Which category you fall in depends on how much control an employer has over when, where, and how you work. The more control the employer has, the less likely you'll be classified as an independent contractor. How long and how often have you contracted with one client? If you contract frequently and exclusively with one employer and have done so for a long period of time, it is possible that you'll be an employee in the eyes of the IRS. This classification issue is yet another good reason to diversify your client base. IRS Publication 937 outlines the factors that differentiate between the two definitions.

The Nanny Tax

The 1994 Nanny Tax loosens the tax rules for parents who pay baby-sitters and housekeepers less than $1,000 annually and for all domestic employees under eighteen years of age. Even if your high school baby-sitter earns $5,000 a year from you, as long as she's under eighteen, you're not responsible for paying taxes. However, nannies and au pairs whose main job is baby-sitting are not excluded, so you must withhold Social Security for them.

Where Are You Going?

Evaluate your home business along the way. Have you met your goals? Do you still enjoy doing the work? Does independent contracting still provide you with the flexibility you desire? Are you achieving a work/family balance that's acceptable to you? Can you handle the workload alone or do you need to add support staff? Are you generating sufficient profit considering the amount of time you're putting into it?

Many independent contractors become interested in changing from the person who does all the work into the person who subcontracts it all out. Using other contractors to help you out can give you tremendous flexibility and some relief from the sometimes unrelieved brutality of grinding out the work. Kathleen Dixon also feels a lot of financial pressure to build up her business. Says Dixon, "I've gotten to the point where I say, 'Okay, do I continue to just work by myself or do I start hiring subcontractors?' If I do it all myself, I'm assured of the quality. But as a single mother, I need to think about growing and finding subcontractors whose high standards match my own."

Joan Silver, biotech support consultant, thinks she probably should be marketing her company in other fields, but she enjoys the comfortable familiarity with a narrow niche of business. Working about twenty-five hours a week is just right, says Silver. "My clients like to deal with me because I can do everything for them. I'm even willing to sully my hands with paperwork. I'm happy because I'm away from hands-on tech stuff—moving blood and urine around—and I get to manage people, which I enjoy. What's more, I love the intellectual stimulation that comes from working with scientists." Joan says she isn't making "tons of money," but at least she's making more than if she were teaching high school science, a job for which she holds a credential.

Consultants frequently receive offers for full-time work from their clients. Mace almost always gets an offer, but she doesn't want to give up being a part-time professional. Says Mace, "I tell them no. Why? Because I don't want to be limited by their vacation plan. I like to think I'm beyond that. For example, if I wanted to, I could take six weeks off a year and work very little in December. If you told a big company that's what you wanted to do, they'd laugh in your face.''

That's why independent contracting is so ideal. Whether it's working with scientists, taking extended summer or winter vacations, or taking the kids to the beach in the middle of the week that turns you on, it's your choice and it's certainly nobody's business but your own.

PART FIVE

MAKING IT WORK

Not Taking Anybody's Garbage:

An Interview with Sandy Geist

Sandy Geist hopes the transition to part-time won't be as difficult for the second part-time professional at Progressive Insurance Company in Cleveland as it was for her. Geist and the other database programmers in her department trade nights and on-call weekends to keep Progressive's claims processing computers up and running twenty-four hours a day. Given this round-the-clock schedule, it wasn't obvious how to structure a part-time position with the team, but the outspoken thirty-three-year-old Geist and her manager ironed out an arrangement whereby she worked twenty-eight hours a week and her fair share of on-call duty.

Q: *So how do you like working part-time?*

A: It's worse than I expected. I guess I thought the transition would be a lot smoother. There were more pressures and details to work out than I ever imagined. Not only was going from forty to twenty-eight hours hard for me personally—at first I still thought I could do the same amount of work—but the little stuff like time off and being on call didn't turn out to be simple at all.

Q: *What has been the biggest stumbling block?*

A: The new boss I got after six months made it clear in our first meeting that he never would have approved my part-time status . . . but felt stuck with the decision. He'd never managed a part-timer before. At first he was hell-bent on managing my time for me, making decisions about what I could or could not handle. That frustrated both of us. I suggested he treat me more like a full-timer—assigning me whatever projects he wanted to assign me—then I'd tell him whether I could handle them or not. I've learned not to be shy around my boss.

Q: *Give me an example of your new assertiveness.*

A: Well, each team member takes turns working from 2:00 A.M. to 8:00 A.M. on the second Sunday of every month to perform routine maintenance on the claims computer system. When full-timers take this shift, they take a day off the following week to compensate. When it was my turn, I didn't get to. Or, if I did want to take a day, my boss would ask me to come in on Friday.

Q: *Why is that?*

A: He's worried that I'm not around enough. He thinks, "Oh, God, she's already only here three days and now she's taking off another day!" Until recently I would just get mad and walk away, but recently I brought up the issue. I said, "Look, if a full-timer took off Monday and Tuesday would you ask him if he's coming in Saturday and Sunday?" It's ridiculous. I picked this job because a lot of face time isn't required. It's a support job. It's not a job where you're meeting with users and the businesspeople. I really work only with my group.

Q: *So how did you resolve the issue?*

A: My boss relented and offered the day off as long as the workload allowed. In busy times, I'm supposed to take two half days. I thought it was a fair compromise.

Q: *How's the relationship with your boss now?*

A: Well, letting me manage my own time has helped. In fact, he recently chose me for a week-long training session on a new technology. My team was fairly shocked that he chose me, but I felt terrific about it. It was a definite signal that he felt I was paying my dues and making a contribution.

Q: *How are things going with your team?*

A: I'm secure enough now about the quality of my work that I'm not going to take anybody's garbage anymore. I got tired of the same old smart comments and jokes. I've yet to fall short on anything, I have yet to miss a deadline, and until I do, I don't want to hear it anymore.

Q: *Are you actually having intense conversations like that with coworkers?*

A: Oh, yes. As a matter of fact, I had one last Tuesday because there was some talk going on behind my back. You know, sometimes technical people can get pretty petty. Anyway, somebody didn't think I was pulling my weight in one area and they were grousing about that. I had to explain to them that working in that area was no longer my assignment; it wasn't that I was slacking. Then the next thing you know, I got wind of more grousing. So finally I just came out with it and said, "Look, you guys don't seem that pleased with the work I'm doing. But when I ask you for feedback, you're too busy or you have to fix something first. You say you'll tell me later, but you don't. If it's true and you want me off the team, fine. I'll gladly get off. But don't sit there and act like I'm not doing my work without telling me specifically what the problem is."

In the end, being honest with them worked.

TEN

Managing Your Part-time Job at the Office

"It took about four months before I could begin to enjoy the balance."

—Nancy Siegal, part-time physical therapist

Be careful what you wish for—you may get it, goes the saying. Working part-time in a company where full-timers outnumber you a hundred to one can be intimidating. At first a new part-time job can seem more battle than balance, especially when others are watching your every move to see if you fail. Nevertheless, most of the women we talked to hung on like pit bulls, fiercely committed to making it work. They generously shared war stories, strategies they used to overcome obstacles, and the midcourse corrections they had to make. But the common thread in all arrangements and in all industries was that *communications make it or break it.*

GOING PUBLIC WITHIN THE COMPANY

Managers often steer you wrong. After weeks spent sweating out the beautiful details of a part-time arrangement, they tell you to keep a low profile about it, as if the part-time deal is a dirty little secret between the two of you that shouldn't get around. Bad idea. Usually this secretive approach ends up creating more problems than it solves.

177

The best approach is to come out of the part-time closet and address all concerns headon so that everyone involved feels more comfortable about it. Prepare a memo spelling out your schedule, including times you're available at the office and at home. Include your plan for handling meetings, phone calls, emergency situations, and for keeping everyone updated on your work. If possible, make it clear that you're willing to adjust your schedule to help out in an emergency. The memo should be detailed enough to address the primary concern in coworkers' minds: Will her part-time schedule mean I get stuck doing more work? Address potential hot spots head-on. Contrary to popular belief, raising the objections your coworkers might hold does not plant ideas in their minds. Rather, it shows that you are sensitive to the concerns that a nonstandard schedule always raises. In some cases, it may be more appropriate for your supervisor either to write and/or sign the memo.

Don't stop with the memo. Flexibility expert Sandra Sullivan recommends that you put a fifteen-minute agenda item on the board at the staff meeting for your announcement. But an initial public announcement and a memo are not enough, maintains Sullivan. "You've got to keep getting on the meeting agenda, probably every other month is about right. Ask 'Is it working? What's not working? How can we fix any problems?' You need to start off saying, 'Is it working?' and you need to keep saying, 'Is it working?' because new issues crop up that create new problems. This is the only way you can avoid being blindsided by criticisms later or attacked behind your back.''

Furthermore, if your schedule precludes you from attending regular meetings, make your presence felt in your absence by sending memos to be distributed providing thorough project updates and upcoming deadlines.

TELLING CUSTOMERS AND CLIENTS: DISCRETION ADVISED

Keeping a low profile may be appropriate with customers and clients. Ironically, I experienced my own unconscious customer bias against part-timers when shopping for a literary agent to handle *Going Part-Time*. Following up on a lead, I phoned an agent in Atlanta, a location whose great distance from New York, the home of most of the major publishers, already made me nervous. When I mentioned the topic of my book to her, the woman chirped up enthusiastically, "Perfect, I'm a part-time agent." I caught myself in the act of thinking, "Hmm. Maybe I'd rather have somebody on it full-time." Had she gone on to sell me on her superior experience and her reputation for negotiating the best advances in the business, I would still have been open to working with her. Instead, she went on to relate how she was working part-time as a way to "break into the business" (i.e., she didn't have relationships with any publishing houses to speak of) and that she was moving back with her parents until she started to make some money. Needless to say, I was turned off. Two morals of the story: First, don't answer questions you haven't been asked. And second, if you choose to tell a customer you're part-time, you may wish to emphasize that your skills, contacts, and expertise are so strong that your part-time schedule is no problem.

Most of the women we interviewed did not apprise new customers and clients of their reduced hours. Instead, they coached administrative support staff on how to handle phone calls and inquiries. These allies were invaluable in maintaining a full-time front in their absence. They also used technology to make them "virtual" full-timers—call-forward when they were available at home, beepers for constant availability, carefully worded voice mails. Telecommuter Joan Silver was a master at this part-time sleight-of-hand. Technology combined with a practiced professional phone persona gave the impression, Silver says, "That I've been sitting here at my desk all day just waiting to hear from them." She also recommends that you answer the phone "Hello, this is Joan," rather than "Hello," so business callers won't wonder if they've called a wrong number if one of the children answers. Part-time nonprofit marketer Julie Shippee takes the "phone's my stage" concept one further. She gives clients her "stage name," Julie Ann Shippee, rather than just Julie Shippee, so that she is tipped off immediately that this is a business call and can react with her business demeanor (see chapter 9, You, Inc.).

You probably don't need to keep mum with longtime customers already familiar with your work. Senior manager at Ernst & Young Fran Schulz says her clients have been quite supportive of her part-time status: "They know my schedule, they know when I'm not available, and they also know if they need to get in touch with me, they can."

COMMUNICATING WITH YOUR BOSS

Behind every successful professional is a supportive manager. Conversing often and effectively will help you manage the tendency for managers to view part-timers as irksome creatures who make their lives more difficult. Don't allow your boss to go so long without contact that she starts to wonder if you're still on the payroll, and if you are, what you're doing to earn your pay. One-on-one phone or face-to-face conversations as well as faxes or e-mails updating managers on your progress make them feel more comfortable and less anxious about losing control. If you don't work at keeping in touch, it's all too easy for part-timers to get left out of the picture as priorities and projects shift.

During these talks, discuss the part-time arrangement. Solicit feedback about what concerns or problems people are having with you. Ask for feedback about your job performance as well. Explain that as a professional, it's very important that you hear about these things in order to do a good job. In turn, give your own views about what's working and what's not.

PERFORMANCE EVALUATIONS, PROMOTABILITY, AND OTHER CHECKPOINTS

The performance evaluation is the right venue to review the logistics of your part-time arrangement, to show that you were able to meet your goals and also to fix any problems that may have come to light. Few part-time arrangements remain static. Make sure your boss doesn't downgrade your review because he unconsciously expects you to be doing your old full-time job. You may need to remind him of the scope of your new one. Not surprisingly, the most common adjustments involve situations in which the woman has taken on more work than she is being paid for. Sometimes this results in a formal increase in paid hours.

Performance evaluations are also the right time to advance your career. Researchers at Catalyst were surprised to learn that 53 percent of participants in a study of part-timers received promotions while working reduced hours. A widely diverse group, participants shared one behavior: they initiated discussions with their managers about their professional goals, the kinds of work experiences they sought,

and their plans for advancement. Promote your promotability by documenting your achievements, showing how you brought in money for the business or made contributions to the company, and how you met your predetermined objectives. If your company or your boss doesn't do regular performance reviews, it's up to you to ask for one. People are busy, so even if you've made some great contributions, your work may be overlooked.

COMMUNICATING WITH COWORKERS

''I wouldn't recognize some of the part-timers here if they came up and hit me in the face,'' said one disgruntled coworker we interviewed who was frustrated at the lack of regular contact with part-timers. Her observation also illustrates why you shouldn't skimp on communications with coworkers. A realistic appraisal of your various relationships at work is an essential first step. Don't be fooled. Although coworkers may admire your new family priorities, their top priority is how your new balance will affect Numero Uno. A detailed memo combined with a personal conversation, followed up by requests for feedback, works best here. Avoid generic, "How do you think it's working?" questions. They invite a shorthand "Fine," even though there may be small issues that aren't so fine. Ask specific questions that will pull out concrete objections that you can fix.

As with your boss, maintain ongoing communications. Nature abhors a vacuum and so do coworkers' minds. With you not here, negative feelings can fester and take hold. Fill the vacuum with positive communications—updates on your work, "attaboys" for them, and concerns about the work that's being done. Often coworkers hesitate to call you at home even if you've encouraged them to. Have a dry run at the office one day just to see if your communications systems work correctly. Call them on your days off and encourage them to reciprocate.

A PRIME PITFALL: FALLING OUT OF THE LOOP

Most part-time professionals agree that terrible things happen to those who get out of the informal information system that is part of every office. In other words, if coworkers don't resent you, they might ignore you altogether. Both behaviors can prove fatal. Although it might be tempting to hole up in your office cutting out "all the pointless politics" (the people), it doesn't pay to skip the mingling totally. Nancy Anderson recalls that at first, when coworkers wanted to chat, she was so focused on trying to get her work done in the shorter amount of time, "My stomach would start to get tight as I'd sit there thinking about all the things I had to get done." But she's learned to control that. Taking ten minutes in the morning to exchange a few words over coffee is a good investment that has paid off for Anderson, who has very strong relationships with colleagues. Anderson adds, "My basic strategy is to try to behave the same way I'd behave if I were here all day."

When computer programmer Karen Gage was working part-time, mostly from her home, for a software company, the communication loop broke down completely. This culminated in a showdown between her and coworkers that left "blood all over the floor." Gage's workgroup was composed of people "notorious throughout the company for mishandling people—actually they were notorious for being jerks," says Gage, "so my expectations were low, but nowhere low enough."

She had made it clear that other team members were welcome to call her at any time, but the phone didn't ring much. Her home office was equipped with a fax machine and e-mail, but e-mail and faxes didn't show up either. The "arcane" piece of system software she was working on involved a lot of details that "you had to get right," explains the thirty-seven-year-old mother of two. Accordingly, she submitted a thorough and complete engineering report on her work for their review. When no feedback was forthcoming, she pestered them, eventually receiving a copy of her own report with "minimal notes in the margins." Gage dutifully made all the changes addressed in their notes and resubmitted. It was at that point that, as Gage puts it, "I got shot with a cannon." The accusations came fast and furious: "You didn't fix the things we told you to fix, the problems we edited." The 1975 Princeton graduate, accustomed to superstar status, was stunned. She said, "Wait a minute, we must have some sort of serious communication problem here because I addressed every single one of your concerns." It turns out, Gage relates, "they had had a major philosophical problem with my part of the project as a whole, but they hadn't bothered to tell me about it. Or perhaps they discussed it so much among themselves, they were sure someone had told me. But in fact, no one had."

An at-home mother for several years after the incident, Gage is now philosophical about the fiasco, and she has learned a thing or two about how the disaster could have been averted. Besides being pickier about finding compatible colleagues, if she had to do it all over again she would build in ongoing communication checkpoints. She says, "Believe me, I'd advertise that I'd be in the office one day a week, and I would always be there on that day. You can save so much time by just popping in to someone's office and getting an idea for how to do something better or for hearing when plans are shifting completely. It's amazing how quickly you can get out of touch."

June Langhoff, author of *The Telecommuter's Advisor,* recommends that if you're working from home you should communicate with the office at least twice a day, preferably including one "real-time voice conversation." She also advises sending a weekly status report to your boss or coworkers with such headings as: "This Week's Accomplishments," "Next Week's Activities," "Let's Talk About," and "For Your Information."

■ **IMAGE ENHANCING IDEAS**

If being part-time is your public relations problem, these tips were overheard at the water cooler.

"I never brag about or advertise how great working part-time is. I only bring it up when it relates to business."

"Every once in a while I'd volunteer for a project that no one else wanted to do, or take a trip that no one else wanted just to let people know that I'm still a part of the team. Knocking yourself out now and then sends the message that the job really matters to you."

"When I was working full-time and came in on a Saturday, I'd hide in my office so I could just work. Now I want everybody who comes in to see that I'm putting in extra hours. I make sure they see me."

"I make a point of attending certain social functions, and I never duck contributions for gifts."

"My after-midnight faxes become my signature at work. I loved that because it gave the impression that I was still killing myself after hours to get the work done."

"If I'm running behind a due date for a project, I make sure that I'm physically in the office during that period because I think it is very important that people see you were working hard. If you miss the deadline it isn't because you weren't working, it was because of external factors or changes in the system."

DEALING WITH COWORKER RESENTMENT

Sometimes despite your best efforts to cover all the bases, coworker problems set in like mildew in a damp carpet—you can't put your finger on it, but you know it's there because the sour odor flares up now and then. Usually, coworkers won't tell you what's wrong even when you ask. Most likely you'll just sense there's been some talk. Here's a short list of negative attitudes commonly harbored by coworkers toward part-time professionals and some strategies for dealing with them.

Attitude: It must be nice working part-time. What's happening on *One Life to Live?*

The jokes about part-time being a cakewalk or a vacation are rankling to part-time professionals. Truthful explanations of how you're exhausting your savings in the process or that, believe it or not, things are just as crazy now but in a different way will probably fall on unsympathetic ears. You should also probably stifle the impulse to respond as one particularly cantankerous part-timer did when she felt harassed. She relished the opportunity to come right back in their faces with variations of the following: "Yeah, it's great. We're having a ball. I'm so fortunate that my husband earns a six-figure income so I can afford to cut back." Or "Yeah, and if you'd give up your Lexus and designer clothes for the whole family, you could do it too!"

Advice: Blow it off. Use standard rejoinders for such remarks including, "Yeah, but you wouldn't think my paycheck is so nice," or "Tell that to my financial planner."

Attitude: Since you're not pulling your weight anymore, the rest of us have to do the heavy lifting.

Don't blow off this one. First of all, you need to find out more about the weight you're supposedly not pulling. Are your coworkers really doing a disproportionate amount of work because of your schedule? If part-timers exit promptly at three and the full-timers stay until seven or eight and the extra work always falls on the full-timers, you've got to fix it. Or if Friday is the day the workload seems to pick up and Friday is the day you're off, your coworkers' resentment is understandable. Ask questions that encourage the other person to be specific, such as "Gee, it sounds like that's a problem for you. Could you be more specific?" or "Can you give me an example of this?" Make it clear that you are willing to be flexible, that you're more than willing to stay late occasionally or come in on a day off now and then. Point out the work you're accomplishing at home. If you ascertain that, in fact, the complaint is unreasonable, perhaps you need to have a candid conversation in which you explain what the new scope of your job is and exactly how you are doing it.

Attitude: So why are you getting such special treatment?

First of all, professional jealousy is not limited to coworkers of part-timers. Human resources vice-president David Kennedy of New England Electric notes that any time any employee gets assigned to a special project, gets a promotion, or in any way is allowed to do something different—not just work a flexible schedule—it stirs up some resentment. Explain that the only reason you have the "special" arrangement is that it fits in with the business needs—not because of your personal needs. You might point out that the more successful this arrangement is, the more likely it is that others will have the option if they need it. Cast yourself in the role of a mentor: Here's how I did it, here's how you might do it, too.

Attitude: It's too much trouble to try and schedule meetings around you.

For one senior executive at a Silicon Valley high-tech firm, scheduling meetings has been one of the few negatives in an otherwise smooth part-time experience. "Although nobody has the audacity to come right out and say they resent my working part-time," explains this thirty-five-year-old manager who wants to remain anonymous, "the resentment manifests itself in their disregard for my schedule. For example, everyone in this whole office knows I don't work on Thursdays, yet people constantly schedule meetings for Thursdays even though they have four other days to pick from." When this kept happening, she decided to address the issue directly. She said to one coworker, "I've noticed you consistently pick Thursdays for meetings. Since you know I don't come in on Thursday, I can't help but wonder if you're trying to send the message that you don't want me to attend your meetings."

Although most managers and coworkers we interviewed admitted that meetings were a sore point, almost all found the problem to be relatively minor. The solution: Make sure everyone is aware of your schedule and that you stick to it. Ad hoc meetings are more problematic, but solvable. In some cases, you could come in for the meeting. In others, you could volunteer to teleconference in, if necessary.

Attitude: I've got enough trouble taking care of my own stuff without handling your customers or projects when you're not here.

Again, a good part-time plan should not foist extra work onto the shoulders of coworkers. Perhaps the communication logistics need more fine-tuning or even a major overhaul. With voice mail, call-forwarding, and beepers, coworkers should be able to get in touch with you easily. Ellen Bravo, executive director of the organization 9to5, advocates a team approach to help solve this problem. With this approach, each member is familiar with each others clients, thus allowing everyone greater flexibility. Says Bravo, ''Think how many times you call a full-time lawyer and she's not available—she's in court or whatever. Wouldn't it be great if there were some other lawyer who could say, 'Oh, yes. I'm familiar with your file. I can answer that particular question for you.' ''

In some cases, however, the customers make it difficult to satisfy their needs on a part-time basis. A part-time computer saleswoman with Hewlett-Packard who sells products to a large discount retail chain is finding it almost impossible to keep the huge customer satisfied on a part-time basis. The buyer from the chain doesn't know she's part-time. He doesn't respect their appointments and breaks them almost half the time, and he expects her to be on-site when he calls, available continually. Because the information she needs to answer questions and change orders is only available at the office, coworkers end up scrambling on her days off. She's currently investigating making a switch to another product line that's more conducive to a flexible work arrangement.

Attitude: I get tired of bending over backward for people with families. They chose to have kids, so let them deal with the consequences.

As family-friendly benefits grow, so does the resentment on the part of childless workers. It's not fair, they contend, for an employer to act as if their time is less valuable than that of coworkers with kids. Why should they pay the price for the flexible policies? They don't really pay the price, asserts Charles Rodgers, a principal at the Boston-based Work-Family Directions. In fact, they come out way ahead in terms of salary and career growth over their coworkers who are the primary caregivers. He points to a survey of twenty-five Fortune 500 companies that shows that only 10 percent of men and a third of women in management are primary caregivers for young children. Clearly, based on the low percentage of primary caregivers in top positions, working mothers pay a big career price for having families. Furthermore, Rodgers counters, the needs of working parents are legitimate. You cannot assume that individual managers will look out for the family needs of their employees. They don't have time and it's not their job. Hence, the need for family-friendly policies.

> ■ If a man leaves at three to watch his son's softball game, he's seen as a good father. If a woman does the same thing, she's perceived as being unprofessional.
>
> —Cindy Bitner, former part-time banker

FLEXIBILITY WORKS BOTH WAYS

You will be bitterly disappointed if you expect to adhere to your new part-time schedule. Lunches and meetings run over, the computer system goes down when you've got a twenty-five-page document to finish, an out-of-town client needs to see you on your day off. If there's one piece of advice that came through loud and clear in our research it was that flexibility works both ways.

> ■ Ninety-four percent of part-time employees work beyond their agreed-upon schedules. Half were compensated.
>
> —Catalyst survey

First, child-care arrangements need to be flexible enough to accommodate the unexpected. Nurse practitioner Michele Helmuth builds in an extra hour to handle the overflow. Intel's Mimi Thomas has her husband, who runs a landscape business from their home, and her mother, who lives forty-five minutes away, back up her day-care arrangements.

Second, expect that the workload will spike to full-time from time to time. When you structure your part-time job, don't just factor in three-fifths of the regular workload. Factor in three-fifths of the surplus workload as well, advises Carol Meyer of Andersen Consulting. "For part-time to work at Andersen Consulting, you need to do whatever it takes—and those are important words—to get the work done. That spirit has to be there." In the business consulting industry, Meyer notes, people end up juggling both personal time and business, swapping a day here or there, or staying late one day or working on the phone one night. "What doesn't work is when part-timers structure their days so they must leave every day at the stroke of five because the sitter leaves at five-fifteen."

Setting Limits

On the other hand, turning into the incredible bending woman is not exactly the balancing act you need. Learning to say no and setting reasonable limits are necessary skills for making part-time work over the long haul. For example, Hewlett-Packard part-time financial analyst Beth Swenson has left promptly at four on most days of the last eight years. Pacing herself has been the key to achieving such an unusually long part-time stint. Says Swenson, "It's so easy to get sucked into staying late all the time." Swenson has strong feelings about not putting her children in day care after school, and for this reason she wants to stay part-time for several more years. This doesn't mean Swenson stops working at four—she just goes home. And at home she's got a coveted ISDN line where she can do most of what she does at work from there.

Another strategy is to give up trying to do everything perfectly. When banker Cindy Bitner worked full-time at the Bank of Boston, she felt she had to go over every piece of paper that crossed her desk with a fine-tooth comb. "As a part-timer, I learned to pass things on or up. I remember asking a member of my staff to draft a 1990 marketing plan. When he had it done, I just passed it on to my boss after just a quick once-over. That would have been unheard of for me working full-time."

Minimizing Interruptions

To maintain the "mean machine" efficiency part-timers are famous for means cutting out a certain amount of socializing. It also means mastering the art of what one woman calls "interrupt management." The trick is to find the right mix of interruptions, social activity, and discipline. Kim Reed, marketing communications manager at a San Francisco Bay area software firm, says it took her a while to hit her stride. "After I do a bit of mingling, I actually put headphones on and plug in a CD to drown out what everyone else is doing, and start doing my own job. I can really crank the work out that way."

What's Your Priority?

Prioritizing is a key skill in working part-time. Who is it you must please? What are the most important things you do? Some things can't be cut short. Relationships with customers are a top priority for businesses, so when you start cutting down your "to do" list, don't start there. Nancy Anderson notes that when it comes to customers, "you can't make conversations any shorter." Shannon Larson, a manager with New England Electric, notes that once she went part-time, she decided to focus on the regulatory part of her job (utilities were regulated at that time), testifying before regulatory commissions, preparing documents, and so on. Says Larson, "I make sure I do all aspects of that perfectly. Then I don't worry that much about the rest. I worked out agreements with other coworkers to pick up some leftover parts of my full-time job. But if they don't get them done the way I would do them, or even if some things fall through the cracks, it's less serious."

Workload Creep

All too often, managers slip into the habit of expecting the occasional episode of overtime work to become a regular thing. You negotiated to work for thirty hours, but end up working thirty-five, then forty, then forty-five. Naturally, the workload creep makes you feel exploited. Judy Chang experienced workload creep right before she quit her job in the Afro-American Studies department at the University of Illinois. "I started doing some light programming at home. Soon I found myself regularly putting in a lot of extra hours just to keep the place from falling apart. It wasn't until very late in that job I realized my efforts were not even being appreciated. In my new part-time job I'm trying not to succumb to the same temptation to work at night so much."

Solution: Establish the appropriate workload upfront. Reducing hours must be accompanied by a reduction in the amount of work. This point cannot be overemphasized. Once that's done, establish good feedback mechanisms. If you're already a victim of workload creep, try to shed the overage by renegotiating the division of responsibilities, and pledging that if you volunteer in the future, it will be for a finite period of time.

Hey, This Is Not What I Bargained For

Most of the women we talked to were gradually evolving toward a return to full-time work. Managers may notice a part-timer taking on more work and suggest a formal increase in hours. In others, the woman herself initiates renegotiations. Some women went back to full-time and looked for a job-share partner. Judy Chang is upping her schedule from half to three-quarter time at the University of Illinois. Says Chang, "By the time I get coffee, do the necessary chatting with the clerical staff, touch bases with my boss if he's there, answer my e-mail and phone calls, and deal with the mail, the morning is shot. Gone. And if I'm doing something that takes a lot of thought, for example, writing a program for managing something,

■ DOWN TO BASICS

What it takes from those who know:

"Take responsibility for making it work. I see a lot of people who when they're having problems because they aren't accessible enough or when there's a problem scheduling a meeting, they blame the situation or they blame other people. That's deadly in a part-time position."

—Nancy Anderson, CEO of TRADE

"My approach has always been to underpromise and overdeliver."

—Mary Jane Elmore, venture capitalist

"Develop a thick skin. Try not to be defensive. Instead focus on ways to make it work."

—Pam Craig, Andersen Consulting

"Be a professional. To me being a professional means you keep going till you get the job done. If there's work that needs to be finished for or on Friday, you can't simply say, 'Oh, it's Thursday night. Sorry, I can't do it because I don't work on Fridays.' That just won't fly. Make it up some other way."

—Fran Schulz, Ernst & Young

"Marry the right guy. My husband's been a feminist for as long as I've known him—twenty years. He backs me up around the house and with child care. I couldn't work without his support."

—Judy Chang, University of Illinois

"The extra step of checking voice mail and e-mail from home goes a long way for me."

—Sandy Geist, Progressive Insurance

"I never say, 'No, I don't work Fridays.' I always say, 'No, how about Monday?' "

—Kathi Kaplan, Silicon Graphics, Inc.

I need several uninterrupted hours. Kyle's nursery is a five-minute walk from where I work, and I'm always finding myself suddenly dropping what I'm doing and dashing out the door at the last minute to get there. I'm always in a hurry. I also miss having a lunch hour, which was a big networking time for me. I plan to go three-quarters time when kindergarten starts next fall. That's ideal for me.''

WHEN TO CUT BAIT

Like a transplant operation in which the body rejects the foreign organ, a part-time professional job doesn't always "take." Sometimes wanting a family and a life doesn't fit in with the corporate culture. Usually this is because the work culture can't (or won't) support anything but full-timers. The most highly publicized case of a part-time job-gone-bad is that of Meredith Vieira, CBS correspondent. Vieira worked part-time on *60 Minutes,* producing roughly half of the twenty segments a year full-timers completed. After Vieira struggled for two years—both personally and professionally— Vieira's boss, *60 Minutes* executive producer Don Hewitt, declared her part-time contract DOA. Hewitt's refusal to extend her part-time contract sparked a firestorm of debate on the sexism women who work at the top of their professions face as soon as they become mothers. Hewitt's *60 Minutes* environment was inflexible, but as Vieira herself points out, Hewitt's all-or-nothing work ethic had served Hewitt and his smashingly successful show well for decades. And, after all, Vieira conceded in a 1991 *Working Woman* interview, "It's his candy store, not mine." Vieira had made no bones about putting family first, even bringing her baby with her to negotiations. As for her own role in the unhappy ending, she pleads guilty of ambivalence and unrealistic expectations, fatal to most part-time situations, not just prime-time ones. Vieira confesses, "I don't believe you can have it all, but still I thought maybe *I* could." The lesson? Be realistic about the workplace you're in. Not every part-time job will work in every situation all of the time no matter how talented you are. But most of the time it will.

ELEVEN

Strategies for Managing at Home

"Women are asking the wrong question today. They're asking, 'Will I still be able to get the job done if I work part-time?' What they should be asking is, 'Will I still be able to take care of the kids properly if I work part-time?' "

—Arlene Rossen Cardozo, *Sequencing*

T.G.I.F. It's been a long week and you're ready for your day off. A lazy summer day stretches out before you. You're on top of things. It's not even nine in the morning and you've got two loads of laundry under your belt, you've called into the office twice for messages, cleaned up the kitchen twice, made several insurance and doctor phone calls, and fielded three social calls for your still-slumbering teenagers. The phone rings and this time it's your boss. The adrenaline starts to flow when you look over at your busy three-year-old. Buying yourself thirty seconds, you suggest that you change phones.

What your boss can't see is you and your cordless moving through the house to "secure the phone call." You start scanning for the remote control so that you can put your favorite antiscreaming strategy into action: turning on a kid's video. Since your teenager just got up, you stride resolutely toward her room, toward the undulating blare of Snoop Doggy Dogg, you place your hand over the microphone and contort your face in ways only mothers and Jim Carrey can, mouthing the words, "Turn that down. It's my boss!" Total elapsed time is two minutes. You sit down in your office chair, try to calm down and try to get in a professional frame of mind. Now you begin your business call.

When customers and colleagues reach out and touch you remotely via the phone, catching you right in the middle of the rough and tumble of family life, the effect can be jarring. And this was one of your smoother phone calls.

How can you steer your way through the obstacle course of family and home activities while at the same time keeping a handle on professional commitments? Frankly, it can be a bumpy ride. This chapter should help smooth the way.

MARKING OFF BOUNDARIES BETWEEN WORK AND HOME

By virtue of the accessibility you probably designed into your part-time plan, the crossover between work and home is much more intense. It's important to decide in the beginning how much you will allow work to penetrate your family life. There is no one right answer. You could use an east is east, west is west approach in which you jealousy guard your home turf from work intrusions. On the other hand, a home situation that happily invites interruptions and the free flow of work in the midst of family activities is just as legitimate. Your decision about the balance you choose will depend on many factors. The point is that you need to establish ground rules to support whatever boundaries you choose to set. Here are some steps to take when you determine the way you want to regulate the work/family flow:

Analyze the Type of Work and How Best to Do It

In the first few weeks as a part-timer, track the tasks you actually end up doing at home. Are they mostly jobs that require you to be alone, such as conducting telephone interviews, scheduling appointments? Are they jobs that you could do after the children are in bed or while they're playing with friends, such as reading e-mail or proofreading a draft? Is it mostly phone work such as sharing information with a job-share partner or other colleague who won't be put off by children's noises in the background?

Then analyze your list. Decide how much time you will probably need to spend at home alone, how much work you will need to do with kids around, and what you can do after the kids are in bed. Then see how that fits in with your home life. Researcher Andy Koontz with Syntex generally tried to do voice mails when her daughter Sophie was still napping. Because she was the type of child who was difficult to distract while Koontz tried to do some paperwork, she had to restrict her work time to when Sophie was napping or at night after she was in bed. Says Koontz, "Basically, I couldn't use the phone while she was up.

Decide on an Approach to Work Time

Indianapolis pediatrician Susan Davis who job shares a busy pediatric practice goes into her home office between 7:30 and 8:30 A.M., including Saturdays, for a patient-doctor phone-in hour. Patients can call her home to ask questions, get advice, and to determine if an office visit and examination are necessary. Says Davis, herself the mother of a seven-year-old and a three-year-old, "People love it. And my partner and I love it because it concentrates our calls. My patients know they can call me then, so they don't call that often at noon or at three." Davis is able to set this specific time aside because her baby-sitter, a cousin who has been taking care of her daughter since she was six weeks old, arrives before the phone hour begins and gets her ready for school.

Independent contractor Cynthia Nickerson likes to compartmentalize her day, giving her full attention to work when she's at work, and then turning it off once she's home. Better to stay late to get her work done at the office in order to avoid bringing something home. Only in extreme circumstances does she bring work home. Mimi Thomas with Intel says she can't get anything substantial done at home because she gets totally immersed in her kids and doesn't have the self-discipline to drag herself to the computer to work.

On the other hand, if you do your work at home on a more informal, casual basis, you might not feel honorbound to maintain a professional facade. Says Henci Goer, part-time medical abstractor, "If my boss is calling me at home, he has to expect to hear some kid noise in the background." Seattle communications consultant Laurel Prokop loves to "mix it up." She loves her days "off," when she goes through the day making choices like "Do I want to bake a cake right now or do I want to format the next volume?" Prokop even has a triple timer, a special gadget that times three things simultaneously. Says Prokop, "I always do three things at once. I balance the laser printer with the laundry. If I have forty pages coming off the laser printer, that's the right time to take those slightly damp shirts out of the dryer and hang them up or to empty the garbage cans. If I'm taking the kids to the park, I stop in at Starbucks for some coffee and a scone, take the hundred pages I need to proof and sit there and work and enjoy the scenery.''

Lori Johnson mixes work and family on the road. Says Johnson, ''While I'm waiting for my daughter to come out from ballet, I take my cell phone and call in for messages and knock off some of my own calls. Some people may not think it's appropriate to work from the car, but it's been a lifesaver for me.'' Independent contractor Suzanne Ely takes her portable computer out in the grass and logs in some time while her children play outdoors. She avoids interruptions by the neighbors and passersby by keeping her head down and refusing eye contact.

Defending the Work/Family Border: Five Tips

1. DEDICATE A SEPARATE ROOM OR STRATEGICALLY PLACE A PARTITION

Keep all your work materials, supplies, and equipment in a clearly demarcated space. Tell your kids and husband your office supplies are off-limits and suggest the consequences if the stapler, tape or the Exacto knife turns up missing when you need it. Don't allow your kids to play on your computer if you can help it. If it's your only computer, have them ask you before they turn it on so that you can save all unsaved documents. But just in case the unthinkable happens in your home and your child (gasp) accidentally moves your files into the trash, practice extra careful computer safety by backing up everything and storing it with a neighbor or at the office. You might also consider protecting your system with a log-on password.

2. MAKE THEM READ YOUR LIPS

Spell out exactly what you want from your family members in order for you to succeed. For example, make it clear you do not want to be interrupted when you go into your office or corner office to work. Some women hang a sign, ''Do not disturb'' or ''Woman at work'' or ''I'll be available at 5:00 P.M.'' to let people know. Explicitly explain that the only interruptions you'll accept are Dad, doctor, and school.

3. ALERT THE MEDIA THAT YOU'RE GOING TO WORK

Announce the fact that you're going to work even if this means you just walk across the room to your desk. Make sure to explain to your children what you will be doing and why it's important that you do it.

4. KNOCK IT OFF

On your day off when you have to work in your home office, call it quits after a reasonable amount of time, if your children are home. Kids can understandably feel cheated if you're always on the phone or on the computer. Small children especially have a hard time understanding why Mom won't talk to them even though she's within range. After putting away your work, come out and give them your undivided attention. Go through some ritual for ending your workday. Push in your computer chair, clean up your workspace, announce that you're done, watch the news, change your clothes, inspect the garden, kiss your children as if you've just returned from the office, start dinner, or my favorite close-down ritual, pouring a ceremonial glass of chilled California Chardonnay.

5. TREAT YOUR WORK WITH RESPECT, AND OTHERS WILL TOO

Talk to your family about the work you do and why it's important to you. Let your friends know your schedule and if they happen to call you then, tell them you're working at the moment. Using the "not now, but when" approach will condition them not to expect to chat with you when you tell them you're at work.

6. TIPS FOR KIDPROOFING YOUR PHONE CALLS

The "how to handle business phone calls at home" problem persists regardless of how old your children are. Each age brings with it unique phone pros and cons. While young children can't reach and pick up the receiver to answer the phone, they can cry and whine relentlessly whenever they see their mother with a phone attached to her ear. Older children can answer the phone, but when they do, they often irritate and confuse business callers with their barely articulate speech. Teenagers race to the phone but their voices might show irritation that it isn't one of their buddies. No one of any age seems capable of taking messages dependably. You would probably never hire one of your own children to be your receptionist, yet that's exactly the service they perform for you every day at home. And the truth is that even husbands forget.

- *Set firm phone guidelines for the family.* Tell everyone that if you're on the phone, write you a note if it's absolutely necessary to disturb you. If you have call waiting, make sure your children understand they are to respond to all call-waiting signals and that your calls always take precedence over theirs. They may groan that this isn't fair. Ignore it. I know from personal experience that callers will eventually let you know if no one answered (i.e., call-waiting beeps were ignored). If this occurs, mete out the appropriate consequence.

- *Have kids practice answering the phone with a greeting that identifies the household.* "Hello. This is the Smith residence" is simple, easy, and effective. If your family has more than one last name, "Hello, Smith and Jones residence," works, too.

- *Make it easy for everyone to take messages.* Place pads and pens (get the stationary type from an office supply if you have trouble with pads and pens disappearing). Make sure to ask periodically, "Any calls for me?" to jog their memories.

- *Group all your pending phone calls together, sit down, and make them in batches.* In case you don't reach people, set aside a chunk of time and request that they call you back then.

- *Put together an emergency phone call survival kit.* Try preparing a "bribery bag" full of interesting stamps, trinkets, and games, whatever fascinates your child, plus a few pieces of candy. Only allow the kids to play with these bags when you're on the phone unexpectedly. Have several videos that are reserved for the same purpose. This way the kids will look forward to your business calls.

- *Work with a cordless phone.* The cordless allows you to set up the movies, to get out the bribery bag, and to turn off loud music at the beginning of the conversation and to relocate to your office where the materials you need are located. Furthermore, if you're going to be outside with the kids or back in the garden, you can take the portable with you so you don't miss an important call. Keep in mind, though, that the cordless doesn't always deliver as clear a sound as a regular telephone and others can listen in up to a mile away.

- *Reschedule a phone appointment if necessary.* If your kids are so tired or so fussy that you can see it's hopeless to try to conduct a phone conversation, dodge the bullet by saying you can't talk right now, you have another phone appointment, or say that you are in a meeting, would 4:00 work? Be sure to be available then.

- *Cite business reasons only for rescheduling.* When someone calls you on business, never respond that you can't talk because you're just sitting down to lunch with the kids or that you have some kids over playing. These reasons sound weak to the uninitiated.

The Most Kid-Proof Solution

A separate business line is the only child-proof (well, almost) method and the one that you probably should choose if you have an official telecommuting job or a job where you will be accessible to customers or other clients to whom it is essential to present a professional front. The only downsides are the expense of the line installation (about $80), the monthly service bills (about $20), and the cost of the extra phones (each about $100).

Set up a separate business line located far away from the household distractions. An answering machine, voice mail, or answering service handles incoming calls when you're not there. Tell your children they are never to answer your business line, but just in case, teach them how to answer the phone and take messages properly. Emphasize they are not to provide any personal information about your location in the shower or at the shopping mall.

PART-TIME CHILD CARE

Flexible day care is critical to your success at home. The unavoidable give and take between work and home—a client will only be in town on your day off, your child is sick and can't go to school one or two days—means you need child care and it needs to be flexible. Surprisingly, child care that is part-time and flexible and affordable turns out to be more difficult to come by than full-time because quality caregivers often prefer full-time work. Also, many day-care centers limit their clientele to full-time because of staffing and scheduling issues. Here are the options and pros and cons of each.

A Good Day-Care Center

Besides being cheaper and saving wear and tear on your home, some centers accept children for a few hours or part-time. Hewlett-Packard job sharer Susan Lovegren delivers her two preschool children to day-care centers before work. She thinks the effort is well worth it. Lovegren likes the fact that it's a business. She feels more comfortable bringing issues up in a business setting with established procedures. Says the thirty-five-year-old human resources manager, "An in-home day-care provider would mean one more person to supervise and to keep happy. And when managing people is what you do all day long, you don't want to come home and face more people issues."

The big negative with day care comes when children get sick. Sick children often present a bigger problem for part-time professionals than for full-timers. If a part-timer stays home for a day or two to nurse a sick child, she's missing over half of her workweek. Her absence not only keeps her from completing work, but intensifies the perception that she's "never" in the office. A secure back-up system for sick days goes a long way to overcome this problem. Special day-care centers for sick children are one option. Lovegren and her husband have managed to work it out between them. Last year when the household was hit with chickenpox, for example, she and her husband split the days spent at home.

Get full-time day care anyway, if you can afford it. Besides the peace of mind for emergencies, you can use the extra hours for meetings, getting work done at home uninterrupted, or for pursuing a personal interest. Computer programmer Sandy Geist who works three days a week, opted for full-time day care. Her son's day-care center allows her to pay either $25 a day or $100 a week. Paying the extra $25 allows her to take her son to day care when she wants to clean her house without him running across the freshly mopped floors or to shop when the malls are less crowded. Says Geist, "We don't have a lot of that one-on-one time anymore, so when we want to play golf together, Bob takes the day off and we don't have to worry about getting a sitter. Plus when I have to go in on a Friday, I'm not frantically looking around for my mom or someone else to cover for me. Or if, God forbid, I get sick. For an extra $25, it's definitely worth it."

Caution: Make sure your day-care center's scheduling is flexible enough to accommodate you on short notice. Several women we talked to said their centers needed advance notice. Administrators schedule day-care workers based on the number of real bodies that will attend every day. This means they have to scramble if you call at the last minute to say you'll be bringing in your child.

The Part-time Nanny

In-home child-care advocates argue that the extra cost is worth every penny because their children escape the germ exposure and subsequent upper-respiratory tract infections that seem to run rampant among the day-care population. Certainly children particularly susceptible to disease probably fare better in their own homes. Furthermore, in-home care also frees you from the brutal early-morning drill of rousting the kids out of bed and hurriedly dressing, feeding, and loading them into the car before you start your workday.

Finding a qualified nanny who is willing to work part-time can be daunting. Karen Gage interviewed twenty-seven candidates before she found one she liked and who was as flexible as she needed her to be. But once she found her, Gage said the arrangement worked well. Her sitter came in for fifteen hours a week, usually in the mornings. The kids would be there with the nanny when Gage went upstairs, walked into her office, and shut the door. She wouldn't reappear until she was done working. Says Gage, "If my daughter had a problem or was feeling low, she'd come up and visit for a minute or two and then leave. After three to four hours in my office, I'd knock off at lunch and go play with the kids. I'd get the rest of my work done at night after they were in bed."

Paying for full-time in-home day care, including live-in nannies or au pairs, can be a worthwhile strategy to relieve your juggling act on your days at home. Lori Johnson advocates the full-time in-home route: "It's definitely worth it to look long and hard to find somebody who has the kind of flexibility you need. My nanny's there from eight to six, but she has full-time flexibility so when my husband has to be late and I'm gone, she can stay."

Baby-sitters for When They're Not Babies Anymore
Child care for school-age children gets cheaper, but also more complex. Unless your job stops at 2:30 sharp, you'll still need after-school care and holiday and summer coverage. Here's the rub: Older (and by now more vocal) children often object to the after-school arrangements you patch together. You want them to concentrate on homework. They want to play with friends, and participate in extra-curricular activities, and often they chafe at being "baby-sat" by the same older woman they used to love back in kindergarten. To complicate matters further, the after-school child-care details requires driving children around to keep them on schedules so complex and busy they resemble O'Hare airport on a late Friday afternoon. The scheduling and chauffeuring keeps getting heavier and doesn't let up until the children can drive themselves where they need to go.

Here are the after-school options:

REGULAR BABY-SITTERS

Baby-sitters can stay home with younger siblings and supervise the homework and extracurricular schedules of older ones if you're lucky enough to find someone interested in that narrow time slot. High school students or local college students make good short-term sitters but often quit at the end of the semester. It is essential to make sure that their judgment, driving skills, maturity, and dependability are all they should be.

ON-SITE BEFORE-AND-AFTER-SCHOOL DAY CARE

Many schools today offer before and after school daycare. My youngest daughter regularly attends her school's "Clubhouse" program and loves the summer camp–type atmosphere. I love it because unlike many such after-school programs, it's totally flexible, allowing her to attend whenever she wants with no advance notice required. However, it doesn't come cheap. It costs $4.99 per hour per child, making it almost cost-prohibitive if you have more than one child in the program. Another negative with on-site school care is that your child care is shackled to the school schedule. Those unexpected days when the program closes down can throw a huge monkey wrench into your work plans.

FAMILY AND FRIENDS

Using on-site school day care or regular sitters combined with help from family and friends is the most prevalent child-care system for part-timers. Older siblings, neighbors, and friends, what Betty Friedan calls "the extended family of choice," provide an indispensable pool of after-school care for school-age children. They can serve as your backups when you're between sitters or when school Christmas vacation lasts three weeks and you're only off for one. It can also work on a more regular basis.

Mother of three Lori Johnson, for example, prefers that her two-year-old stay home with the baby-sitter and not be "dragged around" to her older children's after-school activities. In order to keep the sitter at home, Johnson does a lot of carpooling. "One way I deal with my children's schedules," says Johnson, "is to trade off with other parents. I invest time in forming relationships with parents whose children go to school with my kids." If she has a tough week and can't be there to pick up at dance class, she asks one of these parents to cover for her. Then during the weeks when she's more flexible, she reciprocates. That way her husband doesn't have to take off work to do car pools. Besides, her older kids are happier if they don't have to stay home with the sitter. "The downside," Johnson explains, "is that this solution calls for a logistically significant amount of juggling and requires that I know these parents very well."

A Correlation Between Part-time Work and Manipulative Behavior

Our research on part-timers unearthed only one psychological pitfall for children. Martha Hahn Sugar, psychologist and author of *When Mother Works, Who Pays,* conducted research for her Ph.D. thesis on the psychological effects on children of having mothers who worked. She found that children of part-timers had the highest scores in manipulation, especially in hypochondria. The daughters of part-timers in particular scored significantly higher in manipulative behavior than the children of full-time working mothers and at-home mothers. She speculates that the reason for this is that part-time mothers are a self-selecting group who by virtue of choosing to work part-time, put extra value on supporting their children. Because they are inclined to bend over backward for their kids and because they have flexible schedules, their children take advantage of them. If the child wants to go to a basketball game, part-time moms are often willing to make a change in their schedules. "The child becomes conditioned to keep pressuring until she can get the response she needs. The full-time working mom clearly can't accommodate the wish. Her response is 'Sorry, not possible. You'll have to deal with it.' " The part-time mom feels guilty saying no and gives in.

Hahn suggests the following to eliminate this manipulative behavior:

1. *Discipline children consistently.* Don't excuse children's poor behavior and then escape to work to ignore it. Quality time often consists of discipline.
2. *Stop feeling guilty about the time you spend working.* Children sense your ambivalence and manipulate it. Remember, all others feel like this from time to time, regardless of their work hours. Many part-timers may feel unconsciously that they should be rearing children full-time.
3. *Keep a regular schedule.* Be quite firm about when you will be working and setting clear boundaries. Don't fall into the trap of constantly interrupting your work in order to take on additional chauffeuring or homework that children can probably do themselves.

HUSBANDS MAY NOT GET IT RIGHT AWAY

"My husband will do anything that needs to be done," said one contented part-timer, "the house and laundry are my job on the days I'm off. But he pitches in on giving kids baths, making lunches, cooking dinner, and cleaning up the kitchen." This husband gets it. He sees himself as a job sharer of the child and house-care duties of home and automatically does his fair share. Unfortunately, in many cases husbands may unconsciously start operating according to a new set of hidden assumptions when their wives cut back their hours. First of all, a husband who shared the workload when you held down a full-time job may regress. He may start treating you like a modern-day June Cleaver who is expected to keep the house spotless with the smell of home-baked goodies wafting from the kitchen and take over all child care and housework responsibilities while he is freed up to pursue his interest in golf. Second, now that you're earning less, a subtle power shift may take place. He may feel you are no longer entitled to complain about his not sharing the "second shift" at home. He may chafe at the idea of household help since your earnings are down, or he may expect you to start clipping coupons and growing and canning your own vegetables to save money. Third, you may sense a lack of respect for your new, down-sized job. It's as if now you have a professional hobby, instead of a profession.

If you accept these assumptions and are happy with them, terrific. If you don't agree with these assumptions, then you and your husband probably have some issues to work out. You should expect a period of personal growth and adjustment before the two of you settle into a new, mutually agreeable pattern.

Tips for Helping Husbands Make the Transition

• **Acknowledge your husband's concern about money.** Although your husband may enjoy the reduction in stress, the reduction in income may be a frightening prospect in these tough economic times. He may surprise himself and you with the negative feelings that surface when the reality of becoming the only full-time breadwinner hits. Plan how to keep expenses down and then follow through with the plan. Make him aware of the enormous hidden benefits he now enjoys because of your part-time work and stop feeling defensive about how much your job is "costing" him. Don't fall into the trap of thinking that just because it is your paycheck that has decreased,

■ A FEW MOANS AND GROANS

Part-timers air their complaints about their spouses:

"My husband supports my work, but he still doesn't really have a clue after all these years about how many things I'm really juggling. But if I complain, his response is, "So quit your job." He doesn't understand that's not where I'm at. I'm going to do my job no matter what."

> —Michele Helmuth, nurse practitioner and college instructor

"I watched his attitude change after I started working part-time. I'm not expecting him to get down and wash the floor. But he could do a load of laundry or do the dishes, the things he did before we had children. When I went part-time, all of a sudden it stopped. He said, but you're only working twenty-eight hours a week, and I said, No, I'm only getting *paid* for twenty-eight hours a week."

> —Sandy Geist, computer programmer

"When I started my business, my husband didn't realize that when I lose two hours of my workday because of some emergency with the kids, I have to recoup those hours, which means I have to work at night and he has to watch the kids."

> —Ellen Langas Campbell, communications and time-management consultant

"My husband is a fifty-two-year-old engineer and doesn't seem aware there's been a women's movement. In the last fifteen years he has stayed home with the kids for an emergency exactly one day."

> —Sara Jamison, *Sunset* magazine

"I am always the one who has to drive it in order to keep our life organized. Taking the initiative sometimes doesn't really occur to him."

> —Wendy Gibson, marketing and public relations consultant

that any slack in the budget should go for expenses that make his life more pleasant. You decided together that the reduced schedule would be better for the family as a whole, so discretionary spending should be based on an equitable sharing. Sometimes he wins; sometimes you win. If you can afford to hire a lawn service, car washes, snow shoveling, carpet cleaning, painting, redoing kitchen cabinets—traditionally male jobs that are contracted out—you can probably afford a bi-weekly cleaning service.

• **Don't assume your husband understands how hard you're working to juggle your part-time job and family matters.** It would be expecting too much of human nature to think that your husband won't secretly be hoping the new schedule will get him off the hook for a lot of the household drudgery he shared when you worked full-time. You need to make him aware of your schedule and the fact that if you spend two hours running errands during your day off, you'll need to make that time up in the evening and will need him to help with the kids. Job sharers Susan Lovegren and Nancy Kelly have struggled to get their husbands to understand the juggling they do to work the hours they do and to make sure that everything in the home is nice. Says Lovegren, "You really have to lay it on the line. You have to tell husbands, 'This is what I need from you in order to be successful.' "

• **Use the Sunday-night meeting.** Sit down on a Sunday night with the big calendar and go through the week. Discuss what's on everybody's schedule: your hours, what activities the kids need transportation to, when the kids aren't covered, what each of you would like to do for fun, meetings, house projects, food shopping, and cooking. Then prioritize and divvy up the work. Ask your husband, "Which of these things can you handle?"

• **Devise a plan for dividing the workload.** Some couples alternate weeks for chores. Sandy Geist and her husband divided the meal preparation so that he cooks on every day that has a *t* in it, Tuesday, Thursday, and Saturday. Says Geist, "I don't care what he does as long as he's responsible for dinner and then helps with a couple of loads of laundry here and there. I don't expect him to keep the house as clean as I do. Just picking up after himself would help immensely." Make it clear to your husband that you need to be able to count on his accomplishing his end of it so that you can schedule that time for work. Random acts of kindness are nice, but won't help the planning process. If you know that he has signed up to bathe the kids, read to them, and get them to sleep, you can schedule time to sit down at the computer and catch up. After you've divided the work, write it down and post it in a conspicuous spot.

• **Develop a healthy sense of entitlement.** Treat yourself and your work with respect. You are a professional who has made a choice to cut back hours to make a valuable contribution to your family. Convey confidence about your position, otherwise your husband may question your authority and right to ask him to pitch in. Feel entitled to work out an equal sharing of home and child-care responsibilities. Make sure he doesn't always get the "fun" stuff like bedtime stories and bathing. It doesn't matter that you're earning less now, nor does it matter what you're earning compared with what your husband earns.

• **Point out other role models who are married to part-timers.** Capitalize on the fact that fathering and helping at home are now considered macho activities among the dual-income population.

• **Give your mate (and yourself) time to adapt to your new role.** Don't come to any drastic conclusions about yourself, your mate, or the part-time job during the initial transition period. Realize that many difficulties are only temporary.

• **Consider hiring out the housework.** Many women use a cleaning service every other week combined with the strategic use of professional services such as window cleaning, carpet shampooing, and sending the shirts out. After Sara Jamison had been working part-time at *Sunset* magazine as a photo assistant for several years, she went in for her annual physical complaining of stress and fatigue. Her doctor asked her what she did on her day off. "Cleaning," Jamison replied. The good doctor wrote her out an official prescription for a cleaning lady and instructed her to present it to her husband. She still has the prescription from 1985 on her refrigerator. Over ten years later and Sara is still at *Sunset,* and every other Friday two women come to clean. "I love it. I sit and drink my coffee on the porch and feel like I'm living the life of Riley." She adds that her husband suggests periodically that they eliminate the cleaning ladies, saying, "Why don't we just get the kids and me together, and we'll all help out. We don't need a cleaning crew." I tell him, "No way, besides, it's cheaper than a psychiatrist."

YOUR EMOTIONAL HOME LIFE

Switching to part-time is a major lifestyle change. Some women experience a bit of an identity crisis after they make the switch, feeling like they're neither fish nor fowl. "It's sometimes hard to know which world I really belong to," says Susan Lovegren. This is a common sentiment among part-time professionals. On Fridays she belongs to a playgroup in which most of the mothers stay home full-time. When she's there, a part of her feels the need to cover up her work life for fear of being viewed as not giving child rearing enough attention. ''I wonder if they're critical of me because I'm not doing as much as they're doing. On the other hand, I can't say to them, 'Gee, it's been a stressful week.' '' Instead, Lovegren finds herself purposely downplaying her job, giving them the impression that she balances both quite easily, that what she does is just a little part-time job. ''Then when I'm at work I downplay my kids for fear I'll look like too much of a mommy,'' says Lovegren.

The slightly schizophrenic personality changes the part-time professional undergoes on her days at home can be exhausting. It is draining to adjust your personality back and forth from the brisk, no-nonsense businesswoman to the tender, loving, empathic mother (on some days we never make the transition). It's easy to become inordinately irritated and impatient when children make demands or start whining when your mind's still on the office. Says Alexis Rubin, ''I have to tell myself to lighten up. I lecture myself saying, Remember, you were the one who wanted to be home when Jay's schoolday was over. You wanted to be the one to help him with his algebra. Don't blow it now!''

Strategies to Help You Find Your Own Inner Balance at Home

• **Let them eat popcorn.** Set reasonable expectations. On days that you go into work, don't expect that things will run more smoothly than they did when you worked full-time. Says Nancy Kelly, ''We don't have great expectations for days I go in. Often I don't cook when I spend all day at the office. It's okay for the kids to eat popcorn for dinner. At least they're with their father. They're not hungry and they're enjoying it. They get regular food the next day.'' Both Nancy Kelly and her job-share partner Susan Lovegren think a no-fuss no-muss hairdo is key to their success.

• **Save some projects for later.** Marlaine Griffin, a training consultant in San Jose, California, tried to squeeze five years of backlogged projects into her first six months of part-time work. She organized and hosted a reunion of college friends, supervised a household renovation, did some landscaping, started going to Weight Watchers, cleaned out all her closets, got bids on redesigning her home office, and took on the grade school graduation slide show and the PTA tee-shirt sale. Neither Griffin nor her husband were having fun. Says

Griffin, "My husband started throwing a shoe in the door when he came home at night. He never knew whether I would bite or not."

• **Put child-rearing jobs on your to-do list.** Helping with algebra homework, researching a good piano teacher, teaching your child to sew or how to ride a bike are activities just as time-consuming and as important as checking e-mail, writing performance evaluations, or performing other work-related activities that you automatically write down on your agenda. Including these on your list encourages you to accomplish them, and it also gives them the legitimacy they deserve.

• **Keep the two ''P principles'' in mind the next time you wonder where all the time goes.** The first *P* is Parkinson's Law, which states that work expands to fill the time available for its accomplishment. Don't fight this at-home reality. You don't need to prove how quickly you sail through a project with your children. Try to keep your home immune from the office ethic where ''he with the most hectic schedule, the biggest list of achievements, and the most toys wins.'' It's the process you're at home for, not the product. The second *P* is the Pareto Principle, which means most of the results you achieve are produced by a few critical activities. Figure out what those critical activities are that make you feel like your life is under control. Plan your days to include those high-yield activities. For example, part-time businesswoman Karen Garappolo, who runs a custom painting business from her home, has found that getting up at 5:30 and going on a three-mile run helps her feel in control for the rest of the day. Think about what behaviors produce positive effects in your days at home and focus on doing those things regularly.

• **Bigger calendars are better.** Use an oversized calendar with plenty of writing space and keep it by the kitchen phone. Art museum curator Inez McDermott carries a small calendar in her purse and is religious about transferring items to her big calendar. She also checks in with her husband's secretary once a week to add in items from his calendar because once in a while he forgets to mention that he's going to be out of town for a few days.

• **Leave unscheduled time.** Large blocks of unscheduled time can absorb unexpected events. Have at least one full day when you don't schedule any work at all.

• **Practice saying no.** Learn to say no to well-meaning neighbors and friends who step up their requests to watch their kids, drive them to the airport, let in their repairmen, or just hang out for long periods of time. Unless, of course, you want to do these things. Don't feel you must answer the door to salesmen and drop-in visitors or chat with every friend that calls. Protect your time—you've paid dearly for it.

Managing the Volunteer Load

Part-timers often want to give something back to the community and want to set a good example for their children. They are also usually quite interested in the children's schools. However, as Inez McDermott has found out, it's easy to get burned out and overcommitted. She's on the board at her daughter's preschool. She's a director on the Friends of the Library Board. She's also in charge of the artists-in-residence program for the New Hampshire council of artists. Says McDermott, "I tried to hold back for as long as I could on major school volunteer work. For a long time I tried pretending I didn't know how to type, hoping that would keep the requests for committee work down. But once I helped them write a grant, the word was out." She loves having her children see that one person can make a real difference, but making that difference is very time consuming. When it seemed that she was out to meetings every night, she and her husband made a deal that she would be gone only one night a week for volunteer work.

Ellen Langas Campbell of Philadelphia was over her head in volunteer work, so she's decided to say no unless it involved activities where she could direct her own time. She now reads and records books for the blind and offers pro bono public relations work. Says Campbell, "I get a lot more satisfaction if I can see someone getting something out of it versus being on an organization's spring banquet committee." Susan Lovegren stays in control by scheduling her work in the classroom for a specific slot of time. Lovegren works at her daughter's third-grade class once a month for an hour and a half. She pays a sitter to take care of her other three children and is careful not to exceed that.

Sunflower Houses and Savoring the Special Times

When I went to computer programmer Karen Gage's house for our interview, several empty cardboard refrigerator boxes occupied the front porch, obviously forts and homes for child's play. I admired her ingenuity and relaxed attitude. She then told me about a project she and her children were currently working on, one that she had initiated when she was working part-time at the software company. She and her two kids were growing a sunflower garden house. Every foot sunflower seeds are planted. In between the sunflower seeds go morning glory seeds. Once the sunflowers reach the height of six feet, you tie a string across the top so the morning glories fill in, forming the walls and the roof. You then trim out the doors and windows. The first year Gage and her children tried the project, some of the sunflowers failed to germinate and so the houselike effect was never achieved. This year they would try again.

The sunflower garden house seems to me to capture the essence of what part-time professionals are trying to achieve at home: having as much quality and quantity of time as possible. Time and only time can set the stage for good feelings, wide-open learning, and deep and lasting relationships. Such grand and glorious projects as a sunflower house are the stuff memories are made of. What child could ever forget the enchantment of such a fairy-tale cottage deep in summer? The effects of such time are like money in the bank from which children can draw security and stability throughout their lives. The lesson: Manage your time at home so that you can plant some sunflower houses of your own.

PART SIX

IN THE FUTURE

We Need More Invisible Champions:

An Interview with Karen Nussbaum

Karen Nussbaum, the director of the Working Women's Department of the AFL-CIO, has been a longtime advocate for working families. Formerly the director of the Women's Bureau of the U.S. Department of Labor as well as the director of Work/Family Directions in Boston, Nussbaum was active in the eight-year fight for the Family and Medical Leave Act.

Q: *How would you assess the state of the workplace today in terms of part-time professional opportunities for women?*

A: When I talk to a random group of working women—not all professional level—about flexible work arrangements, they tell me, "Sounds like a good idea, but I've never seen that in a job of mine." Family-friendly policies do not exist in the vast majority of companies. That's the problem. Today many good policies have been pioneered and have been found valuable. Flexible arrangements have been tried once or maybe a hundred times in perhaps a thousand companies, but there are six million enterprises in this country and there seems to be no diffusion. We've hit a plateau.

Q: *Who will champion changes in the workplace that will make flexible jobs more available?*

A: Women workers—the grass roots approach rather than one that focuses on a handful of innovative companies who always hear: "Oh, you are the great pioneers of our society. Let's award you again." Yes, there are highly visible champions, but the real pressure comes from below. From the people within companies who pressure for those kinds of changes, either through unions, professional associations, or just individually in their own workplaces.

Q: *What about changes in public policy?*

A: That's what we're trying to do with the Women's Bureau Honor Roll. Our new program gets pledges from employers, organizations, and individuals that go toward improving pay and benefits, building a family-friendly workplace, and for training and advancement for women. We think these are reasonable expectations for families, including the need for either partner or both to work part-time for a period. This shouldn't be extraordinary. And the reasonable company will design policies as a result of pressure for these reasonable needs. I think things are at the breaking point right now, and the way things will change will be in several ways. One is legislative. Fortunately, we saw the first step in this direction with the passage of the Family and Medical Leave Act in 1993, a piece of legislation that finally recognizes that parents work and workers have families. And it has functioned well for those whom it affects. People need to continue at the state level, which I think is going to be more fruitful than the U.S. Congress. Another way is that women will work for themselves instead of trying to cope with hostile corporate environments.

TWELVE

Professional Part-time: Beyond 2000

"In the future, most women won't work full-time."

—Patricia Aburdeen, in an address to a skeptical audience of Silicon Valley women in 1992

These are extraordinary times for part-time professionals. Adjusting for speechmaking hyperbole, Patricia Aburdeen's prediction that most women will step off the full-time treadmill at one time or another in the future is probably accurate. Flexible work arrangements in general may have hit a plateau, as Karen Nussbaum suggests in the introduction to Part Six, but part-time professionals will increasingly push for better options than the punishing (both for us and our families) stranglehold of full-time work. The quiet rebellion is just beginning.

The bulk of this book has been devoted to describing strategies that depend on your own gumption and ingenuity and operate in the absence of genuine workplace support. The workforce is changing more rapidly than the workplace is. Opportunities for good professional part-time work are better than anyone dreamed of a mere decade ago. Yet the opportunities we have are still too few and the price for taking advantage of them still too high. In order for both individuals and business to flourish, we need to reshape public and corporate policy.

WHAT NEEDS TO CHANGE

Make Children a Priority

Penelope Leach, the distinguished British expert in child development, writes and speaks eloquently and forcefully of the need for new mothers and fathers to have access to entitlement programs and social support systems. She urges us—in our legislation, in our policy making, and in our individual choices—to think of children first. In *Children First: What Our Society Must Do—And Is Not Doing—For Our Children Today,* Leach attacks the antichild nature of American culture, a culture so at odds with what constitutes good parenting, that good parenting in the 1990s has become exceedingly difficult, if not impossible. Leach argues, "Children don't make money; worse, their upbringing demands time, that equally precious marketplace commodity. So, politicians pay parenthood lip service, calling it the most important job in the world, while at the same time contributing to a society in which adults cannot be solvent, self-respecting workers and parents." She calls on us as individuals, as leaders in corporations, and as a nation to make good on the endless rhetoric about the importance of family by creating family-based policies.

How Do Other Countries Accommodate Part-time Needs?

Yes, Sweden again. Get this: In Sweden a baby's birth entitles either parent to eighteen months of parental leave at 100 percent pay. Funded by a universal tax on employers, parents may take maternity leave all at once, or they may extend it by combining it with part-time work. At the end of the leave period, both parents may choose to work a six-hour workday until their youngest child turns eight.

This idyllic setup remains a fantastic dream for the foreseeable future in this country. Still, it is not too much to expect some observance of the basic principle involved. At least one parent should reasonably expect to be able to develop him- or herself exclusively to the nurturing of infants in the critical early years. They should also reasonably expect to share that responsibility with the other parent. And they should be able to do all this without a loss of career status. In fact, the most generous employee benefits come close to the Swedish experience. Some U.S. companies already provide extended maternity leave and phase-back options and the opportunity to work part-time for up to three years. They prove it can be done—even here.

Improve Business Attitudes Toward Families

When you pitch your part-time proposal, you do so based on business needs. Yet your business life does not exist in a vacuum. Consultant Barbara Miller couches this concept in business terms. She calls for employers to start viewing the family as a strategic partner, in much the same way that businesses in the last decade have begun to think of their customers and vendors as being strategic partners. And it is true that the family *is* a strategic partner to business. It is the supportive family that provides businesses with workers who are stable, well-fed, hard-working, ethical, and educated, says Miller. The family serves as the refuge where workers recharge so they can devote as much energy and creativity as possible to the job.

Expand the Family and Medical Leave Act

The FMLA, which went into effect in August 1993, guarantees workers twelve weeks of unpaid leave—with no risk to their job—to take care of a newborn, a newly adopted child, or a sick family member, or to tend to their own personal illness. It's great as far as it goes. Unfortunately, according to Ellen Bravo and other experts, the FMLA affects only 43 percent of working women and 48 percent of working men. We recommend expanding it in the following ways.

- Expand the coverage from those who work at least twenty-five hours a week to include those who work less than twenty-five hours a week. These people have family needs and should be eligible for their fair share of benefits.
- Cover branch offices that are more than seventy-five miles from the main work site. The current law unnecessarily excludes people in more remote branches from FMLA protection.
- Lower the threshold of eligibility gradually so that employers of fifteen or more employees are included.
- Offer some protection for employees in the very smallest firms.

Explore Ways to Expand Benefits and Protections for Part-timers

The tempting phenomenon has raised public awareness of part-time inequities. The sensational growth (according to detractors, the "insidious" growth) of the contingent workforce has focused media attention on how most temporary workers don't get pensions, sick leaves, vacations, health insurance, and often any prospects of upward mobility. Media hype has sensationalized the issue calling the

■ THE FAMILY AND MEDICAL LEAVE ACT PASSED AND THE SKY DIDN'T FALL

Many large businesses fiercely opposed the FMLA because they feared it would dramatically increase their costs. A two-and-a-half-year bipartisan study of the law, however, showed that only a small percentage of companies experienced the dreaded cost increases. The flood of women taking advantage of the unpaid maternity leave never materialized. In fact, in the first year of the FMLA, only 25 percent of all the people who took leave did so because of birth or adoption; 59 percent of all those who went on leave did so for personal health reasons that were not related to pregnancy. Another 10 percent went out to care for seriously ill parents or spouses. Far from being bad for business, the study showed that employers found their workers were responding to the more liberal policy with increased productivity and loyalty, proof that business and family are not irreconcilable.

temp workforce "the new migrant workers," "the disposable workforce," and most notably by Rick Belous of the National Planning Association in Washington, "the workplace equivalent of a one-night stand." The Clinton administration responded by directing the Department of Labor to conduct a study of federal regulations on pensions, unemployment insurance, and other programs that leave gaps in coverage for contingent workers.

Federal labor laws that protect traditional (i.e., full-time and in an employer-employee relationship) employees from discrimination, sexual harassment, and hazardous working conditions do little for part-time workers. No laws currently guarantee that part-timers must be paid the same base rate or be given prorated benefits. There has been some legislative activity addressing the issues, but efforts stalled. Congresswoman Patricia Schroeder introduced legislation that would mandate prorated health and pension benefits for anyone working 500 hours a year or more. She also introduced a bill called the Part-Time and Temporary Workers Protection Act, which would require states to pay unemployment comp benefits to part-time workers without requiring them to accept offers of full-time work. Senator Harold Metzenbaum introduced the Contingent Worker Equity Act. But don't hold your breath: Schroeder and Metzenbaum are leaving the Senate and the current conservative mood in Washington makes the passage of such labor legislation highly unlikely.

You may be thinking that such legislation doesn't matter to you because you *want* to work on a part-time temporary basis or because you have more than enough coverage through your husband. But this is shortsighted. In the blink of an eye a divorce, your husband's death or disability, or financial reversals could make you the sole breadwinner and in desperate need of more benefits. It has happened to others and could happen to you.

You may also be thinking that having benefits through your husband's employment gives you a competitive edge over employees who need benefits. If so, it shouldn't. It's illegal to discriminate on the basis of marital status and the fact that a job candidate is a single woman who needs benefits should not affect an employer's hiring decision. Unfortunately, such discrimination is a fact of workplace life, but you shouldn't encourage it. It may come back and bite you someday.

Close the Gap Between Family-Friendly Policy and Practice

Many organizations that have family-friendly policies are surprised that employees rarely take advantage of them. But employees won't exercise their options when they don't think managers will support them. And all too many companies are managed by flexibility Luddites. These managers could champion work/life programs, reaping the benefits of enhanced productivity, easier recruitment, and increased employee retention. Instead, they block the path of progress.

The solution is manager training. Not surprisingly, all the companies that have reaped the greatest rewards from their work/life programs have built in training programs for their managers. Managers need to learn a new management style that values employees based on their contribution, not exclusively on the number of hours they work. They need to learn the business needs and strategies for successfully managing a flex workforce. Further, companies need to structure a clearly defined set of responsibilities for managing a flexible workforce into the manager's own performance evaluations.

Encourage Continued Development and Technology Use to Support Flexible Work Arrangements

Investment in new technologies could make managing part-timers a no-brainer. The replacement of antiquated systems of accounting and managing would remove one major obstacle. Adopting the full-time equivalency system would remove another. New benefits and compensation plans could be individualized to the needs of each worker. Telecommunications technologies could facilitate communication between people, making accessibility a nonissue.

Support Part-time Professional Public Policy

- *Support women government representatives at every level.* Studies of state legislatures by the center for the American Woman and Politics located at Rutgers University in New Jersey show that women of both parties spend more of their time than men of either party on matters that directly affect the health, education, and economic well-being of women and families. They also influence national policy. Says TV columnist Cokie Roberts, "When lawmakers in Washington dispatch federal programs to the state legislatures, you can be sure that it will be the women in those assemblies who will be looking after the children."
- *Join a national group like 9to5 or the Association of Part-Time Professionals.* These networks have newsletters that will keep you informed of new legislation being introduced or the status of pending bills. Pass what you learn on to friends and coworkers.
- *Follow the issues.* Write a letter to your representative about your own experiences and what you want to see change, and follow up by asking candidates for office about their support for specific bills.
- *Follow an electronic bulletin board or chat group dealing with family/work issues.* The beauty of the Internet is that you can get advice, support, and information from people with similar concerns without leaving your work station.

Support a Pro–Flexible Hours Change in Your Workplace

- *Discuss your choice to work part-time with other women.* Fran Rodgers, president of Work/Family Directions, thinks that too often a "conspiracy of silence" surrounds workers who choose part-time for lifestyle reasons. Family issues are not viewed as legitimate concerns that should be addressed in the workplace. It almost doesn't matter how or what you say about your decision. The fact that you bring it up at all gets the subject out of the closet and validates its importance.
- *Volunteer to work on a task force dealing with work issues that have an impact on part-time professionals.* Provide your perspec-

tive on benefits and compensation packages, training needs, and new software systems. Perhaps your company has a diversity task force or a women's network. If the company offers no formal means of addressing work/life issues, network with others informally.

- *Challenge traditional workplace practices that act as barriers to nontraditional workers.* The 7:30 A.M. meeting, the ''optional'' evening dinner meeting, relocations, weekend travel, all-night work sessions. Point out that those practices can put people who have elder care or family responsibilities in a bind. Discourage the all-too-pervasive myth that time on the job equals productivity and commitment to work.
- *Educate management on the business advantages of family-friendly policies.* The research and experience show that companies win when they adopt policies and practices that meet the needs of their employees.

Make Part-time Professional Work More Than a Women's Issue

Men haven't exactly overwhelmed managers with requests for part-time (although a respectable number do work part-time). Still, according to *Fortune* magazine, large-scale surveys of employees at American Express, North Carolina National Bank, and Levi Strauss suggest that fathers are just as distressed as mothers over the difficulties of balancing work and families. Says Towers Perrin consultant Margaret Regan of the hours people put in just to be seen: ''In focus groups, managerial men are saying, face time is killing us.'' This is good because, as Leslie Smith, associate director of the National Association for Female Executives (NAFE), points out, ''as long as the guys over fifty with wives at home to handle the family and home are in charge, things won't change that much.'' Nancy Austin dreams of a time when part-time professional work is neither a women's nor a men's issue. Says Austin, ''It should be a straight performance issue.''

A GOLDEN AGE

We hope we have armed you with the tools you need to pursue part-time professional work: an understanding of the options available, where the trends are taking us, and what you need to do to optimize your opportunities. We have been inspired by the women in this book who showed us how it's done and hope they inspire you. If, like them, we can manage to earn money, engage in satisfying work, and meet the needs of our families, it doesn't get much better.

Victory—defined as broad acceptance and large numbers of practicing part-time professionals—will not come overnight. It will take place over the next several decades. Whether or not the twenty-first century turns out to be a Golden Age for part-time professionals depends in large measure on us as individuals. For part-time professional work to gain broad acceptance, it is crucial that we all participate in the debate about our right to practice our professions at a high level while at the same time fulfilling our obligations to our families. Ultimately, time plus gentle but persistent pressure from women and men who demonstrate their competence and commitment to work while insisting on having a life outside of work will make the difference.

▪ Notes

INTRODUCTION: THE NEW PART-TIME PROFESSIONAL

3 *A lot of people are already doing:* Kathy M. Kristhof, "Redefining Success: Part-Time Professionals Are Shaping a New Work Ethic," *Los Angeles Times*, 6 February 1995, Part-Time Careers special sect.

3 *While the overall workforce:* ibid.

3 *Catalyst . . . surveyed thirty-eight companies:* Catalyst Consulting Group, "Flexible Work Arrangements, Part II: Succeeding with Part-Time Options" (New York, 1993).

3 *97% of those using flexible policies:* Catalyst Consulting Group, "Flexible Work Arrangements."

3-4 *7 to 10 percent of Work & Family Policies: Options for the 90s and Beyond* (Washington, D.C.: Business and Professional Women's Foundation, 1993), p. 4.

4 *Some experts suggest that 28%:* Maria L. LaGanga, "Men Who Break Out of Mold Find New Dreams to Chase," *Los Angeles Times*, 6 February 1995, Part-Time Careers special sec. If one third of part-time professionals are men, 88% by choice, therefore, 88% of one third is 28% since we're only interested in voluntary part-time professionals.

5 *Uncle Sam:* Nancy Henderson, "Tactics That Win Good Part-Time Jobs," *Changing Times* (May 1990): 61–63.

8 *By the year 2000:* Lisa Genasci, "Flex-Time Improves Productivity," *San Francisco Examiner*, 20 Sept. 1993.

8 *Already, a full one-third:* Dana E. Friedman and Ellen Galinsky, "Work and Family Trends," Families and Work Institute (1991): 2.

8 *Catalyst president Sheila Wellington:* Sue Shellenbarger, "Work and Family" column, *Wall Street Journal*, 13 Dec. 1995.

8 *The fastest growing segments of the workforce:* Ronald L. Krannich, *Change Your Job. Change Your Life! High Impact Strategies for Finding Great Jobs in the 90s* 5th ed. (Manassas Park, Va.: Impact Publications, 1995): 19.

9 *More than 400 U.S. corporations:* Catalyst Consulting Group, "Flexible Work Arrangements."

10 *Education Secretary Richard Riley:* San Jose Mercury News, 8 Sept. 1994 Sec. A.

10 *A meager 2%:* Annie Nakuo, "Making Families Count at Work," *San Francisco Examiner,* Tuesday, 1 Feb. 1994/Sec. B.

10 *While the good ideas are already there*: Catalyst Consulting Group, "Flexible Work Arrangements."

1: PART-TIME PROFESSIONAL OPTIONS, FINANCES, AND VALUES

19 *Nationwide, 57%:* Families and Work Institute, "The Families and Work Institute Facts About Flexible Work Arrangements" (New York, 1994).

20 *Of 505 corporations polled:* Marla Cone, "Compatible Partners Make Job Sharing a Win-Win Option," *Los Angeles Times,* 6 February, 1995, Special Part-Time Issue.

21 *It wasn't long ago:* Catalyst Consulting Group, "Flexible Work Arrangements, Part II: Succeeding with Part-Time Options" (New York, 1993).

23 *According to Work/Family Directions:* "AT&T to Employees: Stay Home." *San Jose Mercury News* 18 April 1994, sec. C.

23 *According to a 1994 LINK:* Sandra Sullivan, "Flexibility as a Management Tool," *Employment Relations Today* 13 (Winter 1994): 393.

23 *LINK further estimates:* ibid.

24 *According to LINK:* ibid.

24 *In Microsoft CEO:* "An Excerpt from *The Road Ahead* by Bill Gates," *Working Woman* (January 1996): 35.

26 *The following questions:* Brad Schepp, *The Telecommuter's Handbook* (New York: Pharrow Books, 1990).

27 *In 1992, 23.8 million: New York Times,* 18 April 1993, sect. 3.

27 *women are forming small businesses:* Wendy Zellner, "Women Entrepreneurs," *Business Week,* 18 April 1994: 104.

29 *According to Richard Bolles:* Richard Nelson Bolles, *The 1994 What Color Is Your Parachute?* (Berkeley, Calif.: Ten Speed Press) p. 120.

29 *And it is worth noting that according to:* Zellner, "Women Entrepreneurs": 105.

31 *Manpower, Inc., the largest temp:* Ann Crittenden, "Temporary Solutions," *Working Woman* (February 1994): 32.

31 *According to the National:* ibid.

31 *The temporary worker population:* Tom Peters, *Thriving on Chaos* (New York: Harper & Row, 1988), p. xiv.

33 *Beyond these few obligatory:* A Survey of Part-time Benefits by Hewitt and Associates, 1995.

2: PART-TIME CAREER TRADE-OFFS

40 *A Johnson and Johnson study:* Families and Work Institute, *An Evaluation of Johnson & Johnson's Work-Family Initiative* (New York),: p. 15.

40 *Catalyst reports:* Catalyst Consulting Group, *Flexible Work Arrangements for Managers and Professionals,* (New York, 1993), p. 36.

41 *In a compelling 1993 study:* Deborah Swiss and Judith Walker, *Women and the Work/Family Dilemma* (New York: John Wiley & Sons, 1993).

45 *Forty-one percent of companies:* Catalyst Consulting Group, *Flexible Work Arrangements,* p. 36.

47 *Business consultant Barbara Miller:* Barbara Miller (speech given to the Stanford Institute for Research on Women and Gender, Oct. 11, 1995)

48 *You can't have it all:* Felice Schwartz citation. Catalyst Consulting Group, *Flexible Work Arrangements,* p. 51.

3: WHY YOUR COMPANY SHOULD SAY YES

52 *Standard industry estimates:* Chubb Corporation, "Managing Flexible Work Arrangements" (October 1994).

52 *Pacific Bell, for instance:* D. Nye, "Alternative Staffing Strategies," CompuServe.

52 *Chubb Corporation:* Chubb, "Managing Flexible Work Arrangements."

52 *According to the international:* "Hiring Costs Much More Than It May Appear," *San Jose Mercury News,* 21 Jan. 1996, sec. E.

54 *Seventy-one percent of people:* Families and Work Institute, *An Evaluation of Johnson & Johnson's Work/Family Initiative,* April 1993, p. 4.

54 *A random sample of IBM employees:* Diane Harris, "Big Business Takes on Childcare," *Working Woman* (June 1993): 50.

54 *A 1990 survey done:* Dana Friedman "Linking Work-Family Issues to the Bottom Line," study done for *Working Woman* (New York: The Conference Board Report 962, 1991) p. 18.

54 *After the First Tennessee:* Julia Lawlor, "The Bottom Line on Work/Family Programs," *Working Woman* (July/August 1996): 55.

54 *In the early 1990s:* ibid.

55 *Forty percent of the workforce:* *Work/Family Policies: Options for the 90s and Beyond* (Washington, D.C., Business and Professional Women's Foundation, 1993), p. 8.

55 *A compelling study:* Helmut Hagemann, *The McKinsey Quarterly* 4:10 (Autumn 1994): 19.

57 *The night banking service:* ibid.

58 *Budgets for work/life programs:* Michelle Levander. "Helping Employees Balance Work and Life Puts Execs on Seesaw," *San Jose Mercury News,* 6 Feb. 1995, sec. F.

4: HOW TO BEAT THE TOP FIFTEEN MANAGEMENT OBJECTIONS

60 *Ask any work-life:* Catalyst Consulting Group, *Flexible Work Arrangements for Managers and Professionals* (New York, 1993), p. 4.

61 *The Chubb Corporation addresses:* Chubb Corporation, "Managing Flexible Work Arrangements," October 1994.

66 *Of 14,000 workers questioned:* Lena Williams, "Childless Workers Feel Put Upon," *New York Times* (29 May 1994) Sect. 5.

70 *In a much publicized Fortune:* "Bill Gates and Paul Allen Talk," *Fortune* (October 2, 1995).

5: Turning Your Full-time Job into a Part-time One

77 *a 1993 Catalyst survey:* Catalyst Consulting Group, "Flexible Work Arrangements, Part II: Succeeding with Part-Time Options" (New York, 1993), p. 30.

77-78 *. . . is the retention of high-performing:* Catalyst Consulting Group, "Flexible Work Arrangements, Establishing Options for Managers and Professionals" (New York, 1993), p. 30.

81 *Career guru Richard Bolles:* Richard Nelson Bolles, *What Color Is Your Parachute?* (Berkeley, Calif.: Ten Speed Press, 1996).

82 *In their book on flexible:* Maria Laqueur and Donna Dickinson, *Breaking Out of Nine to Five* (Princeton, N.J.: Peterson's, 1994), p. 99.

92 *According to a recent article:* Ellen Shapiro, "Negotiating for Something New," *Executive Female* (Jan/Feb 1996): 16.

6: Job Sharing

101 *Janice Chaffin:* Dean Takahasi, "HP's Tag Team," *San Jose Mercury News,* 9 June 1996, sec. E.

110 *Of 505 companies:* Marla Cone, "Compatible Partners Make Job Sharing a Win Win Situation," *Los Angeles Times,* 6 February 1995, Part-Time Careers special sec.

7: Coming in from the Outside

127 *A program called OPM Connection:* Maria Laqueur and Donna Dickinson, *Breaking Out of Nine to Five* (Princeton, N.J.: Peterson's, 1994), p. 168.

127 *Over 70% of job openings:* Richard Nelson Bolles, *What Color Is Your Parachute?* (Berkeley, Calif.: Ten Speed Press, 1996).

128 *According to Jackie Larson:* Jackie Larson and Cheri Comstock, *The New Rules of the Job Search Game* (Baltimore: Adams, 1994).

129 *According to out placement consultant:* "Networking-Developing Important Market Intelligence," Manchester Partners International," Princeton, N.Y., CompuServe.

8: Sequencers Reenter the Workforce After Staying Home

136 *According to* Newsweek: Barbara Kantowitz, "Mommy Trackers," *Working Woman* (February 1993): 81.

139 *"SITCOMS":* Faith Popcorn, *Clicking* (New York: HarperCollins, 1996).

141 *Over 38% of temp jobs:* "Profile of the Temporary Workforce," *Contemporary Times* (Spring 1994).

143 *As many as three-quarters:* (Sherwood Ross, "Resume Barrier Scanners," *San Jose Mercury News*, 1 Oct. 1995, sec. PC.

144 *During a job interview:* Charles Logue, *Outplace Yourself and Secrets of an Executive Outplacement Counselor* (Baltimore: Bob Adams, 1995).

9: You, Inc.

145 *A survey by Paul and Sarah Edwards:* "Telecommuters, Entrepreneurs Fuel Home Office Boom," *Valley News Dispatch*, 31 July 1994, sec. C.

148 *According to Joseph Anthony:* Joseph Anthony, *Working for Yourself*, rev. ed. (Washington, D.C.: Kiplinger Washington Editors, 1995), p. 42.

150 *A survey by* Home Run: Brian Collett, "Women Lead the Field in Working from Home," *The London Times*, 3 Oct. 1995.

150 *According to Ellen Parlapiano:* Patricia Cobe and Ellen Parlapiano, *Mompreneurs* (New York: Perigee, 1996).

153 *According to consulting expert Lynne Hobbs:* "Advice to Consultants," Association of Part-Time Professionals *Working Options*, vol. 16, no. 4, April 1996.

153 *According to a Roper poll:* Paul and Sarah Edwards, *Working from Home* (New York: G.P. Putnam, 1994), p. 27.

155 *Karin Abarbanel, author of:* Karin Abarbanel, *Overcoming the Emotional Roadblocks of Starting a Homebased Business* (New York: Henry Holt, 1995).

160 *Your proposal is the most obvious marketing tool:* Ron Tepper, *The Consultant's Proposal, Fee and Contract Problem Solver* (New York: Wiley & Sons, 1993), p. 76.

10: Managing Your Part-time Job at the Office

180 *Researchers at Catalyst:* Catalyst Consulting Group, "Flexible Work Arrangements, Part II: Succeeding with Part-Time Options" (New York, 1993), p. 39.

183 *June Langhoff, author of:* June Langhoff, *The Telecommuter's Advisor* (Newport, R.I.: Aegis Publishing Group, 1996), p. 130.

188 *94% of part-time employees:* Catalyst Consulting Group, "Flexible Work Arrangements, Part II."

192 *In a 1991* Working Woman interview: Lynn Povich, "Did Meredith Vieira Expect Too Much?," *Working Woman* (September 1991): 40.

11: Strategies for Managing at Home

203 *. . . children of part-timers:* Martha Hahn Sugar, *When Mother Works, Who Pays* (Westport, Conn.: Greenwood Publishing Group, 1994).

12: PROFESSIONAL PART-TIME: BEYOND 2000

216 . . . *Leach attacks:* Penelope Leach, *Children First—What Society Must Do—And Is Not Doing—For Children Today* (New York: Alfred A. Knopf, 1994).

217 *The FMLA:* Ellen Bravo, *A 9 to 5 Guide: The Job/Family Challenge* (New York: John Wiley & Sons, 1995), p. 197.

218 *Many large businesses:* Rachel Jones, "3 Million Workers Used Family Leave Law," *San Jose Mercury News,* 2 May 1996.

220 *When lawmakers in Washington:* Cokie Roberts and Seven V. Roberts, "Women and Children First," United Features Syndicate.

220 *"conspiracy of silence":* Kathy Cramer and John Pearce, "Work and Family Policies Become Productivity Tools," *Management Review* (November 1990): 42.

▪ Resources

NATIONAL ASSOCIATIONS

American Association of Retired Persons (AARP)
1909 K Street, N.W.
Washington, D.C. 20049
202-434-2277
Offers programs and services for persons fifty years and older.

Association of Part-Time Professionals
Crescent Plaza, Suite 216
7700 Leesburg Pike
Falls Church, VA 22043
703-734-7975
Provides research information, job leads, and other support for part-time professionals. Also publishes Working Options *newsletter.*

Business and Professional Women USA
2012 Massachusetts Avenue, N.W.
Washington, DC 20036
202-293-1200
Provides research and publications on women's financial work issues.

FEMALE
P.O. Box 31
Elmhurst, IL 60126
630-941-3553
Offers local support group membership for sequencing women and publishes monthly newsletter.

Forty Plus Clubs
Provides job search assistance and referrals for people over forty

through local Forty Plus organizations. Check the telephone directory for one in your area.

Gil Gordon Associates
10 Donner Court
Monmouth Junction, NY 08852
708-329-2266

Provides telecommuting consulting services and publishes a newsletter, Telecommuting Review.

National Association of Female Executives
30 Irving Place, 5th floor
New York, NY 10003
212-477-2200

Offers information, training workshops, and programs for professional women and publishes Female Executive.

National Association for the Self-Employed (NASE)
1023 15th Street, NW, Suite 1200
Washington, D.C. 20025-2600
800-232-NASE or 202-466-2100

Represents over 300,000 small business owners nationwide and offers members health and dental plans at group rates.

National Association of Temporary Services and Staffing
119 S. Saint Asaph Street
Alexandria, VA 22314
703-549-6287

Sponsors industry studies and workshops.

FAMILY-FRIENDLY POLICY EXPERTS

Catalyst Consulting Group
250 Park Avenue South, 5th floor
New York, NY 10003
212-777-8900

Works with business to promote the advancement of women in business through research, advisory services, and communication.

Conference Board, Inc.
Work and Family Information Center
845 Third Avenue
New York, NY 10022

212-759-0900
Provides information and research on work and family issues.

Families and Work Institute
330 Seventh Avenue, 14th Floor
New York, NY 10001
212-465-2044
Provides information on work/family issues and develops training programs and materials for government and business.

National Council of Jewish Women
Work/Family Project
53 West Twenty-third Street
New York, NY 10010
212-645-4048
Helps employers assist employees with work and family issues.

New Ways to Work
785 Market Street, Suite 950
San Francisco, CA 94103
415-995-9860
Offers a publications list, seminars, and training to companies in order to promote flexible work arrangements.

Center for Research on Women
Wellesley College 106 Central Street
Wellesley, MA 02181-8295
617-283-2500
Conducts research and develops programs for improving the status of women, including the work and family area.

Work/Family Directions
930 Commonwealth Avenue
Boston, MA 02215
617-278-4000
Offers consulting services about work and family such as workplace surveys, work/family policies, and management training.

Legal Information

National Organization for Women (NOW)
Legal Defense and Education Fund
1000 Sixteenth Street, N.W.

Suite 700
Washington, D.C. 20036
202-331-0066
Works on cases defending women's rights in many areas; also publishes the "Employment—Pregnancy and Parental Leave Kit."

9to5
National Association of Working Women
238 W. Wisconsin Avenue
Suite 700
Milwaukee, WI 53203-2308
Job Survival Hotline 800-522-0925
Offers information on legal rights in the workplace and personal support.

BENEFITS/COMPENSATION

Employee Benefit Research Institute
2121 K Street, N.W.
Suite 600
Washington, D.C. 20037
www.ebri.org
Employee benefits publications are available for purchase.

Hewitt Associates
100 Half Day Road
Lincolnshire, IL 60069
847-295-5000
Conducts research and provides programs on compensation and benefits for companies.

International Foundation on Employee Benefit Plans
18700 West Bruemond Rd.
Brookfield, WI 53008
414-786-6700
Employee benefits publications are available for purchase.

National Committee on Pay Equity
1126 Sixteenth Street, N.W.
Suite 411
Washington, D.C. 20036
202-331-7343
ncpe@essential.org
Offers two fact sheets to the public: "Tips for Negotiating Wages and Salaries" and "The Wage Gap."

STARTING YOUR OWN BUSINESS

American Woman's Economic Development Corporation (AWED)
71 Vanderbuilt Avenue
Rm 320
New York, NY 10169
212-692-9100
The organization provides training, counseling, and technical assistance to women who own or would like to start their own businesses.

National Association of Women Business Owners
1100 Wayne Avenue
Suite 830
Silver Spring, MD 20910
301-608-2590
Offers information and programs for women business owners.

U.S. Small Business Administration
Office of Women's Business Ownership
409 Third Street, S.W.
Suite 6200
Washington, D.C. 20416
202-205-6673
Small Business Answer Desk
800-U-ASK-SBA
www.sbaonline.sba.gov
Offers support and programs for small business owners.

GOVERNMENT AGENCIES

The Census Bureau
301-457-4608
Provides statistical information about women and work.

Institute for Women's Policy Research
1400 Twentieth Street, N.W.
Suite 104
Washington, D.C. 20036
202-785-5100
www.iwpr.org
Offers information to the public.

U.S. Department of Labor
The Women's Bureau
Washington, D.C. 20210
202-219-6652
Through regional offices, women can obtain information about job training, discrimination, referrals, and statistical and educational data.

■ Books for Further Reading

WOMEN'S ISSUES

Grace Baruch, et al. *Lifeprints: New Patterns of Love and Work for Today's Women*. (New York: New American Library, 1985).

Mary Catherine Bateson. *Composing a Life*. (New York: Penguin Books, 1990).

Ellen Bravo. *The Job/Family Challenge*. (New York: John Wiley & Sons, 1995).

Carol Buckley and Anne Weisberg. *everything a working mother needs to know*. (New York: Doubleday, 1993).

Faye Crosby. *Juggling: The Unexpected Advantages of Balancing Career and Home for Women and Their Families*. (New York: The Free Press, 1991).

Carol Gilligan. *In a Different Voice*. (Cambridge, Mass.: Harvard University Press, 1982).

Arlie Hochschild. *The Second Shift*. (New York: Viking, 1989).

Susan Faludi. *Backlash: The Undeclared War Against American Women*. (New York: Crown, 1991).

Cathy Feldman. *Two Years Without Sleep: Working Moms Talk About Having a Baby and a Job*. (Santa Barbara, Calif.: Blue Point Books, 1993).

Betty Friedan. *The Second Stage*. (New York: Summit Books, 1981).

Sylvia Hewlett. *A Lesser Life*. (New York: William Morrow & Co., 1986).

John Naisbitt and Patricia Aburdeen. *Megatrends 2000*. (New York: William Morrow & Co., 1990).

Felice Schwartz. *Breaking with Tradition*. (New York: Warner Books, 1992).

Marjorie Hausen Shaevitz. *The Superwoman Syndrome*. (New York: Warner Books, 1989).

Jane Swigart. *The Myth of the Bad Mother*. (New York: Doubleday, 1991).

Deborah Swiss and Judith Walker. *Women and the Work/Family Dilemma: How Today's Professional Women Are Finding Solutions.* (New York: John Wiley & Sons, 1993).

FLEXIBLE WORK ARRANGEMENTS

Charlene Canape. *The Part-Time Solution.* (New York: Harper & Row, 1990).

Susan Bacon Dynerman and Lynn O'Rourke Hayes. *The Best Jobs in America for Parents Who Want Careers and Time for Children, Too.* (New York: Rawson Associates, 1991).

Maria Laqueur and Donna Dickinson. *Breaking Out of 9 to 5.* (Princeton, N.J.: Peterson's Printing, 1994).

Barney Olmstead and Suzanne Smith. *The New Job Sharing Handbook.* (San Francisco: New Ways to Work, 1996).

Susan Shellenbarger. "Work and Family" column, *Wall Street Journal,* published every Wednesday.

FAMILY FRIENDLY POLICIES

Catalyst. *Flexible Work Arrangements: Establishing Options for Managers and Professionals.* (New York: Catalyst, 1990).

Catalyst. *Flexible Work Arrangements, Part II: Succeeding with Part-Time Options.* (New York: Catalyst, 1993).

The Conference Board. *Work-Family Roundtable: Flexibility.* (New York: The Conference Board, Dec. 1991).

Families and Work Institute. *The Corporate Reference Guide.* (New York: Families and Work Institute, 1989).

Families and Work Institute. *An Evaluation of Johnson & Johnson's Work-Family Initiative.* (New York: Families and Work Institute, 1993).

Dana E. Friedman. *Linking Work-Family Issues to the Bottom Line.* (New York: The Conference Board Report Number 962, 1991).

Dana E. Friedman, Ellen Galinsky, and Veronica Plowden, eds. *Parental Leave and Productivity.* (New York: Families and Work Institute, 1992).

Ellen Galinsky, James T. Bond, and Dana E. Friedman. *The Changing Workforce: Highlights of the National Study.* (New York: Families and Work Institute, 1991).

Hewitt Associates. *Survey of Benefits for Part-Time Employees.* (Lincolnshire, Ill.: Hewitt Associates, 1991).

Women's Bureau, U.S. Department of Labor. *A Working Woman's Guide to Her Job Rights.* (Washington, D.C.: U.S. Dept. of Labor, 1992).

Temping

Richard Belous. *The Contingent Economy: The Growth of the Temporary, Part-Time and Subcontracted Workforce.* (Washington, D.C.: National Planning Association, 1989).

Peggy O'Connell Justice. *The Temp Track: Make One of the Hottest Job Trends of the 90s Work for You.* (Princeton, N.J.: Peterson's, 1994).

Working from Home

Lynie Arden. *The Work-at-Home Sourcebook.* (Boulder, Colo.: Live Oak Publications, 1992).

Kathleen Christensen. *Women and Home-Based Work: The Unspoken Contract.* (New York: Henry Holt, 1988).

Paul and Sarah Edwards. *Working from Home: Everything You Need to Know About Living and Working Under the Same Roof.* (Los Angeles: Jeremy P. Tarcher, Inc., 1990).

Jack M. Nilles. *Making Telecommuting Happen: A Guide for Telemanagers and Telecommuters.* (New York: Van Nostrand Reinhold, 1994).

June Langhoff. *The Telecommuter's Advisor.* (Newport, R.I.: Aegis Publishing Group, 1996).

Jeff Meade. *Home Sweet Office.* (Princeton, N.J.: 1993).

Brad Schepp. *The Telecommuter's Handbook: How to Work for a Salary—Without Ever Leaving the House.* (New York: Pharos Books, 1990).

NEGOTIATING

Roger Fisher and William Ury. *Getting to Yes.* (Boston: Houghton Mifflin, 1981).

STARTING YOUR OWN BUSINESS

Joseph Anthony. *Kiplinger's Revised and Updated Working for Yourself.* (Washington, D.C.: Kiplinger Washington, Editors, Inc., 1995).

Jane Applegate. *Succeeding in Small Business—The 101 Toughest Problems and How to Solve Them.* (New York: Penguin Books, 1992).

Patricia Cobe and Ellen Parlapiano. *Mompreneurs.* (Perigree, 1996).

Jolene Godfrey. *Our Wildest Dreams: Women Entrepreneurs Making Money.* (New York: HarperCollins Publishers, 1992).

Ron Tepper. *The Consultant's Proposal, Fee and Contract Problem Solver.* (New York: Wiley & Sons, 1993).

Laurie Zuckerman. *A Woman's Guide to Building a Business.* (Dover, N.H.: Upstart Publishing, 1990).

CHILDCARE

Nina Barrett. *I Wish Someone Had Told Me: Comfort, Support and Advice for New Moms from More Than 60 Real-Life Mothers.* (New York: Fireside, 1991).

T. Berry Brazelton. *Working and Caring.* (Reading, Mass.: Addison-Wesley, 1985).

Penelope Leach. *Children First: What Society Must Do—And Is Not Doing—For Children Today.* (New York: Alfred Knopf, Inc., 1994).

CAREERS

Richard N. Bolles. *What Color Is Your Parachute?* (Berkeley, Calif.: Ten Speed Press, 1996).

Ronald L. Krannich. *Change Your Job, Change Your Life! High Impact Strategies for Finding Great Jobs in the 90s,* 5th edition. (Manassas Park, Va.: Impact Publications, 1991).

Jackie Larson and Cheri Comstock. *The New Rules of the Job Search Game.* (Baltimore: Bob Adams Publishing, 1994).

Laura Morin. *Every Woman's Guide to Finding a Job: New Rules for Tough Times.* (Baltimore: Bob Adams Publishing, 1994).

Barbara Sher. *Wishcraft.* (New York: Ballantine Books, 1979).

RE-ENTERING WORKFORCE AFTER STAYING HOME

Arlene Rossen Cardozo. *Sequencing.* (New York: Atheneum, 1986).

Darcie Sanders and Martha Bullen. *Staying Home: From Full-Time Professional to Full-Time Parent.* (New York: Little, Brown, & Co., 1992).

Cindy Tolliver. *At-Home Motherhood: Making It Work for You.* (San Jose: Resource Publishing, 1994).

▪ Acknowledgments

Of the many people who have helped with this project, first and foremost, I want to acknowledge the important work of Mary Ann Alwan who collaborated with me in developing and researching the project. Her help with the early drafts of several chapters was invaluable. Without her calm, thoughtful approach, this book would not be as thorough as it is.

An incredible debt of gratitude goes to my writing colleagues, Henci Goer and Alexis Rubin, who put their editing skills at my service and provided feedback on the book's content. Their intelligence, enthusiasm, and accessibility never flagged from day one to the finish line.

Thanks also to my friends Cindy Bitner, Marsha Shain, and Betsy Mace for their careful reading of several chapters and to Karen Garappolo for the cartoon rendering.

I would also like to thank my literary agent Diana Finch, a real professional, for her constructive criticism and warm support. Thanks also to Chris Condry, Rachel Klayman, and their associates at Avon Books who have made the production of *Going Part-Time* both possible and pleasurable.

A special thanks to the many busy people who generously agreed to share their insights and personal experiences. Their words and stories enrich every page of this book. Their willingness to talk about how they struggled to achieve balance through part-time professional work supported my belief in the need for this book. To them I offer my deepest thanks and admiration.

And last, a thanks to my family. My husband Mark's pragmatic optimism always encouraged me to take the next step. And to my daughters Maggie, Anne, and Elizabeth for the sacrifices they made to the cause, my love and appreciation.

—Cindy Tolliver

Many thanks to Nancy Austin, an oft-quoted source in our book and my friend and mentor. Nancy, always the visionary, put me in contact with Cindy knowing our experience with and approach to women's work issues would be a perfect match for *Going Part-Time*.

Additionally, all of my former colleagues at *Working Woman*, especially Diane Harris, have contributed to the spirit of this book. I believe we all hope that alternative work arrangements do not remain only a women's issue.

I thank my family and friends for their high expectations, reassurances and pride. Most of all, I wish to express my love and appreciation to my chief cheerleader and coach, my husband, Kevin Urbonas, who stalwartly suffered through my panic attacks and several lost weekends. Kevin is the ultimate work-life partner.

—Nancy Chambers

▪ INDEX